# RUN WITH the VISION

## Bob Sjogren
## Bill & Amy Stearns

# BETHANY HOUSE PUBLISHERS
MINNEAPOLIS, MINNESOTA 55438

The stories in this book are true, although for security reasons many accounts have been disguised with altered details or fictionalized by inserting the reader into the story.

Published by Bethany House Publishers
A Ministry of Bethany Fellowship, Inc.
11300 Hampshire Avenue South
Minneapolis, Minnesota 55438

Printed in the United States of America.

**Library of Congress Cataloging-in-Publication Data**

Sjogren, Bob
    Run with the vision : a remarkable global plan for the 21st century church / Bob Sjogren, Bill Stearns, Amy Stearns.
        p.   cm.
    Includes bibliographical references.

    1. Missions. 2. Evangelistic work. 3. Christianity and other religions. 4. Christianity—21st century. I. Stearns, Bill. II. Stearns, Amy. III. Title.
BV2061.S527   1995
266'.001'12—dc20                                    95–7498
ISBN 1–55661–321–0                                      CIP

*Run With the Vision* is dedicated to:
Megan
Erin
Carrie
Ami
Brett
Zachary
—some of the special ones who are inheriting
our twenty-first century.

—Bill & Amy Stearns

and to

All the children and adults who catch
a vision of God's global heart for the nations
through the ministry of Destination 2000,
as well as the unsung heroes,
the home staff of countless mission agencies serving and sending out
those who are making history—His-story.

—Bob Sjogren

BILL & AMY STEARNS are with World Christian, an association of "global activists for the cause of Christ." They travel worldwide and work with churches and mission centers to implement the message of this book. Bill is publisher of *World Christian* magazine and author of fourteen books. They make their home in Colorado.

BOB SJOGREN is the Co-Founder of FRONTIERS, an interdenominational faith mission agency seeking to establish churches across the heart of the Muslim world, and the President of Frontiers Associates, a sister agency to FRONTIERS seeking to involve lay people in ministering to missionaries serving in the Muslim world. Along with recruiting individuals to join their established teams, he is the author of *Unveiled at Last*, and regularly teaches seminars designed to educate Christians on the high priority of missions. He and his wife make a home for their four children in Arizona.

# Contents

*Record the vision and inscribe it on tablets,*
*that the one who reads it may run.*

HABAKKUK 2:2

# Part I

## Get the Big Picture

### Our Brave New World

## CHAPTER ONE

# The Twenty-First Century Slugfest

*The future won't be easy! But it will be exciting.*

*"Something really big is going to happen very soon."*

—David Wang

MAY 1987, BAJA CALIFORNIA, MEXICO — Fine-grained white sand squeaks beneath your bare feet in the 90°F, 90% humidity as you drag a clanking trash bag toward the water. Clear, hot sun is everywhere— burning your arms, reflecting from the billions of mica chips in the sand, glinting off the warm blue-green water along the beach. A field of boulders had halted your three mufflerless VW-derived dune buggies, and now you and your team of ten have trekked the last half mile on foot, dragging black trash bags full of bottles.

"Is this any way to build the Kingdom?" you muse. Your feet begin to blister in the hot sand; if you'd known the water was this far, you'd have worn sandals. A middle-aged teammate in a huge pair of yellow Hawaiian shorts with matching shirt stops to wipe sweat off his sunglasses. He hops in the hot sand and yells, "How beautiful are the feet of those who bring good news!" All ten of you stop and stand on the edges of the bags you're dragging. The Hawaiian-outfitted man continues, "They announce salvation and say, 'Our God reigns!' "

Together you sing a chorus and charge on through the sand: "Our God reigns; our God reigns." Cool saltwater stings your feet as you reach the waves; you can almost hear the hiss of steam as your sun- and sand-burned body lurches out into the surf. The bag of bottles floats now as you bob through the seawater out past the small breakers. The rest of the team are soon all treading water, stretched in a line a hundred yards from shore. You open your trash bag, pull out two or three soda bottles at a time and toss them out to sea. You find yourself praying as you toss each one: "Don't return void. Please, God, don't let your Word return without accomplishing its purpose." Your bag empty, you swing it overhead to catch air, clasp the top closed and rest against it as if it were a life raft. What a crazy, tiring idea.

Later you slosh to shore. "That," you say to your middle-aged teammate, "was definitely the fun part."

"The fun part," he replies, "is when they arrive."

AUGUST 1990. BAMUMBA, MINDANAO ISLAND, PHILIPPINES — Wycliffe missionaries debate just how demented their report will sound at headquarters. It would read something like this: "This has been the most remarkable week! Sunday morning hundreds of bottles began washing up on shore near the Muslim village of Bamumba. The bottles have manufacturers' markings from the USA. And inside each one is a small tract or Scripture passage written in the local trade language—Cebuano! Several village leaders have gathered every night to discuss this strange occurrence. After months of trying to approach the village, we've been invited over to explain the meanings of several tracts. We had never been allowed to even speak with the elders before! The whole people group is buzzing! We don't know who did this; all we know is 'Our God reigns!' "

The people who blistered through a weekend on the Baja coast with the crazy idea to float Scripture and tracts across 5,000 miles of open ocean to the Philippines were members of Current Evangelism. The group studies the currents and launches their Scripture-packed bottles across the open ocean.

No, this isn't exactly the latest, laudable model for accomplishing world evangelization! In fact, the Wycliffe missionaries asked that no one be encouraged to toss bottles in any body of water regardless of their good intentions. But the tactic does provoke a thought: God is willing to use crazy ideas to accomplish His task of world evangelization. So is it time for you to get radical? Time for your church fellowship to zero in—even through unconventional strategies—to impact your community, your culture, your world?

Life won't go on as it has, you know. Something huge is happening in the big picture of God's plan for this planet. As an early 90s pop song put it, we're "watching the world wake up from history."

## The Twenty-First Century Slugfest

If there's anything we should have learned from the past few years, it's that the near future holds everything but what we expect. Our era on this planet will not be "business as usual" politically, economically, socially, or personally! The old prophet Habakkuk put it this way:

Look among the nations! Observe! Be astonished! Wonder! Because I am doing something in your days—you would not believe if you were told (Habakkuk 1:5, NIV).

Any world-watcher smells something blowing in the wind. In only a twenty-four-month period of 1990–1991, fully 25% of the countries of the world changed governments. These weren't changes of political parties, but whole governments! Within a six-month period from the end of 1991 to mid-1992, seventeen new countries formed. Map makers are hard-pressed to keep up with the changing political face of the planet.

Even today's political change is tinged with spiritual overtones. For example, some thirty years ago Tanja Khodkevich wrote in a poem: "You can pray freely, but just so God alone can hear." For this she received from the dreaded KGB, the Soviet secret police, a sentence of ten years of hard labor. Yet in 1991 a new director of the KGB welcomed a delegation of Christians. *Christianity Today* editor Philip Yancey recorded the KGB director's speech:

Political questions cannot be decided until there is sincere repentance, a return to faith by the people. That is the cross I must bear. In the study of scientific atheism, there was the idea that religion divides people. Now we see the opposite: Love for God can only unite.[1]

In late 1995, in Ivanovo, Russia, directors of a museum honoring the first band of "Soviets"—factory workers who rebelled against the czar—asked a ministry for Christian materials to rededicate the museum to spiritual change in Jesus Christ.[2]

But politics is only a superficial indicator of the surging heart-changes in our world. If the Lord gives it to us, the twenty-first century is going to be a time of spiritual significance. It will probably evidence the best and worst of religion in an all-out spiritual slugfest. The rattling events of the past few years should clue us in. (The following breakthroughs and statistics are documented in *Global Reports* listed in Sources Cited, found in the back of the book.)

- It took from the beginning of the Church until 1900 for committed believers to become 2.5% of the world population. It took until 1970, just 70 years, for that percentage to double. By then, committed believers were 5% of a much larger world population.

- Then it took just 22 years to double again. In 1992, committed believers grew to become 10% of a still larger world population!

- At least 260,274 people are now being presented the plan of salvation every day worldwide.

- In each of the past 20 centuries, Christian growth has consistently exceeded world population growth. Right now the number of committed, Bible-believing Christians (560 million!) is doubling every ten and a half years while world population is doubling only every 35 years.

- In 1992, George Otis, Jr., president of the Sentinel Group research agency, estimated: About 70% of all the Church's outreach since its beginning until today has been accomplished in this century alone. About 70% of what's been accomplished in this century has taken place since 1945. And of all the combined outreach of the Body of Christ since 1945, about 70% of it has happened since late 1989.

- An Asian specialist says of response to the Gospel in Asia: "The traditional word 'harvest' no longer seems adequate to describe what God is doing. I would describe it as 'the great ingathering.' These are breakthroughs of an unprecedented nature."

- A Japanese government survey reported that when the citizens of Japan were asked who was the greatest religious leader of history, 67% replied, "Jesus Christ." In 1992, the best-selling book in Japan was the Bible.

- Estimates of the number of believers in China range from 30 million to 100 million!

- Even under intense governmental repression during the 1980s and early 90s, Vietnam's house churches grew rapidly. After the arrest of its pastor in 1991, one church renewed its commitment and planted 300 new churches in Vietnam over the next two years. The congregation saw nearly 10,000 come to faith in Jesus Christ! Meanwhile, in prison, the pastor led 25 of his cell mates to Christ!

- It is estimated that in India, believers may now account for 10% of the country's population! With the total number of Indian citizens past the 900 million mark, it's obvious the Church of Jesus Christ is well represented in India. In this country where baptism is a solid sign of conversion, researchers report an average of 15,000 new believers baptized every day across India!

- In Nepal in the fall of 1991, 100 believers were publicly baptized—an event that would have brought imprisonment just nine months before. In a 1995 Luis Palau rally, 26,000 attended in Kathmandu, and 1,400 made public commitments to Christ. From a few persecuted believers in the 1950's, the Church in Nepal has mushroomed to 150,000.

- In some areas, Muslims are turning to Christ by the thousands. For example, in Bulgaria, more than 3,000 Turkish Muslims came to Christ in 1992–1993. In 1992 a Coptic priest and an Assemblies of God missionary surprisingly teamed up as an evangelistic team in Egypt. As a result, about 25,000 Muslims were brought to faith in Christ—in a country where Christians are often persecuted.

- As Croatia became an independent country in the early 90s breakup of Yugoslavia, its government mandated Christian education training in all public schools. Croatia thus joined an impressive list of countries allowing Bible teaching and/or Bible distribution in public schools—countries including some of the Commonwealth of Independent States, Romania, Bulgaria, Papua New Guinea, Panama, and Bolivia, to name a few.

- In West Africa, the number of believers in Gambia, Guinea Bissau, Mali, and Guinea is now growing at twice the population rate. Across Africa, about 20,000 are daily added to the Body of Christ!

- It is estimated the entire continent will be 50% Christian by the year 2000.

Why aren't many Western disciples aware of the awesome move of God across our globe? Perhaps because much of the West's view of God's work in His world no longer matches reality.

While Western Christians are now only one fourth of the worldwide Body of Christ, North Americans constitute perhaps less than 15% of the worldwide Church. Westerners without real communication links to the Two-Thirds World are missing at least 85% of what God is really doing! For example, George Otis, Jr., says of the North American church, "Today, mounting evidence forces us to acknowledge that North America has been largely bypassed by the great spiritual harvest occurring in other parts of the world." If believers look only at their own quiet corner of Christendom, it is no wonder they are often discouraged!

A simple world population chart tells us something is up in God's global program.

## Population Growth

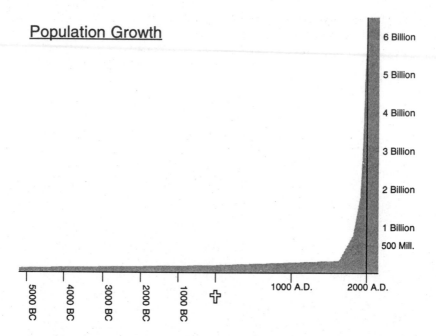

That abrupt upturn on the chart frightens many with its grim implication of a disastrous global population explosion. But what does it mean from God's perspective?

Of all His creation, God most highly values the souls of humans. And right now God is suddenly packing into one place at one time more human souls than at any other time in history. And He is allowing those billions of new babies to be birthed mostly into the Two-Thirds World—which, naturally, is where the Church is now growing like wildfire! What a harvest!

And there are more mind-boggling breakthroughs:

- In late 1992 Zimbabwean church leaders from 70 denominations gathered to commit themselves to plant 10,000 new churches by the year 2000. Results so far? One of those denominations, the Free Methodists, had developed a total of thirteen congregations in their previous *100-year history* in Zimbabwe. Within six months of the commitment, the Free Methodists planted thirty new churches of new believers—more than doubling 100 years' growth in half a year! A leader reported, "We've finally come to life!"

- In all the bad news about South Africa over the past decades, the good news about the current South African mission movement has seldom been publicized. For example, a 1992 November baptismal service took five pastors five hours, and the line of those waiting to be baptized was five kilometers long. In that one afternoon 7,000 new believers were baptized! Similar reports of even 10,000 being baptized in a single day come from Angola during the height of its bloody civil war.

- In Cuba, a three-week Gospel crusade in 1988 reported more than 22,000 commitments to Christ. Since that time, this island nation is seeing phenomenal growth of evangelical faith. A Cuban pastor recently reported, "There is an explosion of evangelism in Cuba today. It's beautiful!" One pastor alone established 50 house churches in a three-month period. The churches average a total of 900 in attendance and report about 50 responding to salvation in Christ weekly.

- In Guatemala, the capital city now has five churches with more than 5,000 members each. Evangelical believers have increased to become nearly 30% of the population—a trend seen throughout most of Central America. One prayer meeting held in the National Soccer Stadium of Guatemala City was attended by more than 45,000 believers.

- The evangelical church in Argentina has grown more than 800% in the past ten years. Three congregations led by pastors Omar Cabrera, Carlos Anaconda, and Hector Jiminez each have memberships of more than 100,000.

- In Russia, about 22% of former atheists now believe in God, and another 25% say they have always believed in God—even throughout the repression of atheistic communism.

  In the former Soviet Union, more than 15,000 educators have now been trained to use a new curriculum to teach biblically based morals and the life of Jesus Christ.

  More than 96% report reading the Bible regularly and discussing it in their classes! Imagine the classroom of nine-year-olds at School #10 in Vladimir poring over Russian-English New Testaments, racing to find John 3:16.

- About 120,000,000 people are presented the Gospel for the first time each year.

- The Body of Christ now owns 158,725,000 computers worldwide! What an opportunity to link them up for the Kingdom!

- In May 1995, 80,000 Korean students publicly dedicated themselves to world evangelization. Another 25,000 later signed commitments to send or go as missionaries.

- About 1.7 billion people now listen to Christian radio or watch Christian TV on a monthly basis!
- Christians now spend 388,000,000 man-hours every year proclaiming the Gospel in evangelism!
- Fully 10% of the earth's population has now viewed the life of Jesus Christ depicted in *Jesus*, a film based on the book of Luke.
- David Bryant, an experienced world-watcher with Concerts of Prayer, International, says, "The landscape of the Church today leaves no question in the minds of many leaders that the Body of Christ is poised at the threshold of a coming world revival. God is raising up in the Body worldwide a prayer movement that is unprecedented in the history of the Church, and that is set on nothing less than an army of revived and mobilized Christians."

Something is definitely happening out there! The Gospel is spreading like wildfire. But we must not be ignorant of the fact that there is a cost in seeing this harvest gathered. This is a second trend that suggests a twenty-first-century slugfest for the Church.

## Take Off Your Kid Gloves

AUGUST 1992. NORTHEASTERN NIGERIA — You're sitting on a warm, round rock at the edge of the village well, mopping your face, terrified. The dry, cracked buzz of cicadas in the scrub oaks around the dusty village square is the only sound. Hausa villagers stand in a silent circle of heat waves around a white-robed warrior. His muscled arms poise the sword high over a kneeling young man who now gently places his right arm across the wood stump in front of him.

The young man's wife and sister stand trembling just behind him as he kneels in the dust. Around the inside of the circle, the children cringe in silence, fingers in mouths. You sit paralyzed, nauseated.

The Hausa warrior shouts slowly in his language, then in English for your benefit: "This pastor Selchun was carrying a Christian Bible!" He glares eye to eye around the circle of breathless villagers, then at you. "This is the punishment for all infidels!" And he grunts as the sword slashes through the hot air to thump through the wrist and into the wood stump.

Pastor Selchun chokes in pain, but without blinking an eye, he raises his left hand and begins to sing. You recognize the melody: "He is Lord, He is Lord. He has risen from the dead and He is Lord."

The dusty villagers stare wide-eyed in silence. Even the Hausa warrior seems struck dumb. Your heart is in your throat as the kneeling, bloody young man sings: "Every knee shall bow, every tongue confess that Jesus Christ is Lord."

Pastor Selchun is just one of the victims of the mounting do-or-die spiritual battle for this planet. At the time of this true incident, almost 60,000 Christians were homeless in Pastor Selchun's area of Nigeria, driven from their homes by violent mobs. About 300 Christians had been murdered over a three-month period, some of them burned alive in their meetinghouses as over 100 churches were torched. Overall, the Body of Christ is taking some hard knocks:

- More missionaries have been martyred for their faith in Christ in the past 20 years than in the previous 200 years.[2]
- Every year since 1950, the average number of those killed for their faith in Christ worldwide is at least 150,000. That's 150,000 *annually!*[3]

Take your own "State of Your World" poll of even a handful of Christian zealots—committed laypeople, pastors, missionaries, parachurch ministry staff. Ask if the past couple of years of ministry have been more difficult than usual. What you'll invariably find is that, personally and corporately, the Church's battle against the gates of hell seems to be intensifying.

If there is an on-target symbol for our era, it's probably:

These Chinese characters together mean "crisis." The first character alone means "danger." The second character, by itself, means "opportunity." Here's the message: Especially at our crisis point in history, it seems that every opportunity is increasingly dangerous. Yet every danger holds more and more opportunities for the Church: *Crisis Equals Opportunity.*

The apostle Paul put it this way: "A wide door of opportunity has opened to me." Then he added, "and there are many adversaries" (1 Corinthians 16:9). Increasingly in our day, unprecedented ministry opportunities are accompanied by bad-to-the-bone opposition. Sin seems to be less subtle in its onslaught against the good. Something big is at hand in the cosmic war of good vs. evil.

If there is a chapter of Scripture that fellowship after fellowship across the globe seems to allude to these days, it's the twelfth chapter of Revelation. Hardcore believers challenge each other with these passages about the accuser of the brethren, about overcoming the enemy by the blood of the Lamb and the word of our testimony, about the devil "having great wrath, knowing that he has only a short time," about iron-willed believers who do "not love their life even to death."

As believers in Jesus Christ, our reputation is that we're harmless but nice. And we go to lots of meetings. But it's time for us to take off our kid gloves. We as a Church just might be at the flash point of history, and God is looking for a few good men and women who are tough enough for such a time as this.

What's your part in God's big-picture plan? As a believer, it is far more significant than being nice and going to lots of meetings. Because of God's great love, woven together in His global plan is a personalized plan for your life. Your challenge is simply to see where God wants you to fit in.

## Goers, Welcomers, Senders, Mobilizers

The Current Evangelism tracts-in-a-bottle brigade are a radical bunch. In our study together, you'll meet more Christian radicals— some a bit more reserved in their big-picture strategies, some even wilder. All these people exemplify specific roles in the whole mission of the Church:

1. They're *goers*. God has designed them to go to foreign locations, to cross-cultural barriers in order to minister the blessing of redemption in Jesus Christ.
2. Others stay in their own hometowns as *welcomers*, ministering to the internationals God has brought to their city.
3. Some of them are *senders*. They find fulfillment in obedience to God as they stay on the home front, exercising their gifts in ministries that strengthen the Church for its task, in ministries that impact their own culture for the sake of His name among the nations. They're the base for launching the Church's global mission.
4. Maybe they specialize as *mobilizers*. Like military recruiters, they encourage and exhort other believers to fulfill their strategic roles in the life-or-death big picture of what God is doing these days.

Or maybe they're a combination of these roles. These models—

goers, welcomers, senders, mobilizers—aren't cut and dried. Christians making a difference in reaching the world are often a combination of these roles, and may be in these roles at different times in their lives. Yet these four categories can help you define *your* role in this exciting era of the mission of the Church. And they'll provide tested models for how you as an individual and you as a local church can take action

That's what this book is all about. Helping you determine God's role for your life as you go through the eighty or so years that God gives to you.

But first we'll need to get a good grip on the big picture. Then we'll work through the practicalities of where you fit in.

Fasten your seat belt. There's something coming at us, something going on out there among ordinary Christians that has everything to do with the significance of our age. You just might find your to-do list filling up with bizarre activities like tossing pop bottles into the ocean at Baja or praying for one-handed pastors in Nigeria.

## CHAPTER TWO

# From Baltimore to Bulgaria

*An overview of God's global plan*

*"I am witnessing a growing awareness among church leaders that the end of the age is upon us. It's time to believe that the Church of Jesus Christ can complete its mission on earth."*

—J. Philip Hogan

BALTIMORE — The summer evening air is saunalike as you walk the half mile from a parking lot to Stamps Student Union on the campus of the University of Maryland. You step through the building's huge white doors and the air conditioning slaps your sweaty body with chills. Summer school students scurry around you down cool marble hallways as you look for the Grand Ballroom. You finally ask a Gypsy-looking student if he knows where the auditorium is. "You one of those gnarly missionaries?" he asks.

"Well, I was invited to see a sort of play they're putting on," you say. He rolls his eyes and points toward the Ballroom door. It swings open as you approach and Jay Randall bursts out, script in hand. Director of the Caspian Project, he strikes you as a grown-up, dark-haired Bart Simpson. "You're late!" he grins, and plops in your hand a rolled-up script titled *A View From on High*. "Your name tag's inside the front cover," Jay says. "Rehearsal in two minutes."

"What part do I play?" you call after Jay as he rushes off down the hallway.

"Satan," he yells back.

You step into the dim, empty auditorium to find yourself in a maze of exhibit booths. One has bold letters announcing "We're Reaching for the Unreached." Another booth's slogan is "Extending the Ripple of Truth." You stand a bit befuddled and pull out your name tag, headlined in burgundy letters: "ACMC."

The door slams behind you, and Jay rushes by. "Put on the name tag and follow me." He leads you through a maze of mission displays as he explains. "ACMC used to stand for the Association of Church Mission Committees, but they've broadened it to—let's see—something like Advancing Commitment in Mission among Churches. No, that's not it. Advancing Churches' Mission Commitment. Whatever. Any church with any vision needs to belong. This has been a great conference so far!"

You're hurtling down the aisle now between hundreds of chairs. "But why me?"

Jay stops. "Whining, are we? Well, this is about the quickest way we think you can get up to speed on an overview of the mission of the Church. If you studied through Frontier's *Destination 2000* or *Unveiled at Last* course or *Catch the Vision 2000* or the *Perspectives on the World Christian Movement* course, you're all set to jump into the next chapter, to run with the vision. But we weren't sure if you'd gone through one of those studies and wanted to give you an overview. Besides, you can use this in your own fellowship. The script is in your hands."

"No, that's not what I meant," you say. "I figured we'd need to do some kind of overview so that we're tracking together on the rest of this study. What I meant by 'Why me?' was why do *I* have to play Satan?"

Jay smiles condescendingly as he guides you by the shoulders toward the front of the auditorium. "I can't think of a single reason. Can you?" He seats you in the front row. "Seriously," he grins. "All you have to do is watch. We've already got plenty of demonic types."

Two hours later the auditorium is packed with "those gnarly mission types," young and old. You sit down next to a young couple who introduce themselves as Mike and Brenda Kroupa from Michigan. Mike says, "Yeah, I make my living with computers. But in real life we're mission mobilizers—" Suddenly the indigo curtains sweep apart, and the play begins.

## A View From on High

Jay Randall strides to the microphone on stage and says, "Ladies and gentlemen, today we'd like to show you this new drama designed to help you show the non-mission types in your church a fresh way of looking at God's heart for every people. It's humorous, challenging, inspiring, and it doesn't take tons of dramatic talent or time to pull off. We'd like to show the whole thing to you, but we can't. It was written as an entire Sunday morning service and that would take an hour and we've only got twenty minutes tonight. So, with the help of my imaginary VCR remote control, I'll 'freeze-frame' the action at some points and summarize for you. Normally, some of the pastoral staff and other church leaders would fill the main roles, but this evening we've asked some of the ACMC gang and some other buddies of mine to fill in. So here we go!"

Southwest ACMC representative Larry Walker, serving as the host for the evening, gives the introduction: "As we thought of trying to give an overview of God's plan to redeem mankind, we thought the best overview might be from heaven. So, in this worship service we will try to take the heavenly perspective." As he speaks, two men dressed in robes move to the upper right side of the stage behind a pulpit. Larry says, "We join the scene as a senior angel is giving a junior angel his orientation tour of the universe."

The spotlight focuses on the two robed men as they start bobbing and jiggling, giving the impression they are moving in hyperspace through the galaxy. They gradually slow down and begin to speak above the giggles of the crowd.

The junior angel looks at the senior angel with a puzzled look. "Why are we slowing down?" he asks.

The senior angel replies in a hushed voice, "We're getting close to the 'visited planet.' See that second star on the right?" The junior angel nods. "Okay. See the planet with the rings? Just beyond it you can just make it out—okay, that's better. There it is!"

The junior angel stares off in the distance in disbelief. "You're kidding," he says. "That's it? The zillions of planets we've sped past and that's it? I thought it would be bigger or brighter or something, but this is so—so ordinary!"

The senior angel smiles and pats his partner's shoulder. "Exactly," he says. "He delights in using the ordinary. And it was this place, this planet that He visited just a short time ago, what its inhabitants would call two millenniums—which they feel is a long time."

"Why would He visit such short-sighted creatures?" the junior angel says with disgust.

"Careful," the senior angel warns. "Part of the mystery is that someday they will rule over us and the rest of the angels."

"Them?" The junior angel gestures at the audience, then squints. "I see what you mean about His using the ordinary."

"Well, I'm just getting started and I'm already getting ahead of myself." The senior angel starts into a storytelling mode: "A long time ago the Fallen One wasn't fallen. He was the fairest and brightest of all the angels. But it wasn't enough. He wanted to be worshiped. There was war in heaven and, unbelievably, one-third of the angels sided with the Fallen One. They started to set up their own kingdom."

"I find that hard to believe," the junior angel·says.

"Most humans feel that way, too. Anyway, this grieved Father very much, and He began a plan. He chose this small little planet in the midst of the Fallen One's Occupied Territory. He filled it with living things—including some human-kinds. And it was very good. But they too revolted, refusing to listen to Father's instructions—not just once, but over and over."

The junior angel crosses his arms and grunts. "He should have just wiped them out."

"Well, He did—at least most of them. But He gave them another chance. He chose Abraham and his descendants to be central to the plan. The idea was that Father would be close to them. Abraham's family would flourish, and all the tribes of peoples would see these favored people and come to see what was different about them. And they would introduce these seekers to Father."

The junior angel slaps the podium. "What a great plan!"

"Unfortunately," the senior angel continues, "it didn't work. Well, it sort of worked. Sometimes. But as often as not, Abraham and his descendants forgot that their blessing was a privilege and mistook it for a right. So The Holy One stepped out of His infiniteness to be born as an ordinary human into this ordinary human lineage."

"Inconceivable! Sorry—no pun intended." The junior angel looks up from his script and smiles at the audience's chuckles.

Shaking his head disapprovingly, the senior angel continues, "Nevertheless, it happened as I have said. He became the Groom and paid the highest bride-price ever. The perfect life freely given to rebellious men so that even they could be wooed and won as part of the Bride. His followers were deputized with power, authority, and purpose to scour every nook and cranny of the earth to invite some from every tongue and tribe and nation to the Wedding Feast."

"Incredible, but how are His followers doing now?"

"Well, let's look in on an average church. Well—above average."

"How do you know it's above average?" asks Junior.

"Well, the pastor told me so." The crowd snickers. "Of course," he continues, "in most of the planet's peoples everybody thinks they are above average with above-average children, above-average looks, and above-average intelligence."

The junior angel scratches his chin. "But how can all of them be above average. . . ?"

The senior angel interrupts him. "I didn't say it made sense. Anyway, they're about to worship Father in song."

At this, Jay steps onto the stage and points his imaginary remote control switch at the actors. They freeze in their positions. Jay says to the audience, "Now at this point, your congregation would sing their normal songs and take an offering. This would take about ten minutes, during which time the angels are looking on with great interest. Now if I can release this pause button." Jay fiddles with his remote control, pointing it at the angels, and makes a big demonstration of punching a button.

The angels resume motion. Junior nods his head. "Not bad singing, I guess."

The senior angel puts his arm around the junior angel and says, "Like I said, it's an above-average group for human-types."

The junior angel starts speaking, wistfully at first, then with growing exasperation, "But you'd think they could do better than that if they could see the Holy One on the throne in all that radiant splendor, with the river of life flowing out from it and with the four living creatures at His side, with thousands and thousands of angels as far as the eye can see singing His glory with the multitudes."

The senior angel clamps his hand over the junior angel's mouth. "Whoa! Slow down, Junior. That's just the problem: They haven't seen anything yet. But not to worry. They will one day. Then," he smiles rapturously, "watch how they praise Him!"

The junior angel shakes his head and happens to point in your direction. From the platform, Junior says, "Yeah, that blond guy." He's pointing at Mike Kroupa, seated next to you. "When they were passing those plates back and forth, most of them were putting something in. But that blond guy was taking stuff out." Mike's face goes crimson.

With a shrug, the senior angel says, "I didn't say they were much above average."

Larry Walker moves to the front of the audience with a microphone. Junior asks, "What are they doing now?"

"They are reporting on some of the advances that the Kingdom of Light has made against the kingdom of darkness," the senior angel replies.

"Has anyone got a testimony about how God is on the move today?" Larry asks the audience.

Several hands shoot up. He holds the microphone to an excited woman in a red blouse, flowered skirt, and tennis shoes who says, "Recently two million have been brought to faith in Christ throughout Central America through a joint effort of Campus Crusade's *Jesus* film and CBN!"

Others share actual, up-to-the-minute breakthroughs:

"A young group of a thousand Puerto Ricans called 'Las Catacumbas' is mobilizing to reach Muslims!"

"Missionaries in Togo in West Africa saw one preaching point with about 400 worshipers grow in just five years to ten congregations of 4,000 believers!"

"More than 170 million are now praying every day for world evangelization!"

"There were 3,224 new house churches planted in Thailand in the last decade. The church in Laos has grown from 5,000 to 20,000 in just five years!"

"Whole states in India are claiming to be 95% Christian now! Nagaland and Mizoram believers are progressing in their goal to send out 3,000 new missionaries by the year 2000!"

Larry, puffing from rushing all over the auditorium, staggers back toward the front of the audience as the angels begin their next lines.

The junior angel wipes his brow. "Father is really on the move! Those are great snapshots—but I don't get the big picture."

The senior angel motions for him to be silent. "Shh! I think you will if you'll just be quiet a minute."

Larry speaks again: "Can anyone tell me the population of the world today?" In this ACMC audience, most know the correct answer, and several shout it out. Larry continues, "Right. Now we had planned on inviting all of them here today, but the local fire marshal was most uncooperative. So we decided that each of us here this evening would have to represent about 10 million people.

"Now, one out of every ten people in the world is an active Christian with a vital, reproducing relationship with Jesus Christ. So each of you with a sign under your seat that says 'Active Christian,' please stand." You paw under your chair to find a slip of paper that reads, "Buddhist." You whisper to Mike and Brenda, "What in the world—?"

There is a rustle as about a tenth of the crowd stands. They're all located in the right and center sections of the auditorium. "Notice how they're sprinkled throughout this part of the room," says Larry. "You may be seated. Could I have the 'Nominal Christians' stand up?" This time, in the right and center sections, about a fifth of the audience stands.

"Okay. For every one committed believer worldwide, there are two nominal Christians. Now how about the 'Non-Christians Within Reach of the Church'?" Again in the same right and center sections, a huge group comprising about 30% of the entire audience stands.

"For every one committed believer and every two nominal Christians in the world today, there are three non-Christians within reach of the Gospel. Thanks. Now those of you with the 'Hindu' sign, please stand. Now 'Buddhist' and 'Tribal.'" A large group stands in a new section on the left of the auditorium.

"Thank you. You may sit down. Now, would all of you with 'Muslim' signs please stand up?" The audience gasps as half of the left section stands as a group. Larry waits for the reaction to die down and says, "Muslims believe in Allah and Mohammed as his prophet. They believe in Jesus, but only as a prophet like Mohammed. Half of the billion Muslims of the world are under age sixteen, and they are trying to live 'good' lives so that their good works will outweigh their bad works on judgment day. Muslims, you may be seated. Now, for every one committed believer and two nominal believers and three non-Christians within reach of the Gospel, there are four non-Christians in cultures with no church movements at all. These unreached people groups are beyond the reach of normal evangelism."

You remark to the Kroupas that you knew there were plenty of cultures without indigenous church movements, but it is shocking to see this graphic illustration. Larry interrupts you from the front, "We are calling this part," pointing to the center and left sections where the Muslim, Buddhist, and Tribal representatives stood, "the 'unreached part' of the world for simplicity. Not only are these two-plus billion people unreached, they are currently beyond the reach of the Gospel.

"Would all the 'Active Christians' stand again please? Notice that you are sprinkled throughout the reached part of the world—we can easily get to most of the non-Christians. And notice that there are hardly any 'Active Christians' near the Muslims, Hindus, Buddhists, or Tribals. Some of the Christians will need to leave their own cultures to plant the Gospel in a different culture. Let's call them 'Ambassadors.'

"The ten of you with the 'Ambassador' signs come up here and be our work force." Ten people near you in the front row stand, and Larry turns them toward the audience. "Now, you have the world before you. Jesus has said to go into all the world and take the Gospel to all peoples. On the count of three I want you to go and stand by those peoples who most need to hear the Gospel. Ready? One, two, three, GO!"

The ten trot quickly to the center and left sections, which Larry designated as unreached peoples, spreading out among the Buddhists, Hindus, Tribals, and Muslims.

Larry smiles and says, "Isn't this wonderful?! Almost all of our ambassadors went to the 'unreached' part of the world. But you know, I need to make this picture accurate for you. I need most of you to go to the 'reached' part of the world. . . ." He continues moving "Ambassadors" until there is only one left in the "unreached" section, and the other nine are grouped in the "reached" areas near the bulk of Active Christians.

"Today, in reality," Larry continues, "nine out of every ten Christian workers who go cross-culturally go to the 'reached' part of the world. Yes, they go to cultures other than their own, but they go to cultures that already have strong church movements. Now, we're not saying that all of them need to come over to this 'unreached' side of the world. They are doing good work—many people still need to hear the Gospel in the 'reached' part of the world. But we do need to be praying that God would raise up a whole new army of laborers who will go to the remaining unreached peoples. Our challenge to you is to pray with us that the Lord of the Harvest will raise up laborers to go into His harvest fields.

"Thank you; you've been great, and we've saved the fire marshall a lot of grief." Larry sits down, and everyone's focus is drawn back to the stage as four actors take their place center stage. The angels resume their conversation.

"But why is it taking so long?" Junior angel demanded. "Two thousand years should have been plenty of time to get the job done."

The senior angel casts a sideways glance at the junior angel. He nods as if deciding something. "I don't usually make this part of the tour, but since you asked, remember the Fallen One?" He points to an actor walking up to the stage. He is dressed in a black suit, red tie, slicked back hair, and dark sunglasses. The actor then paces, wringing his hands evilly, looking out at the audience.

The senior angel continues, "Look way over there—you can see what was happening at his headquarters just a short time ago. Listen. . . ."

The angels freeze their positions as the lights dim and the spotlight falls on center stage. Satan stands stroking his chin. "Middle East," an actor dressed in white sweatpants, white sweatshirt, and a turban; and "Central Asia," an actress in a black skirt and purple blouse, face forward and at attention, awaiting Satan's summons.

In a raspy, harsh voice, Satan speaks: "Demon of the Middle East, your report!"

Middle East steps forward. "No problem, your unrighteousness," he says confidently.

"It had better be good," Satan warns.

Middle East smiles evilly. "What do you expect? Keeping the Gospel out of Iraq, Iran, Saudi Arabia, Kuwait, Oman, the Emirates—it's been a piece of cake!"

"Elaborate!" Satan growls.

Middle East cackles, circling around his master. "Through isolation and revivals of Islamic fundamentalism, I have been able to hold off our Enemy from my captives. The terror generated by a few zealots has caused those stupid Christians to hate my people—they'll never be concerned enough to send missionaries into my territory! Besides, they're too scared." Here Middle East hesitates and says quickly, "We have had a little opposition, however."

Satan is suddenly alert and concerned. Middle East, backing away, becomes mildly defensive. "But it is really nothing. I wouldn't want to bother you with such a small matter."

Satan glares but gestures for Middle East to continue.

Middle East starts slowly, "Well, somehow a handful of Christians became motivated to start praying. Each year now during the Muslim month of Ramadan, a few—actually, several million Christians—have started praying for Muslims. Then, here and there, a bit of subversive literature slipped past my censors. Now, a few Muslims have turned aside from our deception. But who are they among millions? Just a drop in the bucket!"

Satan fumes and fakes a slap across Middle East's face. "Enough, you blockhead!" he growls. "If only one missionary opens up your land to the Gospel, you're a failure." Satan turns to the actress, Central Asia. "Central Asia, report!"

With a bit of a swagger and a sneer toward Middle East, Central Asia approaches the evil one. "Well, sir," she hisses, "things are as stable as ever. Through the lies of the oppressive Soviet regime I so splendidly established, the Uzbeks, Kazakhs, Turkmen, Tajiks—well, all the peoples of my region—were well beyond the reach of any Christian witness. You see, Western Christians have fallen neatly into my trap: They think all these peoples were Russians! Hah! Pray for them? Hah—unthinkable! They don't even know these peoples exist. And the few German, Russian, and Korean Christians living there are scared to death to reach out to them. What a brilliant piece of work, don't you agree?"

Satan waves his hand, "Get on with it!"

Central Asia continues, "Well, my people are tightly sealed off. Their economies are in such a shambles they'll never listen to spiritual truth. No sir, no chance of them hearing the Gospel. Chief, it's going to take a lot of spiritual warfare to break through my forces. It's going to take thousands of hours of prayer—and that," she chuckles and dusts her hands in finality, "is an impossibility!"

Shaking, Satan yells, "Impossibility? Remember this: Nothing is impossible for Him if those Christians are fully His!"

Pouting a bit, Middle East steps up to the other two and cuts in, "Why all the pressure on us? These people don't even have a church in their culture. Why not come down on our colleagues' territories where our Enemy's gospel is spreading like wildfire?"

"Why am I so protective of your territories?" Satan sneers rhetorically, walking around his two emissaries. "It's true, the people under your jurisdiction have no church that can spread from within. Yet, there are prophecies that concern me. The worst one is this: 'This Gospel of the Kingdom will be preached in the whole world as a testimony to all nations, and then the end will come.' Therefore, our destruction will not come as long as your territories remain closed. Understand?"

Satan faces front and barks, "The West!"

A fourth actor jumps up from the second row of the audience, dressed in jeans and a black shirt. She runs up on stage to join the others.

"Ready to report, your wickedness!" she says crisply as she stands at attention beside Satan.

"The Church in the West—" he demands. "Have they learned to pray again?"

The West smiles evilly, extends her hands, and starts prancing about center stage. "I have them in the palm of my hand. I have convinced most of our Enemy's disciples that prayer is not the most important thing. They think it's a boring venture when compared with the fun activities that don't advance the Gospel. I have enticed them to chase after high-paying jobs for materialistic gain. Through their many possessions, I have lulled them to sleep into lives of comfort and complacency so that now many of them don't even know they are in the middle of a spiritual war! They think they're still on earth for their own benefit! Imagine! Because I have created a humanistic society that denies the supernatural, these puny Christians only give lip service to that awesome means of spiritual destruction—the Enemy's weapon of prayer. Oh, I let them play at prayer, but I never let them get their eyes or their prayers off themselves. So, you see, Mr. B., since I have done such a good job, these peons"—she motions to Middle East and Central Asia who are standing near the back of the platform sticking their tongues out at her—"should have free reign in their regions."

Satan nods his head and scratches his chin, scheming something. "Yes, yes. Good, good. Now who else has a good report? Southeast Asia, where's your report?"

At that, Satan and company freeze. The lights go up and the angels resume movement.

"Jumpin' Jehosaphat!" exclaims the junior angel. "So how does the story end?"

"The Book says that one day there will be some from every tongue and tribe and nation before the throne worshiping Father. Each people worshiping in their own unique way—Zulus leaping into the air to the pounding of festive drums, millions of deep Russian voices rolling across the plains like the very earth of Mother Russia."

The junior angel nods, then points at you in the audience: "And . . . and it will all be done through—? Through them?" He slaps a hand to his forehead.

"Quiet," the senior angel reprimands. "His ways are not our ways."

The junior angel asks, "But how soon will all this take place?"

We don't know exactly, but it could be very soon. It all depends . . ." the senior angel trails off.

The junior angel prompts him, "Yes?"

The senior angel pulls Junior close to him. "The Fallen One is very clever—and his lies are very beguiling. Lie Number One is this: Every human knows in his very bones that Father has created each of them to live in perfection with Him in the next life. But the Fallen One has bent that truth and made them believe that by constantly chasing after that perfection they can fill this life with it. So they squander their lives trying to protect themselves from hurt and pain, expecting their families or friends, their accomplishments or amusements to give them the significance and security that only Father can really give."

Junior has been looking at someone in the right section for some time while the senior angel was talking. Senior notices and pokes him, "Junior, I hope you are getting all this."

"Are you sure they can't see us?" Junior asks.

"Positive," Senior says.

Junior waves and then pulls at his cheeks, sticking his tongue out. Senior steps on Junior's foot and Junior responds with a muffled, "Ow! Whatever you say." He rubs his foot.

Senior continues, "Lie Number Two is equally insidious. For the remnant that get past Lie Number One, the Fallen One has this trap set and it's ready to be sprung. It's 'Guilt.' You see, Father wants His children to do everything they do out of grateful love, by His grace, bringing to Him all the honor and glory. Instead, when they hear the numbers or see the pictures of unsaved people, they feel guilty. So they give money instead of themselves. Of course many of them are guilty and they need to admit to Father that they have believed these lies, then accept His forgiveness and change—but then forget the guilt."

"Let them have it, I say!" Junior says, rolling his eyes.

Senior shakes his head. "No, no. That's not it at all. I feel sorry for them—the Bride is so close to being ready for the Groom. If they stop believing these lies, perhaps they could sense how near the Groom's appearance is. Well, there is one other thing to be done. They must begin to pray; they have not yet realized their power in prayer. In fact, the Fallen One fears this probably more than— Well, let's look in on him again. This is a mystery, but this may well be the scene at his head-quarters in the very near future—if the Bride begins to pray. Watch now."

As he says this, the lights dim. We see Satan spotlighted at center stage. He is pacing and nearly raving. Middle East, Central Asia, and The West are facing the back of the stage a few feet away from him, heads bowed.

Satan almost screams in his anger, "How can this be happening? My leaders said they were in control, and yet the Enemy is gaining! Where is everyone? I want your reports! Who will report first?"

No one answers.

"Well? Leader of Middle East, come forward! What is your report?"

Middle East turns in a military style and marches forward, not look-ing at his master. "Sir," he begins, "they finally discovered their most powerful weapon. The whole Church started praying for my region. A prayer here or there is no problem for me. But *someone* let 22 million pray in October '93, nearly 50 million in '95, more than—. Well, then they went crazy and began sending thousands of laborers. Thousands from Korea, from China, from Latin America, from Africa as well. We were powerless against the awesome force of the Enemy. First, my peo-ple the Kurds slipped from my grasp when they heard the Gospel from Christian relief workers after that Gulf War in '91. Then thousands of our captives began having dreams of—well, you know: dreams of the One Who died and rose again. Then all heaven broke loose, and some in Kuwait, tens of thousands in Egypt, and—now there are more than 12 million of those Christians in my territory—"

"Silence!" Satan screams. Middle East falls to the ground. "How could you let this happen? Don't you know what this means? Central Asia, report!"

Central Asia turns and marches forward, not looking at her master. "Well," she begins, "as you know, while my demons were spreading atheism, those Christians in both the East and the West were praying. Their prayers brought the downfall of communism. I was sure we had generations of atheists held captive. But suddenly, millions started praying. Then a great wave of missionaries flooded my territory. Tens of thousands from every corner of the globe! I don't know how it happened! Now my peoples are abandoning both Islam and communism to follow the Enemy. I don't know what to do! Soon, all my peoples will be history!"

Satan shouts at both of them, "How could you be so foolish? It is now only a matter of time before the Enemy Leader returns. Where is The West!"

The West turns around, bound and gagged, and, stumbling forward, she falls at Satan's feet.

Satan pulls his hair and screams in agony, "Aaggghh! They've bound us with their prayers!" He then crumbles to the floor. All the actors freeze as the house lights go up. The energy is felt all through the room and spontaneously the whole audience applauds—not so much for the actors as for the victory Jesus has over Satan and his minions!

After a few seconds, the junior angel breaks in, "Wow! But will this happen?"

"It all depends," says the senior angel, "on the churches, and the people that fill them."

"I think I understand," says Junior. "Very ordinary people, but empowered by Almighty Father."

With a smile and a pat on the shoulder, Senior says, "Junior, I think you're gonna make it after all." The audience chuckles and claps.

The junior angel points again at Mike Kroupa, next to you, saying, "Hey, why is that guy so nervous?"

"Well," says the senior angel, looking at his watch, "it's fifty minutes into the Sunday service and the pastor hasn't even started his sermon."

Amid the laughter, Jay moves back up onto the stage as the actors exit to their seats in the audience. Jay explains, "At this point the pastor steps down to wrap up and to invite the congregation to think afresh about aligning their lives with God's purpose for all of history. Then he gives the benediction and they are on their way. And we'll let you be on your way as well. Thank you!"

The audience bursts into applause again. You nod as you stand and stretch. "That's the killer passage," you say.

"What is?" Mike and Brenda Kroupa ask.

" 'And this Gospel of the Kingdom shall be proclaimed in all the world as a testimony to the nations.' "

" 'And then the end shall come,' " Brenda adds.

## The Big Picture Basics

God intends for us to read His Word as one book, with one introduction, one story, and one conclusion. The heart of the story is God's
desire to bless us that we might be a blessing to every distinct ethnic
group on the earth, all in order to bring our Father the greatest glory
humankind could give Him. This basic concept is the foundation of all
we do as believers. (If that idea is still hazy to you, then studying *Destination 2000, Unveiled at Last, Catch the Vision 2000*, or the *Perspectives
on the World Christian Movement* course will get you up to speed. See
Materials and Courses under Resources in the back of the book for how
to connect with these materials.)

With that in mind, we'll need to clarify three points to be sure we
track together on the rest of our story.

### 1. It's Time for People-Group Thinking.

The biblical pattern is that God works in individuals within "people
groups"—nations, peoples, or gentiles in biblical terminology—groups
that refer to themselves as "us" and other groups as "them." God's promise to bless His people with redemption in Jesus Christ—and then
through them to bless every people—is the unifying theme of all Scripture (see Psalm 67).

What is usually referred to as Jesus' Great Commission command
states plainly that we are to go and "make disciples of all the nations"
(Matthew 28:18–20). The word "nation" in the original Greek is
*ethne*—the term from which we get the English "ethnic." The day of
viewing the world as a mix of *politically* defined countries is over. It's
time to look at the world as the Bible does, in terms of people groups.

(You can do your own quick-study of "the nations" in Scripture by
looking at the following: Genesis 3:15; 12:1–3; 18:18; 22:17–18; 26:4
and 28:14; 2 Chronicles 6:32–33; Psalm 67:1–2, 7; Malachi 1:11; Luke
2:29–32 and 24:45–47; Matthew 24:14 and 28:19; Romans 1:5; and
Revelation 5:9).

It is estimated that there are about 24,000 nations or peoples on
the planet today. In the past decade, unnecessary confusion about the
big-picture mission of the Church arose because of confusing definitions of the peoples, nations, or *ethne* we are called to disciple. Some
suggested that taxi drivers in Boise were a people group; others thought
the upper-class in Buenos Aires were a group.

Much depends on how a people group is defined. For example, in
the 1993 edition of *Operation World*, a tremendous window on the
world, editor Patrick Johnstone states that India has 482 people

groups. The Institute of Hindu Studies in Pasadena, California, states that there are 2,759. The Anthropological Society of India, after seven years of the most exhaustive people-group research ever done in any country, insists there are 2,795 different people groups in India.

A basic definition that fits the pragmatic needs of most World Christians includes the following from Mission Frontiers:

> A significantly large ethnic or sociological grouping of individuals who perceive themselves to have a common affinity for one another. For evangelistic purposes, it is the largest group within which the Gospel can spread as a church-planting movement without encountering barriers of understanding or acceptance.

A simpler lay-level definition might be one promoted by the Adopt-A-People Clearinghouse:

> A people group is a unit of people that can be identified by a proper name and a location.

That is, although Brisbane teenagers are a category of a population, they are not called a name, not identified by a proper noun. The Dai of southern China and the Bugis of Indonesia (whose piracy inspired tales of the "bogeyman") are obviously distinct ethne.

An emphasis on the biblical concept of people-group thinking affects even our prayer lives. Remember to pray for the peoples or nations within the political countries of our world. For example, when you pray for Latin America, you can pray for the Arabs and Turks in Honduras, the Pakistani Muslims in Guatemala, the Javanese in Surinam, the Urdu from Bihar, India in Belize, and the Palestinians in Uruguay!

A "discipled" ethne has a strong enough church to evangelize its own people. But there are thousands of people groups without a church— the remaining "unreached peoples," or, as some put it, "least-reached peoples." The offer of Christ's redemption is yet to be shared with about 2,400 clusters of cultures comprising perhaps 10,000 distinct peoples, each having no church movement within them.[1]

An official definition of what makes a people group "unreached" is this:

> A people group is unreached if there is no indigenous community of believing Christians with adequate numbers and resources to evangelize their people group without requiring outside (cross-cultural) assistance. In other words a people group is considered "reached" if it has a viable, indigenous, self-reproducing church

movement in its midst. This means a reached people group has strong churches pastored by their own people using their own language, and these churches are actively evangelizing their people and planting daughter churches.

In very general terms, these unreached people groups are characterized by at least one of the following. An unreached people is one that

1. has not been presented the Gospel message and/or
2. does not have God's Word in their heart language and/or
3. does not have access to God's Word—perhaps because of illiteracy and/or
4. has not responded to the Gospel.[2]

Currently Wycliffe Bible Translators, Campus Crusade for Christ, and the Southern Baptist denomination are surveying the entire globe to pinpoint the remaining unreached peoples. These extensive surveys will determine from on-field research the accuracy of the present lists of unreached peoples.

Regardless of the exact number of remaining unreached groups, Patrick Johnstone of WEC estimates that of all the people groups on the face of the earth, possibly only 500 have absolutely no laborers at all in their culture beginning to reach out to them.

Does the growing interest in and focus on unreached peoples mean we believers can neglect the ministries going on and needing to go on within our churches, or within our own cultures, or in people groups that already have churches? May it never be so! In Chapter 5 we'll be thinking through the exciting implications of using the unreached peoples concept to focus and integrate a fellowship's vision of the overall mission of the Church! The end goal of all we do in a local church body, whether we work with children in the nursery or run a youth program, should somehow help result in seeing the nations—reached and as yet unreached—brought into the glory of our Father!

## 2. It's Time for a Closure Mentality.

For decades much of Western Christianity has preached a very personal Gospel. And that emphasis is, of course, biblical: God deals with us One-on-one. But leaving the growth of discipleship to an I'm-the-center-of-the-universe perspective is anything but biblical. It's easy to get lost in the blessings and lose sight of God's purpose for us in reaching our neighbors and the nations. Like the disciples who began following Jesus, we are intent on our next personal step. As Jesus' disciples plodded behind Him through the fields, they—as any farm-bred hiker does—watched their feet to make sure where they were stepping as they followed Jesus. Yet Jesus turned to them and said, "Lift up your eyes!" (John 4:35). When they did, they saw fields ripe and white for harvest.

What happens when we plunge into the harvest?

In Matthew 28 Jesus tells us that while we are going, we are to "disciple." This idea of discipling the nations is crystallized as He tells us to "baptize" them (place them into the Name, identifying with Him in salvation) and to teach them everything He has commanded us. When we do this, churches are born.

In other words, Christ was telling us to go to every distinct ethnic group on the face of the earth and start a church. He wants everyone to have an equal opportunity to know Him. From your neighborhood to the ends of the earth and everywhere in between, Jesus Christ is building His Church. The only question is: Where do you fit in?

But here's the point: One day He'll finish the task.

Any biblical worldview has to grapple with that awesome concept: The Great Commission of discipling the nations is to be *finished*. This "closure" idea can inspire distracted or unfocused believers into surprising action. It can also spur zealous disciples into spouting wild predictions about when exactly the job will be finished—perhaps by A.D. 2000? By the lyrical year of 2020?

But as we approach the end of the twentieth century most of us are already weary of date-setters. When Jesus said that no one would know the day, the hour, the times, or the epochs of the Father's timetable (Acts 1:7), He put His authoritative stamp of "False Prophet" on anyone who claims to know when the Age of the Church will be completed.

Nevertheless, this age *will* come to a close. And we are not simply twiddling our thumbs waiting, doing evangelism, discipleship, and cross-cultural ministry to kill time until Christ comes. All that we do is a distinct step toward the cosmic purpose of history.

### 3. It's Time for Strategic Action.

You noticed in the play that the enemy rages, knowing his time is short. In the specific countdown of God's global plan, in the light of closure, believers must move only in the directions God is going. Now is a time when the good is especially the enemy of the best. We can't afford to spend resources on nice but nonessential ideas or efforts. It's time for solid, careful prayer that will bind the enemy. It's time for unity, for obedience in purity, for researching and understanding more about our harvest field. It's time for each of us to fulfill our personal strategic role.

## Gripped by the Unexpected

With these basics in mind, let's take a closer look at where we're walking as we wade into this immense harvest field. We're entering a world of the unexpected.

Your average day within your own culture, for example, might not have been like that of a Campus Crusade for Christ film team in northern India:

In a staunchly Islamic village in late 1993, the only Christian died and was buried on the cemetery hill overlooking the town. That night, every person in the village saw a male stranger who was weeping walk down the hill from the cemetery to their houses. The figure came closer and closer until everyone saw his face.

The next evening, the *Jesus* film team rolled into town, set up their projector, and propped a screen against the side of their van. As they tested the equipment, they found nothing worked—a fairly common occurrence for these film teams who are pushing back Satan's territory throughout India. After checking everything, they could only pray—during which they sensed the serious spiritual battles roiling through the air of this simple, nondescript village.

The projector kicked into action, and the *Jesus* film based on the book of Luke began. Villagers came from every house to sit and watch in silence. Through the beginning scenes of the film, the villagers seemed distracted, disinterested. Then the scene of Jesus' baptism showed for the first time the actor's face as Jesus came up out of the water.

Villagers screamed, grabbed each other, and pointed to the face of the British actor who portrays Jesus. "That's him!" they shouted. "That's the face of the one who came from the grave!"

The entire village committed themselves to Jesus Christ.

Not a typical occurrence in our neighborhood? Probably not. But even we can get prepared to be surprised and sometimes shocked out of our business-as-usual lives by the God who is calling the nations of the world to himself.

But what does today's world look like?

## CHAPTER THREE

# Discipling What Nations?

## Our harvest field

"Millions of new names can be added to the Lamb's Book of Life as we take advantage of the incredible opportunities for evangelism that lie before us. Together, working in partnership with the Holy Spirit, we can add hundreds of new pages to the Lamb's Book of Life!"

—Dick Eastman

SOMEWHERE IN THE AMAZON — It's midday, but you can't see the sun above the canopy of foliage a hundred feet above you. You're almost panting as the Jeep under you bucks like a wild horse along the track. "It must be the . . . ah . . . heat or something. Can we stop for a break?" you ask. The muffler is broken, and your head rings with the roar of the Jeep.

The tall man in the driver's seat nods and pulls to a stop. He revs the engine and switches off the ignition to the palpable silence of the jungle. He steps off to the side of the four-foot-wide muck he's been calling the road. "It's your jet-lag. Don't worry about it. The heat takes it out of you, too. Let me check you for bugs."

It's probably about 100° F. and 99% humidity in the dripping forest of the central Amazon Basin. You swing your daypack off your shoulders and wish there were a dry place to sit—other than that board seat in the back of the Jeep. You notice your host smiling as he lifts your arms, pulls your khaki collar away to check your neck. Your skin crawls at the prospect of insects burrowing into your skin within a matter of minutes. Your smile probably looks more like a grimace. "Just a breather, all right?" you beg. "My kidneys feel like they've been worked over by Muhammad Ali."

Maybe with the ulterior motive of prolonging your rest break, you ask, "Now, I heard some of the story from your students; but what really happened in this village?"

"What did the students say?" He stretches. You thought missionaries no longer took on the "Indiana Jones" look, but South African Donald Richards looks exactly the part. All he needs is a whip.

You mop your forehead with a sweaty bandanna. "Well, a couple of them said they were riding on a bus after your training session at the school, and a wealthy landowner's personal secretary overheard them talking about ecological principles in caring for the rain forest environment. Then she set up a meeting with the landowner for you."

"Yes," he says. "We met, and we couldn't believe it when he donated 40,000 hectares—a hectare is about two and a half acres. He gave us 20,000 at the north end of his property—which covers about 160,000 hectares—and another 20,000 at the south end. He wants us to maintain these areas. They'll be sort of buffer zones around his property in the middle, keeping development damage to a minimum in the whole area."

Donald Richards is, you think to yourself as perspiration drips into your eyes, warming to the story.

He continues: "So as we started doing some quick fact-finding about the area, we found the government knew of at least two tribal groups in the sections donated to us. No one had ever been granted permission to enter these areas or contact these groups. So of course as we began planning our ecological strategies for the area, we began praying and planning for contact with these unreached people groups!"

"They told me the story of when you got to the village," you say, stretching your rest break. "But I'd like to hear your version."

Donald's face lights with joy. He pulls off his Indiana Jones hat and wipes his hair. "Three of us took this trek, not sure where we were heading. All the aerial maps showed nothing; but we knew there was a tribal group here somewhere." He points up the muddy rut. "After five hours and 27 rivers crossed, it was pitch dark as we drove into the village of the cabana-type huts of the Karitiana. Several of them had been out to trading posts, so a few of them knew some Portuguese. But we were the first outsiders they had seen in ten years.

"We finally understood they were having some kind of gathering in large huts made of mud bricks. All the other huts were of palm branch. Near the door there was fish roasting over a fire, with the smoke wafting inside. Several of them insisted we enter. With no idea what we were getting into, we ducked inside. There were candles made of gum flickering everywhere, shining off the faces of about 30 or 40 men, women, and kids.

"A man sitting in the center spoke in Portuguese and said he would stop what they were doing to tell us a story. So the three of us squeezed in and sat on the ground. 'This is where we celebrate Jesus,' the man said. I know my jaw dropped and my eyes must have bugged out. I asked him to repeat it, and he told me in rough Portuguese that these 35 Karitiana were following Jesus."

At this point Donald plops his hat back on and raises his eyebrows to ask if you're finally ready to get the Jeep back in gear. "We'd better be bumping along if we're going to make it before dark. And we don't want to be out here in the dark." You wearily climb back in. He fires the machine into its growl and yells back over his shoulder as he wrestles the steering wheel: "So he stood in the hut and gave us what amounted to a testimony. He said it was almost a year ago that he had a vision. He said Jesus came to him and took him to heaven. Somehow he knew who it was—Jesus—and knew he was seeing heaven.

"It was beautiful, filled with more people than he had ever seen. But he didn't see many Indians, and didn't see any Karitiana. So he asked Jesus why. And he says Jesus told him, 'Because you are serving demons, not Me.' And then Jesus asked him his name, and he said, 'Francisco.' Then Jesus said, 'No, that is what you are called in Portuguese. What is your Karitiana name?' He replied, 'Rual.' Jesus said, 'I made you a Karitiana. You are worthy of the Karitiana. I made you a nation, and I want you to worship Me as Karitiana.' And immediately he's back in his hut."

"Wow," you say, goosebumps on your arms even in the steaming Amazon.

"So," yells Donald as you bounce on the board-back seat, "Rual has spent the last year telling everyone in the tribe what happened and what Jesus said. And so far 35 of them have quit worshiping spirits to follow Jesus. There are only 156 Karitiana. But there's going to be a good showing of them percentage-wise around the throne of the Lamb, eh? Must be the 'fullness of time' for the discipling of this little nation!"

## Looking Over the World

God is using ordinary people to build His Church, even in tiny people groups today. Before we look at how God may want to use you in the expansion of His Kingdom, we need to get a glimpse of the state of the world. With that knowledge in hand, then—and only then—can you better determine where God may want you. As Proverbs puts it,

What a shame—yes, how stupid!—to decide before knowing the facts (Proverbs 18:13, TLB).

With this in mind, let's review some of the "Global ABCs." There is an easy-to-remember categorization of the harvest field used by many researchers and mission agencies:

*World C:* The 10% of committed Christians and 20% of nominal Christians on the planet constitute "World C."

*World B:* The 30% of the global population who are non-Christians living in cultures that have churches are "World B."

*World A:* The 40% of the world that make up the populations of unreached peoples are termed "World A."

The people of World A reside mostly in a rectangular-shaped box stretching from West Africa to the eastern edge of Asia between the ten- and forty-degree north latitudes. Luis Bush, international director of the AD2000 and Beyond Movement calls this area "The 10/40 Window."

Some points to note:

1. More than 95% of the world's unreached peoples live in this area.
2. The 10/40 Window outlines the heartlands of the major non-

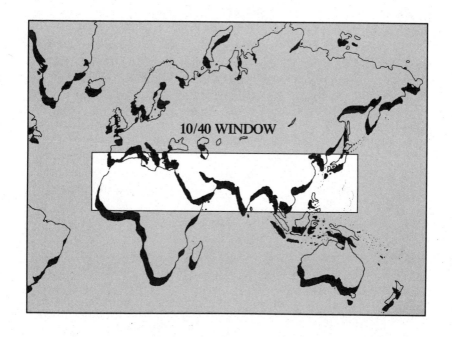

Christian religions of the world—Islam, Hinduism, Buddhism, Shintoism, Confucianism, etc.

3. About 80% of the poorest of the world's poor live in this region, enduring humanity's lowest standards of living. (The 10/40 Window booklet)

Lloyd Carpenter, a video producer based in Pasadena, California, suggests that we can get a good mental image of the spiritual bondage of the people groups within the 10/40 Window from examining any map of the floors of the world's oceans. An unsettling dragonlike shape enwraps this region of the globe. The configuration of the ocean floor along the east coast and horn of Africa appears like the snarling head of the dragon clenching its teeth around Madagascar. "Wings" along the back of the serpent jut up into the Arabian Sea and the Bay of Bengal.

And the back and tail seem to wrap around Southeast Asia and up along the east coast of China. The image, of course, is nothing so well defined as to be biblically symbolic—but it does imprint in the mind the fact that the old serpent—the devil—has a diabolical grip on the peoples of the 10/40 Window!

Whether we categorize the harvest field into Worlds A, B, and C, or into the peoples inside and outside the 10/40 window, or into the reached and unreached peoples, or the "saved" and the "lost," the impression is the same: There is much to be done. The harvest is ripe. And the harvest is vast.

While we don't want to overgeneralize, this huge harvest field breaks rather easily into basic cultural blocs. Looking at those blocs is one way to edge away from our ingrained tendency to think of the harvest field in terms of geographical countries and to remember the real "fields" are people—migrating, increasing, dying, splintering, or combining.

Researchers suggest categorizing the world's unreached peoples into twelve "affinity groups": Turkic/Altaic; Tibeto-Burman; Jewish; Indian/Dravidian; Arab/Berber; Cauczsus/Slavic; Iranian/Kurdish; Chinese/East Asian; Thai/Southeast Asian; Malay; Ethiopian/Cushitic; and Sahel African.

A more lay-level breakdown of these groups comprises five major blocs of unreached peoples. These include four religious groups—Muslim, Tribal-Animistic, Hindu, and Buddhist—and one geo-political group—the Chinese. You can easily remember these five groups by using the acronym THUMB. "T" for tribal, "H" for Hindu, "U" (turned sideways to make a "C"—we had to push that one!) for Chinese, "M" for Muslim, and "B" for Buddhist. Remember, though, that there are other huge blocs of peoples that fit none of these categories.

In each area below we have suggested material for additional reading. One book you will find especially helpful in understanding your world is *The Compact Guide to World Religions*, by Dean Halverson of International Students Incorporated (Bethany House Publishers,1996). Each chapter of the book was originally designed for use by host families of international students. Easy-to-use sections discuss each religion's origins, basic beliefs, and evangelistic obstacles and opportunities.

So put on your "Comparative World Religions" mortarboard and let's run through an overview of each major bloc. Which tugs most at your heart?

## Muslim Unreached Peoples

One night, in the year A.D. 610, a vision came to Muhammad: "O Muhammad, thou art the Messenger of God." Thus the religion of Islam was born.

The word "Islam" means "submission," and "Muslim" means "one who is submitted to God (Allah)." To be a Muslim, one must say with conviction at some point in his life the creed "There is no God but God, and Muhammad is his Prophet." Upholding the five "pillars of Islam" is also expected. These are:

1. Recite the creed.
2. Pray five times daily at specified times.
3. Fast for the lunar month of Ramadan. (The fast includes abstaining from food and drink during the day. After sundown one is able to eat and drink.)
4. Give alms. (Alms constitute 2.5% of one's income and are given for the upkeep of the mosque and to help the needy.)
5. Make the *hajj*, the holy pilgrimage to the city of Mecca in Saudi Arabia, at least once in one's life. (The more times one makes the *hajj*, the more spiritual he is considered.)

A sixth pillar to some Muslims is the *jihad*, or "holy war." When a Muslim dies in a declared holy war, he automatically enters heaven.

Muslims consider their religion to be an extension of Christianity and Judaism, but they believe the Christian Trinity to be blasphemous and they deny the deity of Jesus. Although the Qur'an instructs Muslims to "listen to the people of the Book," (referring to the Bible), Muslims believe that Christians have corrupted the Holy *Injil* (the Gospels of the New Testament), so the Bible today is not accurate.

In more conservative Islam, women have few if any rights and are little better than slaves. "Heaven" for the Muslim man is a place of virgins—as many as he wants, when he wants them. The Muslim man is allowed up to four wives, but he must be able to provide equally for them. In liberal areas of Islam, the woman is allowed more freedom and many have adopted more Western dress without head-covering—a shameful thing to conservative Muslims.

Whenever a crowd of Western Christians is asked whether they've heard that Islam is the fastest-growing religion in the world, hands shoot up to acknowledge this awareness. It is true that Islam is the fastest-growing major religion in the world, growing at 2.9% annually—beating Christianity as a whole, whose growth is 2.3% Yet if we were to break down Christianity into various "groups," the evangelicals and Pentecostals are the fastest-growing major religious grouping in the world—evangelicals growing at 5.4% and Pentecostals at 8.1% annually.[1]

Although Islam is a growing religion, a high birthrate among Muslims is responsible for most of the growth. Nevertheless, says Chicago-area writer Deb Conklin, Islam is claiming many new converts because:

1. *Islam is an uncomplicated religion.* The only thing one needs to do to convert to Islam is to wholeheartedly recite the creed. There are only six major doctrines: belief in one God; in angels; in the Holy Books—including parts of both Testaments as well as the Qur'an; in the prophets—among whom are Jesus and Muhammad; in a day of judgment; and in predestination. The five practices (pillars) of Islam are external and equally simple to learn.

2. *Islam is an adaptable religion.* It has contextualized itself into hundreds of cultures. Since there is nothing in Islam contradicting the existence of a spirit world, it easily absorbs the animistic worldviews and practices of peoples to whom it is brought. In fact, even today, the vast majority of Muslims embrace such "folk Islam."

3. *Islam is a zealously "evangelistic" religion.* The purpose of Muslims is to win the Western world to Islam. If you think that can't happen, think again. Some areas evangelized by Paul are now firmly under the sway of Islam. So are the cities of Istanbul (once Constantinople) and Alexandria, both once thriving centers of Christianity.[2]

One out of every five persons living on the earth is a Muslim. Perhaps more significantly, about 35% of all unreached people groups are dominantly Muslim.

With evangelistic zeal backed by oil dollars, Muslims are willing to go anywhere and spend whatever it takes to win the world to Islam. In

# Growth Rate
# of the World's
# Religious Blocs

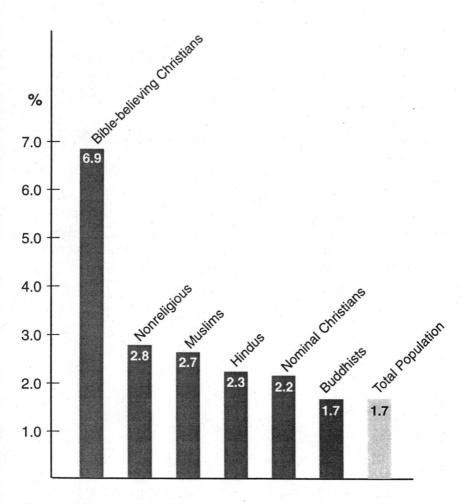

Source: Global Evangelization Movement Database, 1990.

North Africa, the governments of Muslim countries in one recent year spent more to promote missionary activity in eight North African countries than the total Western missionary expenditure for the entire world. In countries with a Christian population, plans are to exterminate Christianity.

Most Muslims are taught several misconceptions about Christianity, including:

- God is one. Therefore, how can Christians say Jesus is also God? To a Muslim, Jesus (*Isa* in the Qur'an, pronounced "Ee-sah") is an honored prophet. The Qur'an teaches that Jesus was born of a virgin, performed miracles, and will come again.

- How can Christians say Jesus is the Son of God? If God has a son, who is His wife? It seems to the Muslim that Christians worship several gods, a very pagan practice. Muslims are often taught that Christians believe in a "trinity" of God the Father, God the Son, and the Virgin Mary!

- Would God allow His faithful prophet Jesus to die on a cross like a common criminal? The Qur'an states that God rescued Jesus and took Him to heaven, substituting a look-alike on the cross.

- Because of the seemingly pagan beliefs and the worldly lifestyle of so many Christians, Muslims feel that Christians have fallen for a corrupted Gospel, distorted from the true, original Gospel of Jesus.

- To the Muslim, Western "Christian" cultures represent Christianity; and the representation is obviously not godly. Yet the Qur'an advises to respect the "People of the Book"—Jews and Christians.

Keep in mind that although the basics of this religion can be sketched out, Islam itself can vary greatly from culture to culture. Islam in Southeast Asia is much more animistic. Islam in the Commonwealth of Independent States is much more nominal. Muslims in the Saudi Peninsula are much more fundamental.

As a result, the means of evangelism to reach Muslims in each of these places can vary. When these Muslims get outside of their own homeland, giving them the Good News will vary even more!

To best learn how to approach Muslims, we recommend the following training programs and books:

*Books:*

C. R. Marsh, *Sharing Your Faith With a Muslim* (Moody Press).
Phil Parshall, *New Paths in Muslim Evangelism* (Baker Book House).

Phil Parshall, *The Cross and the Crescent: Understanding the Muslim Mind and Heart* (Tyndale House Publishers, Inc.).

Phil Parshall, *Beyond the Mosque: Christians Within Muslim Community* (Baker Book House).

Martin Goldsmith, *Islam and Christian Witness* (Hodder and Stoughton).

Bill Musk, *The Unseen Face of Islam: Sharing the Gospel with Ordinary Muslims* (MARC).

Dudley Woodbury, *Muslims and Christians on the Emmaus Road* (MARC).

William J. Saal, *Reaching Muslims for Christ* (Moody).

*Seminars:*

Don McCurry "Reaching Our Muslim Neighbors" (Weekend seminar)

Zwemer Institute on Muslim Studies Summer Training Courses:
Introduction to Islam
Muslim Evangelism
Church Planting in the Muslim Context
Folk Islam

International Mission Incorporated (IMI) Four-week Summer Training Outreach Program (STOP)

Arab World Ministries Summer Training Program

FRONTIERS Seminar: Muslims: The Final Frontier

# Tribal Unreached Peoples

Depending on how a researcher defines "people group," there are from 3,000 to 6,000 unreached groups of Tribals worldwide. They are found in places you would expect, such as Irian Jaya, Papua New Guinea, the Amazon Basin, and in parts of the African continent. But they are also found in virtually every country of the world, according to Dave Sitton, director of the Institute of Tribal Studies, headquartered in Los Fresnos, Texas. Most of the world's 2,000,000 nomads are actually tribals.

Dave points out: "The great mystery of life for tribal clans is: How can we control the spirits? Fear keeps tribal peoples in bondage and usually very resistant to the Gospel." It's obvious from the frowns and grunts of the shaman or witch doctor or holy man that most spirits are evil and unpredictable. They must be appeased. Carefully appeased.[3]

Many of the world's tribal peoples mix in more institutionalized religions to add power to their spirit worship. Tribes syncretize their animism with Islam, Buddhism, and Christianity—often emphasizing the rituals of Roman Catholicism.

How can tribal unreached peoples be approached?

The typical remoteness of tribal groups enforces their distrust of outsiders. Fear of unknown spirits inhibits their exploration of new territories as well as new ideas. But often the toughest problem missionaries to tribals must overcome is "cargoism"—the appeal of outsiders', particularly white men's, gadgets and wealth.

Dave says, "It is important that missionaries understand this hidden agenda when working with tribals. So often their intense interest stems from their hope that finally the mystery of material goods and how to get them will be expounded for them. Sometimes when tribals get excited about the Good News that missionaries bring, it is misunderstood to mean the good news of how to get material wealth. Before long, the people become disillusioned."[4]

In order to find out more about the Tribal peoples of the world, check out the following resources:

Don Richardson, *Peace Child* (Regal Books/Gospel, 1974).

Don Richardson, *Lords of the Earth* (Regal Books/Gospel, 1977).

Don Richardson, *Eternity in Their Hearts* (Regal Books/Gospel, 1981).

John Dekker with Lois Neely, *Torches of Joy: The Dynamic Story of a Stone Age Tribe's Encounter with the Gospel* (Seattle, Wash.: Youth With A Mission Publishing, 1993).

Elisabeth Elliot, *Through Gates of Splendor* (Harper, 1957).

Elisabeth Elliot, *The Savage My Kinsman* (Ann Arbor, Mich.: Servant Books, 1961).

Elisabeth Elliot, *Shadow of the Almighty: The Life and Testament of Jim Elliot* (Harper Collins, 1989).

Mary Beth Lagerborg, *Incessant Drumbeat* (Christian Literature Crusade).

Hugh Steven, *Candle in the Night*—Solomon Islands (Credo Publishing Corp., Canada, 1990).

Isobel Kuhn, *In the Arena*—Lisu of China/Burma, (Overseas Missionary Fellowship).

Isobel Kuhn, *Nests Above the Abyss*—Lisu of China/Burma, (Overseas Missionary Fellowship).

Isobel Kuhn, *Stories of Fire*—Lisu of China/Burma, (Overseas Missionary Fellowship).

Isobel Kuhn, *Green Leaf in Drought*—Lisu of China/Burma, (Overseas Missionary Fellowship).

## Hindu Unreached Peoples

Hinduism is nearly impossible to explain simply since it is actually a conglomeration of ideas, practices, beliefs, and convictions. Hinduism is therefore often puzzling to Westerners; it revolves around a totally different center than does Christianity, asking fundamentally different questions and supplying different answers:

1. *As a philosophy,* Hinduism states: There is a spark of divinity in every human. To call a human a sinner, then, is virtually blasphemy. And there is, of course, no need of a Savior. The writing of Vivekananda says, "It is sin to call anyone a sinner." Good and evil are only illusions. And illusions are dispelled by knowledge. "Salvation," then, is being freed from ignorance, not from our sense of biblical sin. Probably a typical Hindu definition of *sin* would be "causing grief."

Each soul—a "drop of God"—is reborn over and over in higher or lower incarnations of humans, animals, or vegetables according to that soul's *karma.* Karma is the sum of a person's good deeds. These deeds are in a ceremonial sense, not so much in the Western sense of moral good deeds. These good deeds accumulate to allow a person to reincarnate to a higher position in life—for example from a woman to a man—while bad deeds demand a person become a lower form in the next life cycle.

2. *As a world religion,* Hinduism teaches that people are free to choose their own god from among about 330 million. Ultimate salvation is gained through (1) the way of knowledge, (2) the way of devotion, or (3) the way of good ways. This salvation is a release (*Moksha*) of the soul from the cycle of rebirth to reunite with the Absolute—as a drop of water falls into the ocean.

3. *As a popular religion,* Hindus believe that Hinduism is a mixture of ancestral tradition, animal worship, temple cults, magic, exorcism, astrology, and the teachings of gurus (*avatars* or incarnations of gods). General beliefs include: regard of the cow as a goddess; the material world is just an illusion; the world is growing progressively worse; the old is better than the new; and what will be will be regardless of man's efforts to promote or hinder it.

The West has seen a glimpse of Hindu philosophy in many New Age Movement teachings, in the Transcendental Meditation practices of Mahesh Yogi, and in the Hare Krishna converts asking for donations in airports. These mostly negative impressions unfortunately color

Western perceptions of the individuals caught in Hinduism—individuals whose relentless quest for peace (*shanti*) can be God's way of bringing them to himself. Yet most Hindus have no access to the true Gospel; all they know of Christianity is what they have seen in the lives of "Christians."

Dr. Ambedkar, an Indian Hindu, once said, "When I read the Gospels I find there an antidote for the poison Hinduism has injected into our souls. But when I look at the Christians I know, I find they are taken up with seeking their own self-interest and have no concern for their own people." The famous Mahatma Ghandi once said he would embrace Jesus Christ but not Christianity—because of Christians.

In the third century B.C. the Aryans from Central Asia migrated to what is now India. Their search for God resulted in the writings called the Vedas. The Aryan religion evolved into Hinduism, which through the centuries has absorbed virtually all the local religions of the Indian subcontinent.

Today nearly 24% of Asia's three billion people are Hindus. Most live in India, Nepal, and Bali in Indonesia, with large numbers in Bhutan, Fiji, Mauritius, and Suriname and Guyana in South America.

Indian Christians claim that the apostle Thomas brought Christianity to India in the first century. In the sixteenth century, Catholic missionaries such as Francis Xavier and Robert de Nobili—followed by a flood of Protestant missionaries—brought the Gospel to Hindus. These efforts found wide receptivity among the lowest castes of Hinduism. So Christianity came to be known as a religion of outcastes and, during the colonialism of the nineteenth century, the religion of the foreign colonial powers of Europe. Although missionary visas are no longer available to foreigners in India, amazing evangelism and mission efforts are taking place among indigenous ministries.

To the Hindu, God is not personal: "It moves. It moves not. It is far and it is near. It is within all this and it is without all this" is a common statement about the god-force of the universe called Brahma. God—the Absolute—neither loves nor hates human beings, neither helps nor hinders them.

God is to be worshiped in the forms one's ancestors worshiped—in the forms of trees, animals, images, persons, and millions of gods. Two gods are prominent: Vishnu, preserver of the world, and Shiva, the destroyer. Vishnu is usually worshiped through one of his incarnations—Rama or Krishna. Many Hindus live in deep fear that they will invoke the wrath of the *Kula Devata*—the family god—on themselves and their families if they become too interested in Jesus Christ.

Hinduism generally fosters a sense of despair and pessimism, since it is never clear whether one is offending some god, or whether one is effectively progressing or falling behind in the pursuit of salvation. Poverty also easily pervades a Hindu community, since, to the Hindu, holiness and affluence are incompatible. Also, the sacredness of all forms of life—since ancestors may have reincarnated into animals—paradoxically fosters poverty. In India, for example, 30% of each year's grain crop is destroyed by rats, which must be allowed to live, and the sacred cattle that wander the streets of India could feed the entire country for five years if used for food.

As in most world religions, Hinduism is as much a culture as it is a religion. In the Hindu family, women are traditionally the custodians of Hindu rituals and values.

Humans are born into four castes, which have their own social place and occupation. To fulfill that occupation is righteousness. Outcastes are not Hindus. Right actions for an individual are sanctioned by the caste. Generally, the individual is subordinate to the group—such as, in the family a grown man always defers to his family elders.

Hinduism, with its caste system, is a form of social security—everyone knows where they belong. With Christianity's insistence on abolishing the caste distinctions, Hindu converts would lose their standing in society—their privileges, employment, and wealth. Hindu students who convert to Christianity regularly lose their government-sponsored financial aid. Conversion to Christianity often leads to excommunication from the community, damage to the entire family's reputation, termination of marital prospects, and even physical persecution. A recent poll suggested that fully 20% of Hindus would consider becoming followers of Jesus Christ if they didn't have to be cut off from their families and their society in order to do so.

Hindus in general are very open to all sorts of new religious ideas. In Hinduism, all roads lead to God, so all religions are basically good. Generally, any form of worship is right if one's ancestors or one's caste have practiced it. Hindus will often "accept" Jesus as one of their many gods. Because of this eclectic acceptance of all gods, it is difficult to reach out to Hindus. They may readily bow in prayer to receive Christ into their life, but they are simply adding "one more god" to be worshiped. To find out more about reaching Hindus, we suggest you check out the following resources:

Sunder Raj, *Confusion Called Conversion*.
Paul Billheimer, *Destined to Overcome* (Bethany House).
Wesley Duewel, *Mighty Prevailing Power* (Zondervan).
Rabi Maharaj, *Escape into the Light*.

## Buddhist Unreached Peoples

Every morning in Sri Lanka, Tibet, Thailand, Vietnam, and dozens of other Buddhist countries, orange saffron-robed monks move quietly from house to house collecting food. The priests do not say thank you for the offerings, since they feel they are allowing the people a favor, which gains them merit to achieve higher status in the next reincarnation.

Buddhism is based on the sixth-century B.C. teachings of Siddhartha Gautama, later known as Buddha. His focus was on man, not on gods. He taught that life is basically a pattern of pain and suffering that results from desire. The ceasing of all human desires, then, would signal the end of suffering. The goal of life is to move as rapidly as possible toward the absence of desire, known as *nirvana*.

By the third century B.C., Buddhist teachings had been crystallized in written form in a language called *Pali* (related to Sanskrit) on the island of what is now Sri Lanka.

About a hundred years after Gautama found enlightenment sitting under a Bo-tree in 527 B.C., Buddhism split into *Theravada*, a conservative, traditional school, and *Mahayana* Buddhism, a liberal following that modified many traditional practices. Theravada Buddhism, the "school of the elders," is prevalent in Myanmar, Laos, Kampuchea, and Sri Lanka. Mahayana Buddhism is strongest in Tibet, China, Japan, Korea, and Vietnam. In the past few hundred years, Buddhism has splintered into hundreds of varying slants on how to live according to the basic belief system. A splinter group called "Pure Land Buddhism," for example, is the dominant religion of Hawaii.

The nonreligious, philosophical aspects of Buddhism—that it has nothing to do with a Deity—is obvious in the doctrine of *anatta*. This teaching asserts that a person has no soul—no personal center exists. A human, rather, is composed of five *hhandas*, or "aggregates," that give the illusion of identity. That illusion can be swept away only when the tensions of suffering and desire are erased through discipline. Discipline eventually leads to nirvana ("emptiness" or "nakedness"), the state in which the lack of desire allows perfection and pure peace.

In common practice, Buddhism usually takes the form of merit-making acts and Buddhist festivals and ceremonies. Throughout Buddhist countries, citizens invite monks to chant the Sutras, protective formulas for blessing and protection, in all household ceremonies and in funeral and memorial services for the benefit of the cremated deceased.

For the layperson, the principles of Buddhism's Noble Eightfold

Path consist of five don'ts: Don't steal, lie, take a life, engage in illicit sex, or drink liquor.

Most Buddhists also reduce their religious commitment to a simple pattern of gaining merits for good *karma*, the sum of the positive and negative actions in a person's life. Buddhism, as practiced by common folk, is generally an outward activity of doing good to the monks who can give merit, of participating in ceremonies and rituals, and of contributing toward the construction and maintenance of the local Buddhist temple.

Although Buddhism teaches that people are caught in *samsara*, an eternal cycle of birth and death by which a person's karma moves perpetually on to rebirth, or reincarnation, few typical Buddhists place much emphasis on these cycles and levels of future existence or on gaining nirvana because their life is occupied with the simple struggle to survive. Their interest in gaining merit has more to do with an improved life now.

Many laypersons following Buddhism simply feel that no one can protect himself from the eternally linked laws of karma because a previous form of life has dictated one's level of suffering. This fatalism leads most people to practice the forms of Buddhism, while still believing in the existence of various spirits. Beneath Buddhism's philosophy—in which there is no God and man has no individual soul—most Buddhists harbor a deep, ancient belief in spirits, which they fear.

To learn more about Buddhism and how to reach out to them, look through the following resources:

Norman Geisler and J. Yutaka Amano, *The Reincarnation Sensation, A Christian Response* (Wheaton, Ill.: Tyndale House Publishers, 1987).

Losuke Koyama, *Mount Fuji and Mount Sinai, A Critique of Idols* (Maryknoll, N.Y.: Orbis Books, 1984).

Marku Tsering, *Sharing Christ in the Tibetan Buddhist World* (Upper Darby, Penn.: Interserve agent for Tibet Press, 1988).

Tissa Weerasingha, *The Cross and the Bo Tree—Communicating the Gospel to Buddhists* (Taichung, Taiwan: Asia Theological Association, 1989).

J. Isamu Yamamoto, *Beyond Buddhism, A Basic Introduction to the Buddhist Tradition* (Pasadena, Calif.: Sonrise Center for Buddhist Studies, reprint 1990).

International Journal of Frontier Missions, July 1993. Available from Sonrise Center for Buddhist Studies, Pasadena, California.

## Chinese Unreached Peoples

The only major unreached people bloc less defined by religion than by political boundary is the Chinese peoples. What makes it difficult to adequately characterize this bloc is that the Chinese government and, to some extent, the people of China have pursued the idea of the "Great Tradition"—that the Chinese are one people, sharing culture, communication, and ways of conducting affairs. In the light of this view, the Chinese government recognizes one majority people, the Han, and only 55 minority peoples within the borders of the People's Republic of China.

According to Jim Ziervogel, director of the Institute of Chinese Studies, there are, in fact, twelve major people groups among the Han Chinese alone. And most of those twelve Han Chinese peoples have a large number of subgroups set apart by their own dialects and "little traditions."[5] The majority Han is the people group among which the Gospel has exploded in recent years, with tens of millions of believers forming thousands of house churches.

But segments of the Han megagroup and scores of non-Han people groups in the People's Republic of China are unreached; they don't have a strong enough indigenous church to evangelize their own people. In the case of many people groups, they have absolutely no church at all.

In spite of the diversity, some generalizations may be made about the Chinese bloc of unreached peoples. For example, this bloc reflects two influences, ancient Confucianism and modern communism.

Confucius (551–479 B.C.) emphasized the order necessary to society. His teachings urged the Chinese to value social relationships, to live properly in courtesy and common respect, and to admire self-denial as the key means of benefitting all. Confucianism teaches that humans are basically good, although a person's goodness can be weakened and distorted by greed, selfish ambition, or corrupt leadership.

The fact that communism eased into Chinese society on the coattails of Confucianism is no surprise. Although hundreds of millions of Chinese don't really think of themselves as communists, their cultural thought patterns do reflect the communist ideals of (1) submission of the individual to the good of the whole, (2) the evils of a society based on economic classes, and (3) the eventual workers' paradise.

Chinese communistic/Confucianistic thought holds that

Humankind determines its own destiny.
Religion is a dangerous fantasy—"the opiate of the people."
Rational thinking—science—leads to truth.

With this mind-set, many of the people groups of China reject Christianity. That rejection is especially acrid when merged with the anger that many Chinese still feel at the historic blunders of "Christian" countries that meddled in China's affairs.

For example, it is still emphatically taught in the country's history classes that "Christianity is the running dog of imperialism." This phrase arose during the early 1800s when gun ships from "Christian" England forced China to accept shipments of opium. Hoping to addict as many Chinese as possible to the drug to guarantee future markets, the British used in their negotiations the only Westerners who knew both English and Chinese: Christian missionaries.

In many areas, this mind-set of communism/Confucianism is mixed with the popular religious beliefs of Buddhism and Taoism. The teachings of Taoism, credited to a hazy fifth century B.C. figure named Lao-Tzu, outline a philosophy that espouses passivity and harmony with life and nature. But more popularly, Taoism is a religion that has simply absorbed and combined virtually any Chinese folk beliefs and superstitions. And so, as do the popular-level practices of Buddhism, Taoism looks much like any other animistic religion. Fear and appeasement of spirits prompt elaborate rituals involving gongs, amulets, mirrors, candles and incense, bells, charms, and chants. Incantations to the spirit world plead for healing, the telling of fortunes, or the casting of spells.[6]

Classifying more than a billion Chinese citizens is anything but simple. And yet these basic characteristics help explain that, while in the midst of the greatest church growth on earth, scores of Chinese people groups comprising hundreds of millions of individuals are still very much unreached.

Because there are so many diverse peoples in China, be sure what you read will apply to the people you are interested in. We recommend the following resources:

Christopher J. Smith, China, People and Places in the Land of One Billion (Boulder, Colo.: Westview Press, 1991).

Simon Leys, Chinese Shadows (Penguin Books, 1978).

Perry Link, et al, editor, Unofficial China, Popular Culture and Thought in the People's Republic (Boulder, Colo.: Westview Press, 1989).

Geramie Barme and John Minford, editors, Seeds of Fire, Chinese Voices of Conscience.

Zhang Xin Xinard and Sang Ye, Chinese Lives, An Oral History of Contemporary China (N.Y.: Pantheon Books, 1987).

C.K. Yang, Religion in Chinese Society (Berkeley, Calif.: University of

California Press, 1961, and revised 1991).

Tony Lambert, *The Resurrection of the Chinese Church* (Wheaton, Ill.: Overseas Missionary Fellowship, 1994).

Jonathan Chao, edited by Richard Van Houten, *Wise as Serpents, Harmless as Doves* (Pasadena, Calif.: William Carey Library, 1988).

Ralph R. Covell, *Confucius, the Buddha, and Christ: A History of the Gospel in Chinese* (Orbis Books, 1986).

*Mountain Pain*, the life of J. O. Fraser (Overseas Missionary Fellowship, about 1985).

## Keep Up With the World

Studying the harvest field obviously requires more than thinking through the world's major non-Christian religions. As an alert twenty-first-century world Christian, plan to

- Use daily the informative prayer guides to the world such as *Global Prayer Digest* or *Operation World*. (See Publications under Resources.)

- Get the world news behind the world news that's only highlighted in typical news programs. Read regulary *World Press, The Economist, World Monitor, The World and I*, and other secular magazines found in your local library.

- Familiarize yourself with the world's *ethne*. Regularly watch CNN's Sunday cultural programs and *National Geographic* television specials. Read novels set in various cultural backgrounds, befriend internationals in your city, check out English-version foreign newspapers, take a language course.

- Steal an environmental watchword for the Kingdom: "Think globally. Act locally."

All of these resources will help keep you informed about the peoples of the world and may be the source that God uses to direct you where to give your energies.

## The Harvest Is Vast!

Whether staring wide-eyed at global trends or squinting at the millions of lost individuals within the thousands of unreached people groups of the world, we are invariably left feeling pretty intimidated. How can we possibly disciple all these nations, equipping each culture's church to evangelize its own people?

If the task seems insurmountable, remember that God keeps everything in perspective. He created the sun to be 400 times larger than the earth's moon, which is 400 times closer to the surface of our planet. Thus He designed—for some wonderful reason—the possibility of the perfect eclipse. Aren't we of far more worth than a solar eclipse? God planned the growth of His Church in perfect proportion to the vastness of the harvest.

Regardless of how discouraged the worldwide Church sometimes feels about seriously impacting our world, God has prepared an awesome force of harvest workers to keep the job very, *very* do-able!

## CHAPTER FOUR

# The Rag-Tag World Christian Army

*A radical global harvest force*

*"Make a way for me to see the grandeur of the grander scheme unfolding."*

—*Christine & Scott Dente*

SOMEWHERE CLOSE TO THE TOP OF THE WORLD — You nod in the dusk, sitting cross-legged, eyes teary from smoke as the white-bearded little man offers more tea. You're feeling impatient that you entered this hut at the base of the Himalayas forty minutes ago, and yet nothing has been said to you at all. Feeling awkward, you're impatient to be on your way.

"I will tell you a story," he finally says in thick English. "You may tell it to your children, and your children's children."

You have all the time in the world.

He settles across the dark round table, props his cup in both hands, and begins:

Once in a hidden kingdom far, far into our mountains lived a people ruled by a king with all his pagan religious advisers. Almost no one in your country would ever have heard of this kingdom. The king never allowed anyone from the outside to come to the kingdom, and the people were without God and without hope.

On the lower slopes of the mountains lived a group of young people who began to pray for the hidden kingdom. And, as often happens, one fine spring day they understood that they themselves were the answers to their prayers. The young people gathered provisions and began the long, arduous ascent.

Nearing the high reaches of the mountains, they came upon the valley of the Imperial City, with the king's palace glistening in the spring sunshine. Suddenly an old man in regal-looking robes stepped from behind a rock and shouted, "You do not belong here!"

The young people prayed silently and answered, "We have come to serve your king and your people in the love of Jesus Christ."

The old man hesitated. "You are not from other countries; you look as we do. I am an elder in the kingdom. You say you want to serve. We shall see. I will take you to the king."

The young people prayed silently as they were led to the city, to the palace, and into the throne room of the king himself. "We have come to serve your people in the love of Jesus Christ," they said.

The king glowered. The elder who ushered in the young people shuffled his feet. "We shall see," said the king. He gestured to the guards. "Take them to the rubbish heaps!"

So the young people were led to the trash dumps and ordered to haul the refuse of the townsfolk. They carried rubbish, picked up trash from the city streets, and hauled away dead animals from the roads of the kingdom. This they did for seven days. And they sang as they worked.

At the end of the seven days, the king summoned them to appear before him. "So you are here to serve in the love of Jesus Christ," said the king. "We shall see. Take them to work on the walls!"

So the young Christians began to work repairing the walls of the city. They carried rocks from the streams below the palace towers. They mixed clay with straw and water to make bricks. Their hands bled from the rocks. Day after day they were covered with mud and mortar. As the king watched from his palace tower, the young people sang and rebuilt the wall.

After twenty days of making bricks, the young people began to work on the wall. As they did, they looked up to see a solemn line of palace priests in bright yellow robes moving purposefully toward them. The first priest reached the work team and said, "We have come to work with you." The young Christians smiled, sang, and worked.

After thirty days the king looked out his palace window to watch the young Christians singing and working alongside the pagan priests. He summoned them to his throne room. "So you have truly come to serve," he said. "It has been reported to me that my priests each evening go to have tea with you so they can learn about the love of this Jesus. I shall offer a proclamation to the people to gather tonight. You may tell them of the love of this Jesus."

That evening the young Christians sang, and for the first time in the ancient history of the hidden kingdom, the people heard of the love of Jesus. Forty of the citizens became followers of Jesus that night.

Soon the young Christians had to return to their own homeland on the slopes of the mountains. As they left the city of the hidden kingdom, the people cried, "Come back to us. And bring others like you!" And just as they lost sight of the city towers on the beginning of their journey home, the young people heard calls behind them. Rushing down the path came the yellow-robed priests. "We have brought you offerings and gifts," the priests called. "So one day soon you may return and bring others like you."

The ancient man telling you the tale pauses and asks, "More tea?"

You shake your head and say, "Quite a story. Wouldn't it be wonderful if something like that could happen."

The old man rolls his eyes. "Of course."

"You mean it did happen?"

"My friend," the white-bearded man says. "Be assured it happened in the most realistic way. Use your telephone to call one, seven-one-nine, five-two-seven, nine-five-nine-four. Offer a contribution to the young Christians' ministry—to add your support to that of the pagan priests."

"Really?" you say.

The old man rolls his eyes.

## Trends in the Harvest Force

God's pool of laborers is expanding as never before—manned by believers like these young Christians, emerging from cultures that just years ago were themselves considered unreached or resistant to the Gospel.

Let's look at several of the realities of life on the cutting-edge ministry, realities you need to consider as you implement your vision as a member of God's global harvest force

## Trend #1: The Church Is Growing Like Wildfire

Unacknowledged by all too many quiet, discouraged congregations, the Body of Christ is growing "uncontrollably" in most of the world.

- In the late 1980s it was estimated that every day more than 70,000 true believers were added to the Church. In ensuing years of marked global turmoil, that number was deemed far too low. For example, in 1991, the Body of Christ increased by more than

174,000 daily! In 1994, Strategic Frontiers researchers estimated that the daily figure grew to 178,000 daily![1]

- The number of true believers compared to total world population reflects an amazing percentage pattern. Notice the accelerating time frame of these percentages; it took from the time of Christ until just before Columbus' trip across the Atlantic for the Church to grow to 1% of the world population. Yet it took only four years (1989–1993) to grow another 1%!

By A.D. 1430, there was one true believer per hundred (1%) of world population—1 out of 100[2]

1790—Two per hundred (2%)—1 out of 50
1940—Three per hundred (3%)—1 out of 33
1960—Four per hundred (4%)—1 out of 25
1970—Five per hundred (5%)—1 out of 20
1980—Six per hundred (6%)—1 out of 17
1983—Seven per hundred (7%)—1 out of 14
1986—Eight per hundred (8%)—1 out of 12
1989—Nine per hundred (9%)—1 out of 11
1993—Ten per hundred (10%)—1 out of 10

This one-out-of-ten means that worldwide there are 560,000,000 Bible-believing, committed Christians.

If these committed believers were grouped into average-sized congregations of about 100 in each fellowship, there are about 5.6 million congregations of true Christians worldwide!

Including nominal Christians—those who claim faith in Christ but who evidence little of His presence in their lives—Christianity is embraced by one-third of the world's population.

Especially in the West, most Christians don't believe such a global polling of the Church. In fact, some are irritated or resentful about such encouraging news. One pastor's wife commented, "We shouldn't be watching these numbers; we should be serious about our personal relationship with Christ and leave this global scope to God." (Her comments are, of course, eerily reminiscent of the 1790s ecclesiastical rebuff of William Carey's overview of the state of the world at that time. Carey was told by church leaders: "Sit down, young man; if God wants to save the heathen, He will do it without your help or ours!")

Why are many parts of the Church not enthused about the amazing growth of the Body of Christ? Some Western missionaries bristle at these encouraging signs of the growth of the Church because in their own work they have experienced a low response to the Gospel, and so conclude that that must be the norm. Other typical believers in the pew simply don't know what God is doing at all in the big picture. They may be informed about a slice of what their own church or denomination is doing in cross-cultural ministry, but rarely break outside their own circles to learn what others of the 23,000 different denominations or the thousands of ministries worldwide are doing.

Ralph Winter, statistician behind many of the above findings (along with the Lausanne Statistical Task Force), explains that Satan the Deceiver's usual program of misinformation seems to have convinced the Christian West that we're losing the battle. In the United States, for example, he points out:

> Americans are constantly bombarded by negative information. Newspapers, radio and television conspire to pound into Americans that most everything is going wrong all around the world. The total absence of news about the astonishing advance of the Gospel leaves the impression that things are going wrong in that area as well. Thus, few Americans are prepared to believe the amazing positive reports of world Christianity—even though the Christian phenomenon has always been an astounding movement.[3]

Cheer up. You're part of a mushrooming worldwide Family through which Jesus Christ is building His Church. In Him, we are more than conquerors!

## Trend #2: The Two-Thirds-World Mission Force

As late as 1980, several mission spokesmen were still saying that there were perhaps only 3,000 non-Western missionaries in the world. In 1989, the only directory of Two-Thirds-World mission agencies was Larry Pate's *From Every People*, published by Overseas Crusades International.

(Incidentally, the term "Two-Thirds World" refers to those non-Western regions of the globe that contain about two-thirds of the world's population and two-thirds of the world's land mass. It's probably patronizing to still call these cultures the "Third World," as if the West was "first" and the former communist world "second" and everyone else simply "third"!)

Follow-up on the research done in *From Every People* revealed that the non-Western missionary total had risen from 35,924 in 1988 to 46,157 in 1990—in just two years!

Pate further found that in 1990 there were 1,205 non-Western mission agencies—a number that would probably increase to a total of 1,971 non-Western agencies by A.D. 2000.

While 1990 saw 46,157 non-Westerners in mission work—or 35.6% of the total missionaries worldwide, Western missionaries totalled 91,013. That ratio, according to Larry's findings, is expected to shift by the year 2000 to 164,230 non-Westerners to 131,720 Western missionaries. In 2000, Two-Thirds-World missionaries will be 55.5% of the entire harvest force!

In the early 90s, Larry gauged the Western mission movement growth at about 4%. In 1992, he wrote:

> Just as the Western world is consolidating its political power, spiritual power is shifting toward the non-Western world. While the growth rate of the Two-Thirds-World evangelical churches is a remarkable 6.7% per year, the Two-Thirds-World missions movement (which our studies identify as almost entirely evangelical) is growing at 13.3% per year. This projects to a phenomenal 248% increase every ten years![4]

Of course, this is all the official data of the Two-Thirds-World Mission Force. What isn't quantified is the person-by-person "sending" that God is accomplishing through His unofficial channels. For example, no statistics record the fact that in early 1992 a young convert to Christ in Kenya was threatened with death by his Muslim family. But instead of killing him, they disowned him by sending him to a relative's home—in Iran. Today he is suffering and struggling to strengthen the growing church among the many peoples of Iran.

The impact of these Two-Thirds-Worlders is hard for Westerners to comprehend. In the typical church in England or America, for example, it's inconceivable that the congregation could reproduce itself within a few years' time. If it were done, a good percentage of the new church's congregation would simply be disgruntled Christians from other congregations. To see a dozen or even a few new converts each year is exciting to these fellowships. For example, nearly 60,000 churches in the United States annually report no conversions to Jesus Christ![5]

- About 85% of America's churches are either stagnant or dying. Almost 43% of those who identify themselves as Christians in America say that "it does not matter what religious faith you follow because all faiths teach similar lessons about life."

- For the first time in 50 years the number of American career missionaries has dropped from 50,500 in 1988 to 41,142 in 1992. Veteran missionaries who went out after World War II are retiring now in droves, and they're not being replaced.

- Pastor Leith Anderson says, "The North American church already has a diminished role [in global evangelism]. Our mission force is aging and diminishing, while the missionary force from [Two-Thirds-World] countries is younger and growing. South America has 50,000 new churches per year, while 60 churches per week are closing in the United States."[6]

Meanwhile, the Church in Zaire planted more than 10,000 new churches during a six-year period from 1986–1992. Believers of the Garos people of Bangladesh have planted churches in every one of the 20 indigenous tribal peoples of that country. The Garos, with almost 100% of the group claiming to be believers, have sincerely committed themselves to impact peoples in addition to the Tribals until they see "a church among each of the peoples of Bangladesh by the year 2000."[7]

In 1987 the indigenous Evangelical Baptist Church (EBC) of Malawi in southern Africa held a seminar on the need for training new church leadership since churches were growing so rapidly. Each of the six district leaders announced their goals: "Last year," the first one said, "we planted five churches in our district. Next year, we believe God will help us plant 20 churches." Another leader said, "Last year we planted eight churches. This year, by God's grace, we intend to plant 25 new churches." Altogether, the 36 existing EBC churches hoped to plant 67 new churches in the coming twelve months.

Results? Within a week, the EBC workers had planted 20 new churches with 15–18 new believers in each! At the end of just seven months the EBC districts had reached their goal of 67 new churches! Matthias Munyewe, leader of the EBC, smiled, "The urgency to spread the Word has really burned into their hearts. The district leaders have now been asking what their next goals should be!"[8]

The shrinking globe, the loudly ticking clock of history, and the rock-solid biblical emphasis on God's heart for all peoples should clue us in: The West can't pretend to do the job of world evangelization the way it has over the past two hundred—or even the past fifty—years. When one of the most successful mission efforts in South America is a Filipino couple supported by Indonesian churches and sent out by a Singapore mission agency to minister to Indians in Paraguay, you know the mission world is changing!

Missiologists speak of "the third Church." That is, the "first Church" during the first millennium A.D. was predominantly Eastern, centered in Jerusalem and then Rome. In the early days of the spread of the Gospel, the Spirit of God actually forbade the apostle Paul to take the

Good News eastward into Asia (Acts 16:12). Instead, Paul was drawn by his Macedonian call westward toward Rome. Although believers planted new churches across North Africa and eastward into India, the force of the Church moved westward.

The second millennium A.D. saw the focus of the Church in the West—in Europe and its colonies, including the United States. The coming third millennium signals another shift in the vital center of the worldwide Church. Andrew Walls of the University of Aberdeen suggests that we're seeing "a complete change in the center of gravity of Christianity, so that the heartlands of the Church are in Latin America, in certain parts of Asia, and in Africa."[9] Christianity is no longer a "Western religion"!

An Asia Evangelistic Fellowship newsletter points out: "The missionary receiving countries have become the missionary sending countries. The axis of world missionary expansion seems to have shifted from West to East."[10]

Larry Pate concludes from his years of global research that the greatest growth of Christianity will take place as a result of the ministry of indigenous movements in the Two-Thirds World.[11]

This shift is often very unsettling to the typical Western congregation, who can scarcely believe that they are not setting the norm of contemporary Christianity. For example, the fastest-growing segment of the Church, the charismatic movement, is often thought by Western Christians to be centered in America. The American profile of a charismatic is typically a suburban or rural middle-class man. In Europe the charismatic is suburban and likely to be from the upper middle-class. Naturally we interpret life by what we see around us; but many Western charismatics are astonished to find that worldwide charismatic/pentecostalism is characterized as inner-city urban, more female than male, more Two-Thirds-World (66%), more from the poor (87%) and, on the average, younger than eighteen.[12] Professor and researcher L. Grant McClung says, "In terms of resources, most of the communication in the 100-year history of modern pentecostalism has flowed from the Northern to the Southern Hemisphere. That day is now gone and a new reality has come."[13]

The trend isn't just apparent in charismatic or pentecostal circles. Any mission strategy or enterprise that doesn't acknowledge this day of the global interdependence and mutual participation of the entire Church is simply missing the whole-world heart of God. Mission has already evidenced a fundamental shift from its familiar mode of "from the West to the rest." God's global plan of offering His redemption across every cultural barrier is now fully a mission of all of God's Church.

## Trend #3: Short-Term Missions

Doug Millham, who with his wife, Jackie, gives excellent *Discover the World* seminars, recalls his first encounter with the idea he could make a difference short-term:

> One day a few years ago I turned on my TV and was stunned, yet strangely fascinated by what I saw. A news report out of East Africa showed scenes of human suffering that melted my heart. I picked up the phone, and six months later I found myself living in a tent in a refugee camp in Somalia, trying to do anything I could to help bring a little joy to a frightful situation. I returned home a year later as a person completely transformed, totally committed to a life of service to others.[14]

Young and old short-term cross-cultural workers have sold popcorn, dug freshwater wells, played kickball with refugee kids, painted houses, built chapels, fixed generators, handed out literature—the list of possibilities for short-term ministry in other cultures is almost limitless.

In the USA alone, 208 of the total of nearly 700 mission agencies sent out more than 31,000 short-term missionaries in 1988 (last date of reliable data).[15] This was up from about 21,000 just three years before—an increase of about 10,000 short-termers between 1985 and 1988. The ratio today—estimated at about 50% of the North American mission force—is undoubtedly even more amazing.[16]

But short-term mission ministry has a black-eyed reputation among many career missionaries. Short-termers are renowned worldwide for blundering into strategic ministry situations. Through well-meant ignorance or lack of training, some short-termers have warped mission efforts among a people for years to come. Armed with these horror stories some career missionaries snarl that the only reason short-term missions occurs is that today's Christians lack real commitment and endurance.

In North America, the notorious Baby Boomer generation—those born between 1946 and 1964—has been accused of a marked lack of commitment to the long haul. This is nowhere seen so acutely as in the arena of missions. Leith Anderson has traced Western mission agencies' recruiting messages since the early 50s when "response to a divine call" was the chief concern of recruiters and missionary candidates. In the

70s, Anderson found that education rose markedly on the list of qualifications. In the early 90s, the Baby Boom mission candidates were asking questions about health insurance, education of their future children, and retirement benefits.[17]

Leslie Pelt, SIM International career missionary in Nigeria, recalls meeting a fellow missionary arriving in West Africa: "How long are you out for?" she asked. "Well," he replied, "I'm going to try it for six months and see how things work out." His response, says Leslie, was that of many short-termers. "They test the fields like someone smelling, squeezing, and sampling the fruit at the local market. If the climate, language, culture, and amenities are acceptable, then God might be leading them to extend their commitment. However, if things don't go as they hoped, then it must not be God's will for them to stay."[18]

Leslie points out that often it is the national church that cringes most with the growing arrivals of short-termers. The church questions their presence since the motivation of short-termers is sometimes unclear. One Nigerian church leader admitted, "We are realizing that short-termers come mostly for their own experience, not necessarily for what they can contribute to the ministry. The short-term program is a recruitment tool for mission boards. This trend has come at a time when the national church has crucial ministry needs, housing shortages, and limited resources."[19]

Further, many churches on traditional mission fields resent the incredible amounts of money spent short-terming. For example, the round-trip airfare of one American short-termer going to Africa could fully support about six African evangelists or missionaries for an entire year. So when a well-meaning church sends out its youth choir with 40 members to minister for a few weeks, it doesn't take African church leaders long to estimate that 240 evangelists could be supported for an entire year if the funds were spent perhaps more strategically.

Generally, the criticisms are:

1. Results from short-term ministry are unreliable.
2. There is little lasting fruit.
3. The financial costs are high.
4. Short-termers distract career missionaries.
5. They're not real missionaries.

Regardless of the critics, short-term missions is on the rise. Co-founder of Frontiers mission agency Greg Livingstone recalls his part in the germination of today's short-term missions movement:

We called it "Operation Mobilization," rallying 2,000 young

people from 20 countries to visit every village in Austria, Belgium, France, Italy, and Spain. It sounded exciting to many students in the early '60s, but it sounded like bunk to many others. As fast as I could get out the challenge to minister for a summer in Europe, the criticisms came pouring in.

"How can you waste money sacrificed for missions on a summer campaign? That money could go to real life-time missionaries," chided our accusers. This unexpected reproof sent me, the then 22-year-old US coordinator for OM, off to see Dr. Don Hillis, then the general director of TEAM in Wheaton, Illinois. Hillis grinned and set me back on track. "When TEAM started," he confessed, "we simply told people to show up at the dock and bring a Bible and a banjo." Hillis understood something: God is behind a lot of efforts that, though they initially may not look all that strategic, are somehow part of God's process.[20]

Part of the reason for short-term mission trips' success, of course, is what the experience does to participants. Because of a short-term trip he took years ago to the Philippines, one young member of a staunchly non-charismatic congregation is vehement about God's miraculous power in today's world. "There I was in this sweaty night meeting," he recalls. "I had no clue what they were doing. They had helped this old man through the crowd up to the front where I was giving my testimony through an interpreter. So this old man is propped in front of me and the people start saying something and gesturing to me. Then the interpreter tells me they want me to heal his broken ribs! I kind of back off, looking for the pastor, but they keep pushing me toward the old man.

"So what can I do? I reach out and put my hand on the guy's ribs. I could feel how out of place and jagged they were just beneath his skin. And I look up to the rafters and plead something like, 'Please get me out of this, Lord!' And then as I'm praying I feel him breathing hard and. . . . And I feel his ribs shift back into place! He starts jumping, and the whole crowd starts leaping and hugging me, and I'm crying and laughing. I was totally blown away." As the young short-termer finishes his story, he concludes, "I'll never be the same. Don't tell me God can't use anybody. Don't tell me we don't serve a God of awesome power!"

But short-term mission isn't just good for the short-termers. It's also becoming more of an effective strategy in long-range mission efforts. Paul and Suzanne Luciani with Latin American Mission, for example, have worked full time with Latin American Mission in Mexico City expressly to coordinate short-term teams. Instead of random, individual short-term teams wandering into Mexico City from dozens of concerned North American churches, Paul and Suzanne ensure that properly trained teams are channeled into strategic projects of Mexico City's churches. Teams function in the areas of their giftedness—holding basketball clinics for slum kids, or passing out Gospels of John door-to-door for a few weeks—then head home having accomplished something. But the ministry continues through the local Mexican churches, which have supervised and participated in the short-term effort.

In the same way, career missionaries and one-to-two-year short-termers in tough-as-nails Belgium are linking up for exciting success in planting new churches. Johan Lukasse, president of the Belgian Evangelical Mission in Brussels, says, "This way of church planting has stolen my heart!" He explains, "We use teams of young people under the leadership of an experienced church-planting missionary. They are recruited to give a year to this program."

A team moves into a target area and lives in one or two houses as a community. Each team member joins at least one or two social or cultural groups and sports teams—one to a local group. As they develop relationships in these local groups, team members also work on various evangelistic approaches in the area. Further, some do ongoing local research to determine the best long-term approaches for the Gospel to penetrate each segment of the area's society. "While the young people do outreach," says Johan, "they also get training in subjects such as church planting, church growth principles, and effective witness. Heavy emphasis is placed on evaluation and a lot of the learning is by doing."

Results? As the community of short-termers virtually demonstrates a church in the midst of the community, new local believers are simply incorporated into the fellowship. New converts follow the examples of the team—praying, confessing, worshiping, teaching, lovingly resolving conflicts, reaching out to others with the Gospel, giving and studying the Word. By shaping the new disciples into co-workers, the missionaries—both short-term and career—will phase out to leave a discipled indigenous church. The Belgian Evangelical Mission's first church-planting team of short-termers, led by career missionaries, established a church in its first year of ministry. Within two years the church had three elders and two deacons. Two years later that first church planted a daughter church, and another in another four years. And still another daughter church a few years later.

Campus Crusade for Christ sent in a short-term team to Alma-Aty in Kazakhastan during one summer. The Muslims' adherence to Islam there was nominal and the short-term college students reached enough

## Keys to Short-Term Mission Projects

How can short-term trips add to the long-term vision of your fellowship?

- *Look to the fields!* Make sure your project isn't just what *you* want to do, but what is needed in that location and culture. Research what's happening among that people. Plan the project along with workers on the field—missionaries and national ministers alike.
- *Be careful stewards.* The money you'll invest might actually be more effectively spent elsewhere or be a greater asset to the Kingdom by simply giving it to workers on the field—or by purchasing equipment or resources for them. Measure your stewardship by determining if things add up:

    $$\$\$\$\$ \text{ Invested} = \text{Ministry impact on the field} + \text{impact on your short-termers}$$

- *Consider follow-up efforts in your planning.* Don't generate unnecessary burdens for the workers in the field—for example, by blitzing a town with literature that promises personal visits, and then leaving this immense job of visitation to the workers you leave behind as you head home.
- *Prepare carefully.* Meticulous preparation always lessens the need to use your still-necessary contingency/emergency plans.
- *Serve.* Don't even think about sending a team that feels they have so much to offer that they have a superior attitude. As you prepare, use the word *serve* instead of *help*: We're going to serve these people *vs.* We're going to help these poor, unfortunate people. Besides going with a genuine respect for the people to be ministered to, go with a determined attitude to honor those permanent workers who will carry on long after you're gone—no matter how many "better ideas" you have on how to minister.
- *Debrief.* Individual team members need to mull over what God has done in them and how such a trip could be improved.
- *Mobilize.* Put the return short-termers to work helping the home front catch and build their vision of God's heart for every people.
- *Keep the visited people group in the prayers of the whole church.* A short-term trip that is experienced and forgotten doesn't reflect God's heart for the harvest field. Keep your fellowship updated about what God continues to do on the field so they can pray informed prayers.

Kazakhs to start a church. When it came time to leave for the summer, they called up a Frontiers missionary and said, "How would you like to take over this group of believers?"

This trend is big—particularly in the West. And it seems that criticisms of the movement can be quelled by (1) careful, proper screening and training of short-termers and (2) true partnership with on-site career missionaries. Communicator and teacher James Engles notes that even among the notorious Baby Boom generation of North America, "prior short-term service on the field sharply increases interest in a missionary career." Engles studied the short-term phenomenon in the West and found that 22% of all Christian Baby Boomers have visited a Christian organization on site overseas. About 75% of these indicate interest in long-term service. He also discovered that "short-termers are significantly more likely than others to become donors, volunteers, and full-time missionaries."[21]

Seth Barnes, director of the short-termer organization Adventures in Missions, sums up short-term missions in a fitting image:

> Both long-termers and short-termers bring gifts. Long-term missionaries can bring direction; short-termers can bring velocity. We need both. The missionary with a long-term commitment to a community plants a church and disciples its members. The relationships and vision they provide are essential. They can be like the ship's rudder, providing direction, steering the course.
>
> Short-term missionaries can be the wind in the sails, giving thrust and velocity to the enterprise. They bring resources, a prayer base, and tremendous enthusiasm![22]

## Trend #4: Non-Traditional Missions

### Weaknesses

While weakness is hardly a wildly promoted virtue in most cultures, it is a key element in God's program to cross cultural barriers with the reality of the Gospel.

Impressive educational, financial, physical, and mental strengths allow easy access across political borders. That is, governments worldwide see proper credentials and an exemplary resumé as strengths.

But those same strengths are often ineffective in trying to cross cultural barriers. The peasant farming rice in Indonesia is threatened, not attracted, by big credentials.

Greg Livingstone of Frontiers comments, "We wonder if we are sending out overly qualified women. Most of the women in many of the countries we are going to love to sit around and talk about having children and cooking. Throw a woman in there who has a Ph.D. and she can become uneasy, wanting to have a more significant conversation. One of our best women who got to the heart of her people was a hair stylist without a college education. She got into a Muslim country as a nanny. Because her world at home was cutting hair, cooking, and kids, she fit in perfectly. . . ."

In fact, says Dale Ryan of Southern California-based Recovery Partnerships, along with sending out our brightest and best as missionaries, we could learn to work with those who have weaknesses. After all, he says, the thing in life that best passes through cultural or other barriers between people isn't strength or abilities or an imposing publication history. The one quality in any culture that conveys a person's genuineness is an understanding of weakness. And the deepest weakness people can understand, regardless of cultural background, is pain.

For example, in the late 1980s the government of Indonesia decreed that all married civil servants must have only one spouse. Since Muslim men are allowed by Islamic law to have up to four wives, many Indonesian Muslim wives and their children were unceremoniously put out on the street as this decree was enforced.

Most of these women had no marketable skill, and had no background in raising their children as single mothers.

Now, who would be the most strategic members of God's harvest force to send to minister to these outcast single mothers? Marriage and family counselors with framed degrees and whole, happy families?

No. The most effective workers among these women have been believers who themselves are single mothers. They know what it means to have to earn a living and raise children without a husband in the home. They know loneliness, weariness, temptation to bitterness and spite. Divorced, widowed, and often elderly women from the West have been forming support groups with these Indonesian single mothers. The missionaries themselves need a support group, and can embody to these Muslim women the hope and healing of Christ even while they help each other cope.

Painful personal histories that at best raise eyebrows among mission agency recruiters can be what makes a candidate effective—not *defective*—for ministry. Adelene Sicardo Martinez, a Puerto Rican who grew up in New York, felt convicted at Urbana 1990, the InterVarsity student mission conference held every three years in Urbana, Illinois, USA. Her parents had divorced when she was an infant, and her father, who had returned to Puerto Rico, hadn't communicated with her for years. "I had decided that if my father wasn't going to communicate with me, I wouldn't communicate with him either. I shut everything out and decided not to feel."

As she later participated in a short-term InterVarsity Global Project in the Commonwealth of Independent States, she led discussion groups of Americans and Soviets on topics like family, divorce, and guy-girl relationships. "When we discussed family situations, I realized that a lot of the Soviets had the same type of situation as I did. Several people expressed that they never thought that Christians were so human, but that we have a different way of dealing with things. I think that was something really powerful. I could see how my dysfunctionality could even work within ministry."[23]

The day mission agencies begin appealing for recovered alcoholics is the day missionaries will be far more effective in Latin America, where up to 75% of the families are affected by alcoholism. When organizations begin recruiting strong Christians who have suffered through the pain of watching loved ones die of AIDS, missions will take on new impact in Nigeria, with its 20% HIV-positive rates, or in Uganda or Zimbabwe, where 50% of the populations are HIV positive. When the Church is brave enough to ask for women missionaries who have experienced sexual abuse and learned the healing power of Christ, we will see a vast new ingathering of souls in Two-Thirds-World societies, where one of every three women has suffered sexual abuse.

## Women

Women are more than ever a powerful force in world evangelization. Too many male-oriented cultures in the world breed churches that recognize only men's contributions to the mission enterprise. One veteran missionary woman says, "When my husband and I came home from the field to speak to our supporting churches, I was always virtually ignored—as if only he were the missionary and I was just out there to keep house!"

When the People's Republic of China eventually opens more widely to the West, traditional mission groups might have trouble appreciating the incredibly strong role of women among the tens-of-millions of believers in China. In China, where in the nineteenth century everyone worshiped female religious figures such as Guanyin and Mazu, where young girls and older women had the most time of any family members to attend Christian meetings, where female missionaries outnumbered their male counterparts, Christianity early on was considered a religion for women. Further, most Chinese women in the beginning of this century could learn to read only in mission schools, and propriety dictated that women should meet separately from men for Bible study and prayer meetings. Thus a very strong female leadership developed among believers, and itinerant teachers called "Bible women" have become key figures in the amazing spread of the Gospel in China.[24] Leadership over nearly 19,000 cell groups of believers in northern China, for example, comes from a nineteen-year-old young woman!

Women-power has significantly impacted cultures in the West in the past century. And that impact is just now being explored by women among African peoples, women who are beginning to realize that they can have a say in how many children they bear. In Muslim cultures, such as in Nigeria and more recently in Algeria, it was mostly women-power that stalled the political growth of Islamic fundamentalism—which denigrates the status of women. Few onlookers realized the strength of the women's movements in Iraq and Iran during the late 70s and early 80s. In Asia, women are taking on significant roles in commerce. These changing roles of women will affect Christians, and thus affect the harvest force. Western missions have traditionally strategized to train male converts for leadership and naturally expected males to serve as a new church's first missionaries. Just what will God do with the women who form 60% of the global Church, and who are 80% of the Church's prayer warriors!

But male-oriented Western Christianity is catching a more balanced view of the globe as missionaries encounter Two-Thirds-World women-power. For example, missionary and Daystar University College professor Larry Niemeyer admits that his own failure to grasp the impact of a female-oriented society on village life hindered the spread of the Gospel among the Bemba in Zambia.[25]

Jesus Christ, the hope of the world, often chooses weak, foolish vessels, "jars of clay to show that this all-surpassing power is from God and not from us" (2 Corinthians 4:7, NIV). The time has come for encouraging, equipping, sending, and supporting missionaries with life-histories that even a decade ago would have disqualified them from acceptance as a traditional cross-cultural minister. God can use divorcees, recovered chemically dependent believers, non-academics, tradesmen, and grandmothers in His great global plan for our era.

## The Mission Team Concept

Much of the West's mission organization community has traditionally been structured on secular models. For example, traditional American business developed a pyramid style of management, with a chairman and a few top executives giving orders that were carried out by workers at the bottom of the structure. Requests for decisions were passed back up, slowing the process. In this vertical structure, layers of managers supervised the actual work in segmented categories such as research, marketing, manufacturing, or finance, with very little overlap among highly specialized workers.[26]

Mission agencies replicated this familiar pattern. And, unfortunately, Two-Thirds-World agencies assimilated the structure as if it were not only natural for mission work but also the biblical model of organized ministry.

The top-down system worked in Western business in the past; but it doesn't work any longer. A Xerox Corporation executive says, "Before, setting priorities was a top-down process. Now we're turning that process completely upside down." Another says, "This is not an evolution; it's a revolution. This company has been organized in this monolithic approach since 1959. It institutionalized the monolithic approach to management." The reorganized structures of successful Western business are now "horizontal." That is, specialized workers are teamed up to work on specific projects. Engineers, marketing experts, manufacturing workers, and financiers pool their talents, make more decisions to save time, and collectively shape their project to the marketplace.[27]

Fortunately, this shift to horizontal teamwork is catching on in the mission of the Church. Imagine yourself as a member of a cross-cultural team. As in a commando unit, one team member has computer communication skills, another serves as team pastor, another as logistics and mechanical expert. With that in mind the question isn't, "Could I make it on the field as a missionary?" but rather, "Could I add my gifts to a team so that our group effort could plant a church?"

The team concept allows you to take on a specific role within a team. Not all are used in the same way. So what roles need filling?

There are those who are primarily evangelists. They love to talk about Jesus and go to the heart of the sin problem, bringing people face-to-face with an eternal decision. After loving people into the Kingdom, many times evangelists "leave them" to go and evangelize others.

That's where other teammates come in: the disciplers—those who aren't gifted in going out and winning people to the Lord but great at helping new believers grow in their faith! They are the vital link to planting the church well. They do what the evangelists couldn't do on their own.

There are others—what some groups call "facilitators." They are the ones who can't effectively share their faith or disciple, but are great at being servants and helping out the team. They may be there to stand in line for two hours getting groceries for the team while the team itself ministers. They may teach the team's children. They may take trips to the airport for the team, host people while they visit, run to the bank—doing, in short, a variety of things to keep the others doing what they do best.

And this team concept has no age limit!

Frontiers teams, for example, actively recruit retiring couples to join up. They find these seasoned couples to be the glue that holds the team together, saying, "Honey, your husband really didn't mean to say that; what he meant was this, and he still loves you." They are also grandparents to the team's children. As one retired couple says, "We gave up three grandchildren and got seven!" And, very significantly, many Muslims trust them more than the rest put together because of their gray hair.

The apostle Paul, history's greatest missionary, virtually never went into cross-cultural ministry by himself. It's time for us local churches to think teams. Isn't it obvious that sending out single missionaries or couples by themselves isn't a New Testament pattern at all?

Some mission agencies even encourage groups of friends to consider going to the mission field together. A team of old friends already has most of the "bugs" worked out among them; friends know each other's strengths and weaknesses. A group of friends almost naturally solves a team's most common problem—the interpersonal friction that is more often than not rooted in the rigidities of the members rather than in their differences, rigidities that produce resentment, blockages, and hidden agendas. Friends have learned through their years together to see the real issues at stake and to make mutual agreements that stick. It only makes sense that attacking the gates of hell as a team of strong friends is a strategy whose time has come!

## Creative Access

Within the next few years, 80% of the countries with unreached peoples will no longer accept missionaries as missionaries. But that certainly doesn't restrict the Holy Spirit from sending laborers to these harvest fields. Goers just need to gain access more creatively than in the good old days when they entered countries on straightforward missionary visas.

Jesus didn't say, "Go therefore into all the world and preach the gospel—if you can get a missionary visa." Today the gates of hell surrounding the world's unreached peoples are being attacked by cartoonists, water engineers, actors, and agronomists.

A couple of these creative access approaches include:

*Non-Resident Missionaries:* Sometimes a missionary is more effective living outside a restrictive people group than on-site. By living in a nearby unrestricted location, she or he can work more openly in communicating strategies, garnering prayer, and forming strategic partnerships with many organizations.

*Secular Employment:* Tentmaking or "bi-vocational ministry" is a well-known means of entering many "closed" countries. Individual tentmaking—working for a non-Christian employer in a restricted-access region—has drawbacks. Some tentmakers can't share their faith while on the job. And how many of us believers in our own nonrestricted cultures can put in a full day's work, attend to the necessities of family and living, and still have enough time and energy left to impact our community for Jesus Christ?

However, tentmaking in *teams* is a trend on the rise. In this approach the tentmakers establish themselves as a business and employ members of the team and, sometimes, individuals from the community. Some tentmakers operate bookstores that offer both secular and Christian books, video and audio tapes, and other materials. Other teams teach English as a foreign language in their own schools. Others work as teams on solar engineering projects, as medical teams, as construction crews—the list is endless.

One tentmaker says, "Ironically, while tentmaking in part evolved out of limitations, the possibilities for outreach and involvement in the community that are before us through this style of ministry are limited only by our imaginations and resources."[28] One team has organized itself as a new charity project to work among Palestinians. Most of the Palestinians living in what were called the Occupied Territories of Israel aren't allowed to travel into other areas for employment. So this group of tentmakers meets with Palestinians interested in creating needlework products, and the new charity helps them market their wares. "The fact that we are showing a concern for their practical needs is a powerful testimony in itself," one of the team says. "But in addition, this project will by its very nature bring us into close personal contacts over an extended period of time and will provide us with the opportunity to share our faith."[29]

A few years ago another mission team strategized its way into a very restricted Middle Eastern country by assembling a rare group of believers able to design, build, and operate an amusement park! Although the team never finalized the construction of its proposed Middle Eastern tourist theme park, they nevertheless spent several quality years working alongside Muslim counterparts as they conducted feasibility studies.

One caution. Most agencies to the unreached peoples of the world are looking for church planters first, career-oriented people second. If you hold too tightly to your career you may not be an effective church planter. With church planting as a priority, you may find job A, which leads to job B, which may give you job C, which lands you job D, where you work only ten hours a week yet can still obtain a working visa, freeing up maximum time to share your faith with your target people. Many tentmakers still raise support to be able to get a job which requires a minimum amount of work time (therefore less pay) and allows maximum ministry time!

## Trend #5: Global, Functional Unity

Organizations in business and government are finding new ways of partnering and working together. So too is the church!

"Functional unity" is how the Bible describes the oneness of the Body of Christ. Regardless of how an ankle feels about a toe, the two work together in functional unity to take a step. The functions are decidedly different. Similarly, the positions in the body are different. Size, shape, connections, needs, and makeup are different. Strengths and weaknesses vary. But if the ankle joint and the toe are parts of the same body, they can work together in natural, successful unity to get a body moving.

More and more parachurch organizations, churches, on-the-field mission teams, and even denominations are realizing the synergy of functional unity. It is possible for a Christian group to maintain their identity totally and yet to work together with another group of believers. It's increasingly apparent that the time has come for the worldwide Body of Christ to enjoy the reality of "how good and pleasant it is when brothers live together in unity . . . for there the Lord bestows his blessing, even life for evermore" (Psalm 133:1–3, NIV).

One model of functional unity is seen in the current trend of Bible translation and distribution organizations working together. Realizing the urgency of the task and the limits to resources, eight major translation groups (such as Wycliffe Bible Translators) and distribution groups (such as the United Bible Society) met in 1990 to coordinate their efforts. It isn't just a lot more work for each group to try to translate or distribute Scripture for every language on earth, it's also poor stewardship if one group duplicates the work of another. So these organizations decided to let each other know what languages they were targeting so they don't needlessly duplicate millions of work hours of translation and distribution.

In the fall of 1992 others joined this loose-knit coalition, so that now at least eighteen translation and distribution groups are saving work by communicating. The cooperative has announced its objective of working together until every language on earth has the Word of God. Saturation Scripture distribution resulting from this joint effort has already begun among the peoples of Ethiopia.

Another example of functional unity is The World by 2000 Radio, a joint project of the world's four largest Christian radio ministries: HCJB, Far East Broadcasting (FEBC), ELWA (an SIM International ministry), and Trans World Radio. Separately, each radio ministry covers an immense span of the globe with the Gospel. Jointly, they cover it all. Because members share their programs with the other radio ministries, the progress in beaming the Gospel to every people has never been faster.

The opening story we tell in Chapter 9, describing the development of the CoMission, highlights another incredible model of functional unity in the completion of the Great Commission. In this case the leveraging factor that convinced more than 20 key mission groups to cooperate was the overwhelming size of the task. No one organization could faintly hope to impact 300 million people through 120,000 schools in the Commonwealth of Independent States. Sitting down and counting whether one has the resources to complete the building of such a massive tower brought these CoMission groups face-to-face with reality: We can't do it alone.

The AD2000 Movement is another remarkable example of the power in the Body of Christ worldwide as it joins together for the task of our global mission. Growing from a rather haphazard coalition of mission zealots who met in Singapore in January 1990, the AD2000 and Beyond Movement grew country by country, organization by organization, into a global network of thousands of groups determined to make a difference in our world by the year 2000. Headquartered in Colorado Springs, Colorado, in the USA, the AD2000 office simply encourages like-minded churches and groups to find out how each can augment the ministry of the other.

For example, at a consultation in Phoenix, Arizona, in September 1992, key leaders of prayer movements across the USA met with key leaders in urban evangelism and unreached peoples mission efforts. The prayer warriors found that they could channel the power of their prayers specifically in intercession for evangelism and mission efforts. Without building an empire or an institution, Luis Bush of Argentina and Thomas Wang of China are leading thousands of groups across the world and tens of thousands of global harvesters into a working demonstration of functional unity.

In Singapore, more than 35 churches have developed a coalition.

Although they retain their own identities, oversee their own cell groups intermingled throughout this city-state, and represent more than a dozen different denominations, these churches are enjoying halcyon days of ministry in functional unity. As a coalition they have sent out and support more than 85 missionaries worldwide. As a unit they host an annual mission extravaganza. They support a joint seminary-by-extension program in the city that now trains more than 2,000 annually for local and cross-cultural ministry. Similar, smaller coalitions of local churches in the West have formed in Detroit and Philadelphia. Together they support mission teams to unreached people groups "adopted" by the churches in each coalition.

This unity is also reflected directly on the field. In the former Soviet Union, Campus Crusade for Christ, the Southern Baptists, Frontiers, the Navigators, along with Operation Mobilization and the Assemblies of God, are all working together as they target the same people!

Whether seen as a trend of the future or simply a concept of God's heart from the past—functional unity among denominations and parachurch groups is a practicality whose time has come, since the whole Body "grows and builds itself up in love, as each part does its work" (Ephesians 4:16, NIV). That building up will continue until we attain "to the whole measure of the fullness of Christ"—until the Church is finally perfected into eternity (Ephesians 4:13).

So mark it down as a major trend in the historic progress of world evangelization: The Church is destined to more and more work together!

## Come and Join the Reapers

Books could be written on more of the exciting trends of the harvest force:

- *Charismatic renewal:* Renewal movements in virtually every Christian denomination and tradition are impacting world evangelization. Many missiologists feel that as the last bastions of Satan's usurped kingdom—the unreached peoples within the 10/40 Window—are captivated in overt demonic activity, the exploding pentecostal-charismatic movement worldwide is particularly equipped with its emphasis on signs, wonders, and power encounters for such a time as this.

- *Cities:* Harvesters are learning to accentuate city ministry. Today about half the world's population lives in cities. And it could only be head-in-the-sand obstinance that would keep the Church from noting the fact that urban ministry and urban mission is top priority in God's global program. He's doing something in our day—and it often has to do with cities.

- *Clarifying the message:* We as God's people are finally clarifying our message as a whole-person offer of God's redemptive blessing. Mental decisions for Jesus aren't enough; the compassionate bandaging of suffering isn't enough. But ministering to both the spirit and the body seems to be something the harvest force is getting better at balancing.

- *The techno-gospel:* We've got new technologies. The *Jesus* film, for example, by early 1994 had been viewed by more than half a billion people, and more than 33 million had made commitments to salvation in Christ. Electronic communications systems connect the Body as never before. One mission agency's teams, for instance, can communicate on computers freely and in real time via satellite with its headquarters. God is constantly gearing governments, education, and business to provide new tools for Kingdom use!

- *Kid power:* Something's happening among today's 14–24-year-olds worldwide. God seems to be raising up a fresh generation of realists who are superbly equipped to meet the demands of twenty-first-century world evangelization. For example, around the globe there suddenly seems to be a rash of reports that youngsters from ages eight to twelve are taking on adult-level prayer and preaching ministries focused on world evangelization. Called "firebrands," scores of these anointed children are even being invited to world-level mission consultations as full delegates.

And the trends continue. In all kinds of ways, God's harvest force is growing, experimenting, flexing its muscles, getting radical.

According to global researchers David Barrett and Todd Johnson in their marvelous compendium *Our Globe and How to Reach It*, tomorrow's Great Commission harvest force in A.D. 2000 will include:

> 32,000 denominations
> 24,000 parachurch or service agencies
> 103,000 institutions
> Sunday school enrollment of 400 million
> 200,000 new churches planted or opened each year
> 4.9 million full-time Christian workers
> 90 mission councils
> 1.4 billion evangelizing Christians
> 1 billion active Great Commission Christians who take Christ's

command to "disciple the nations" seriously, growing at
6.7% each year
300 million daily intercessors
30 million in full-time prayer ministry
4,800 mission agencies
400,000 career foreign missionaries
60,000 foreign missionaries from Two-Thirds-World countries
250,000 short-term foreign missionaries
500 Great Commission research centers
350 million Christian or church-owned or operated computers in 75 global networks

Today, the harvest force comprises more than 560 million committed believers worldwide in more than 5.6 million congregations. More than 170 million intercessors are praying daily for world evangelization.[30]

Furthermore, rapid change in our world means transformations in our harvest field we can't even predict. As the world faces this "hiccup in history," world-watcher Frank Kaleb Jansen, editor of the mission atlas *Target Earth*, outlines trends to watch that will impact how we do missions:

- Population growth in the southern countries, and population diversity and aging in northern countries—plus an accompanying shift of power from white European-Americans to non-whites.
- Increased mobility—particularly into cities.
- The spread and increasingly free exchange of knowledge.
- A constant threat of collapse in the world economy.
- Scarcity of resources and continuing damage to the environment.
- Not only a new world order of political alliances, but also a developing worldview.
- The quarantining and forgetting of Africa.
- Increasing women's power and importance.
- An increasing onslaught against biblical values.
- The increasing influence of religions.
- The growing power of grassroots movements.[31]

## A Victorious Harvest

With just perhaps 10,000 totally unreached peoples left on the face of the earth, the Great Commission is doable! If the task of planting a church in each of the 10,000 unreached people groups were divided up among our 5.6 million congregations, the ratio would be more than 560 churches for every remaining people!

What would happen if the 56,000 individual believers in those 560 congregations would focus their prayers on that one people group?

What if the 560 congregations were to focus their corporate prayer and their finances to support several mission teams to that people? A church movement could be established in each remaining unreached people; that church could then be discipled to evangelize its own culture individual by individual, and to become a missionary-sending church itself!

As the pace of God's global plan accelerates, we can use our increasing muscle as harvesters to work smarter—bombarding the harvest field with prayer from all over the globe, then partnering together to send in the "ground forces"—and the gates of hell shall not stand against us!

The world can easily be evangelized in this generation IF we begin to think strategically.

But the growing strength of the new harvest force doesn't mean the job is going to get easier. On the contrary, unraveling the false rulership of the enemy of men's souls only gets rougher: "Woe to the earth and the sea; because the devil has come down to you, having great anger, knowing that he has only a short time" (Revelation 12:12). Patrick Johnstone, the gracious researcher, cautions:

> Let us beware, lest the euphoria of the moment blind us to the cost in effort, pain, and even martyrdom that awaits us if we are to achieve our goal of "closure," that is, the discipling of every people/nation. These peoples are unreached because others who preceded us were unable to surmount the high geographical, cultural, religious, and political barriers that keep them isolated from the Good News. . . . To actually achieve our goal will cost us our money, our sons and daughters, our time, our blood, and definitely our lives.[32]

What is *your* role in His harvest? What part does your local church play? What about all the important practicalities of your life and the important ministries of your church that seem to have nothing to do with the planetary picture of blessing every people? In all the choices of life, with all the gifts and ministries open to your church, how can you integrate a single-minded vision of your mission on earth? Read on.

# CHAPTER FIVE

# One Lord, One Faith, One Mission

## Big-picture vision integrates a church's ministries

*"At the turn of the century, the most extensive evangelical awakening of all time occurred. The Sixth Great Awakening began with the Welsh Revival of 1904–1905. The movement swept every state and province of North America. An editorial stated about the revival: 'Its power is felt in every nook and corner of our broad land.' Affected was nearly every brand of evangelical church in North America, Europe, Australia, and South Africa together with their daughter churches and missionary causes in Asia, Latin America, and the islands of the sea. The remarkable awakening led to the conversion of over five million people worldwide. J. Edwin Orr called it 'a blaze of evening glory at the end of the nineteenth century.'"*

—Manny Hooper

TAIPEI — You put down Manny Hooper's treatise on revival and wonder if what you're seeing is a blaze of glory at the dawning of the twenty-first century—except that this time the awakening is first sweeping Asia. Taipei's afternoon traffic blares six stories below your office window as you plow through a pile of letters. The smog outside reminds you of something you read in a lit class at Berkeley: *It sits like a yellow cat along the power poles and congestion of the city.* Now the adventure begins.

You open the first crinkly blue envelope. It's from China, as usual. You remember how confused your classmates were in California, how it took weeks of careful explanation that, yes, Chinese consider themselves as one people, yet that you were from Taiwan, from the Hakka people. And, yes, there are Hakka people on the mainland as well. And, no, those living in Taiwan or Hong Kong aren't a different Chinese; we are all Chinese. But they may be Dai from the south or one of the many Han peoples. And, you supposed, the Hong Kong Han, because of their century-long isolation from the Peoples Republic of China, could perhaps be considered a distinct people. Your gruff classmates never seemed to quite get it. Americans are so inscrutable.

But the American family—who also were difficult to figure out—had understood. You were almost shocked to find that their Christian church actually worked to educate them about other cultures. They had, as they called it, *adopted* the Hakka people. And that family had befriended you, introduced you to Jesus Christ, and their church had discipled you during your years of study.

And now everything—everything—is different.

Like your trip to Hong Kong last week. You couldn't have imagined a thousand Chinese churches gathering for a Concert of Prayer. David Bryant had so skillfully called together in fervent prayer churches that in the past had been so divided. And now they were united in hope. Before you were a believer, you never knew such unity was possible in Asia.

The letters. The first is from a student. He writes that he came to Christ because of a little old lady at a Shanghai train station—and could he ask for study materials? The next letter: a couple asking where they can buy a Bible. They just gave their lives to Jesus Christ. They found out about Him from a children's book—held by an old lady at the train station in Shanghai.

The next four letters are from other areas: Korea, Guam, Japan, Japan again. All thanking Asian Outreach International—the group you work for as a volunteer—and OMS for the *Streams in the Desert* broadcasts. Then a letter from a young girl: She received Jesus as her Savior from a Bible storybook—held by an illiterate old woman at a train station. You're praying and praising through your ninth letter, again from someone who found Jesus because of a train-station encounter with some old woman. Then you remember.

You start to dig, and you find the correspondence in minutes. Two months ago a woman in Shanghai had written:

> I am a very old woman. I do not know how to read or write. My granddaughter writes this for me now. I have been listening to your *Streams in the Desert* and have become a Christian. Now it is your fault: I need a Bible.

You check the follow-up you stapled to the back of the note. Yes, OMS and Asian Outreach, working in partnership, had authorized the sending of a children's Bible with colorful pictures and a few simple phrases below each drawing, phrases like "Jesus is the Son of God." "Jesus forgives my sin." "Jesus is coming back again."

The next letter explains all the other letters. It's from a school-teacher. She says:

> I have watched a woman hobble daily to my commute station in the city. She is ragged and ignorant. But each day she carries a large, colorful book and sits at the same bench. Last week my train was delayed, and so I watched to see what she did. She sat on her bench and simply began leafing slowly through the book. Within a few minutes a crowd gathered to see what the book was. A Bible. The crowd began to read together the words printed at the bottom of each page. The old woman cannot read, so she just turned the pages. At the end of the book, she pointed to your address. She said many people are receiving the forgiveness of Jesus. I am one. And I am writing to thank you and to ask. . . .

You slowly nod at yet another example of what your American host family in Berkeley had called—somewhat irreverently, you had thought—"God-stuff." OMS from the States, joining with David Wang of Asian Outreach International based in Hong Kong, plus you—a be-liever because of the strong ministry of a church in America—handling the radio program's correspondence in Taipei, equipping an illiterate old woman in Shanghai to bring eight or nine people a month into the Kingdom!

## Blessed to Bless Every People

Another U.S. church *adopted* an unreached people with result that will stretch into eternity. Covenant Presbyterian Church of Colorado Springs is focusing on a Central Asian people. Kathleen Both, former member of the church's mission committee, was clicking through her computer's *PC Globe* maps to find a country Covenant's pastor could visit during the October 1993 "Praying Through the 10/40 Window" emphasis. Tens of millions of believers prayed that month for the un-reached in the 10/40 window, and nearly 250 intercessory prayer teams went to the 60 countries in the Window to pray on-site.

"We wanted to pick a country no other intercession teams had yet picked, and we wanted it to be as few time zones away as possible since the trip would be brief." When the search narrowed to Syria and a strange new country of Central Asia, Kathleen took her findings to the mission committee. "I wanted Syria," she admits. But when other committee members began mulling over the possibility of their pastor's visiting such a remote, little-known area as this new central Asian country, their recommendation became obvious.

When their pastor Bill asked, "All right. Where am I going?" Kathleen said, "First, to Moscow. Then by train south for a few days. You need to take your own toilet paper and snacks, and the train costs ten dollars."

"No, really," Bill said.

"Really," said Kathleen.

And thus began the involvement of Covenant Presbyterian with an unreached people on the other side of the globe.

## A Means, Not an End

In the New International Version of the Bible, Acts 1:8 reads this way: "But you will receive power when the Holy Spirit comes on you; and you will be my witnesses in Jerusalem, and in all Judea and Samaria, and to the ends of the earth."

Unfortunately that scripture is often misquoted, changing its meaning. The first misquote goes something like this: "You will be my witnesses *either* in Jerusalem, or Judea, or Samaria, or to the ends of the earth." Thinking that the text reads that way, many say, "I think I'll choose to witness in Jerusalem. Yep. Sounds good to me. Okay, God, use me here." They don't worry about ever having to somehow impact the nations.

A second misquote goes something like this: " . . . and you will be my witnesses *first* in Jerusalem, then Judea, then Samaria, then to the ends of the earth." Thinking of Jesus' command as a progression allows many people to think that they have to become proficient at sharing their faith in their own "Jerusalem" first; then, having mastered that, they can move on to the Judeas, Samarias, and finally the ends of the earth. Few ever make it beyond their "Jerusalem."

The idea behind this text isn't "either/or" or "first/then" but "both/and," as in ". . . you will be my witnesses *both* in Jerusalem, and Judea, and Samaria, and to the ends of the earth."

That helps us to clarify the impact our lives are to make here on this earth. What our Heavenly Father wants us to realize is that no matter what we do individually or corporately as a church, our impact is to be both local (where you are) and international (to the nations). It's not an either/or option or a progressive one. It's simultaneous.

Put another way, whatever ministry God wants you to focus on—again, individually or as a church—whether reaching unwed mothers in downtown Singapore, or being a Christian mechanic witnessing in an auto shop, or being a full-time mom, your ministry isn't an end in itself. It is instead to be a means toward God's goal of reaching the nations! Yes, it's true that you will need to practice sharing your faith locally before you share it cross-culturally (that's what might get you thinking "first/then"), but that doesn't need to keep you from thinking and praying internationally as soon as you come to know the Lord.

Chip Weiant, C.E.O. of a management company in central Ohio, USA, defines a healthy World Christian as "a person who obediently integrates the Great Commission with the Great Commandment—loving God with all your heart, soul, mind, and strength, and loving others as yourself." Put together, the two commands are like the "cross hairs of a long-range rifle helping sight your target," says Chip. "If the cross hairs are off, or one is missing, you will ultimately miss the target."

Too many times, those who have caught a vision for the global world are ineffective (or even blinded) in reaching out to the world in their own backyards, often damaging their day-to-day ministry effectiveness because they lack balance in their overall life perspective.

Sowing the gospel locally to our neighbors doesn't always involve proclamational or confrontational evangelism. *Living Proof*, a must-see video series for every believer serious about being a witness in their local world, clearly helps men and women to see evangelism as a lifestyle of relational evangelism. *Living Proof* effectively communicates that evangelism is not a short-term event, but rather a long-term process. (Order *Living Proof* from NavPress at your local Christian bookshop.)

So, too, becoming a healthy World Christian is a process. Your vision must be on the global world, while being effective and passionate for those in your local world—not becoming so globally minded you're no local good.

The biblical theme of God blessing His people to bless every people provides an inspired structure for our overall mission as the Church, resulting in reaching the unreached nations of the earth.

## A Faulty Illustration!

God blesses His people with His relationship and health and talents and finances and spiritual gifts and skills. And, in the biblical pattern of "Blessed is the nation [the people group] whose God is the Lord," we can joyfully receive God's blessings. We don't need to feel guilty when God pours out His blessing on our lives, our families, our congregation. It's part of what He has promised to do in His plan to demonstrate His character to all the peoples of the world.

But the blessing is for a purpose:

> God be gracious to us and bless us,
> And cause his face to shine upon us—
> That Thy way may be known on the earth,
> Thy salvation among all nations.
> . . . God blesses us, that all the ends of the earth may fear him.
> (Psalm 67:1–2, 7).

How does this twofold program—being blessed to be a blessing—form a structure for integrating ministries? Think through these illustrations of a rocket as the overall mission of a church. You'll find the fault in this illustration soon enough, but for now consider the parallels: The local church is like a four-stage rocket!

*The First Dynamic: God blesses His people to strengthen the church.*

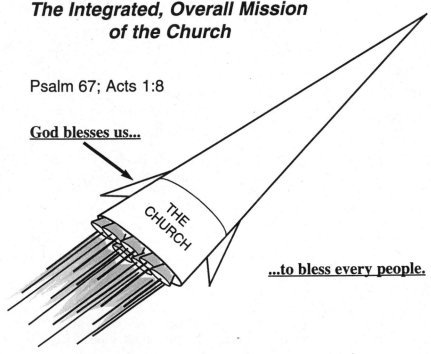

## *The Integrated, Overall Mission of the Church*

Psalm 67; Acts 1:8

**God blesses us...**

THE CHURCH

**...to bless every people.**

*The First Dynamic: God blesses His people to strengthen the church.*

If the church is ever to be a channel of God's blessing to every people, the church itself must first be strengthened. Children need nurture in the admonition of the Lord, families need encouragement and equipping in everything from communication skills to financial management, couples must be counseled, youth discipled, offerings collected, prayers offered in behalf of the fellowship, bodies exercised, sermons preached, walls painted, fellowship enjoyed, and buildings built. All the gifts, skills, and ministries that go on within the church itself can be affirmed and encouraged because the church needs to be strong for its world-level purpose. This is the power dynamic, the "booster stage" of the rocket.

*The Second Dynamic: The church is to bless every people group—including its own.*

Here's where the church begins impacting the world outside its

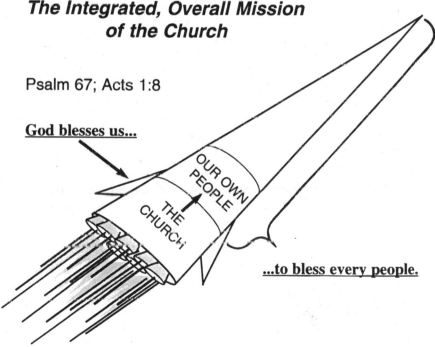

# The Integrated, Overall Mission of the Church

Psalm 67; Acts 1:8

God blesses us...

OUR OWN PEOPLE

THE CHURCH

...to bless every people.

*The Second Dynamic: The church is to bless every people group—including its own.*

walls while at the same time praying for the nations. Going to every people includes going to our own!

The easiest people group to offer God's blessing is, of course, that fellowship's own people group. As part of its overall mission to the world, the local church becomes salt and light to its own community:

*In evangelism.* As a church movement is established in a people group, it is that church's obligation to evangelize its own culture. Mass and personal evangelism aren't just compartments of a local church's ministry; sharing the Good News with neighbors is crucial to the global scope of the Great Commission. This is because the goal is not merely to reach out and save those who are lost, but to bring new souls into the Kingdom to be blessed by God who can become tomorrow's laborers for the nations.

*In ministering to community needs.* Ministering goodness within a fellowship's own culture isn't just being nice. Caring for the homeless, visiting the sick, ministering to those in prison, tending suicide hotlines, giving to the poor, sponsoring an unwed mothers' home, cleaning up trash on the highway, offering free baby-sitting for mothers' days off, raising money for medical research, or singing Christmas carols in the mall for the enjoyment of shoppers are all ways of blessing one's own culture by simply "going about doing good" (see Acts 10:38).

God relieves suffering through His people. But Christians ministering goodness in the name of Jesus Christ also illustrate the character of God for the whole world to see. Christians consistently, sacrificially doing good makes God's love for humankind visible (see 1 John 4:1–12). And besides all that, Christian love in action makes a nice place to live for everybody—including the Christians!

Caring ministries performed by believers impact a culture in far-reaching ways. They witness to the culture and set the stage for evangelism. They are, furthermore, a witness to internationals living in the church's culture and to the nations beyond. This is one of the global reasons behind obeying God's law: "Observe them [the law] carefully, for this will show your wisdom and understanding to the nations, who will hear about all these decrees and say, 'Surely this great nation is a wise and understanding people'" (Deuteronomy 4:6, NIV).

His blessing affects even unbelievers in an ethne through the actions of His people.

*In standing up for righteousness in one's own people group.* A church must often bless its own culture the hard way, by standing for God's character on social issues. When Christians fight pornography, battle drug abuse and child abuse and crime and corruption and injustice, they help bless their own culture.

God's name always denotes His character: He is holy, righteous, and just. So believers don't stand up for God's name on issues in their society only to make their streets safer and life nicer. Blessing one's own culture also broadcasts to every people on earth the character of God and witnesses for His name among the nations. God "guides [us] in the paths of righteousness for His name's sake" (Psalm 23:3). Every ministry of the church pressing for righteousness in society is crucial to the global reputation of a God who doesn't excuse sin.

*The Third Dynamic: The Church is to bless every people group, including reached peoples.*

Here the Church begins to cross cultural barriers into "reached peoples," those distinct ethnic groups with a viable church movement capable of evangelizing its own culture. About half of the world's people groups are in this category.

A fellowship's ministries in this third stage bridge language, social, or other cultural barriers. Blessing other reached peoples entails:

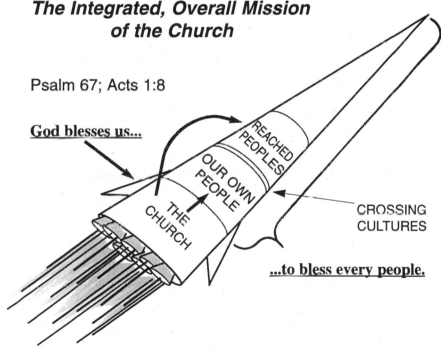

*The Third Dynamic: The church is to bless every people group, including reached peoples.*

- serving their churches
- empowering them to bless their own culture (their own Stage Two) and to equip other reached peoples (their own Stage Three) and
- partnering with them to offer Christ's redemption to unreached peoples.

It is the job of churches in a reached culture to bless their own people through evangelism, doing good, and standing up for righteousness in their society. So it is more than patronizing when another culture's church, from America for example, tries to step in to single-handedly do the job of the church among the people of Romania, who are more than 12% evangelical. It is offensive, since the outside culture suggests the people group's church isn't capable of evangelism, doing good, or salting its own society.

It is also counterproductive to the pattern of God's global plan, since the church in a reached people will not grow strong if someone else is doing its work. And churches in reached people groups need to be strong (Stage One) because they too have a global, big-picture job to do.

*The Fourth Dynamic: The Church is to bless every people group, including the remaining unreached peoples of the world.*

The fourth dynamic of a church is to see that the blessing of redemption is offered to every remaining unreached people group. This has been God's goal from the beginning of Genesis, and it needs to be the end goal of all we do as a Church.

This is the realm of frontier, pioneer missions, where the believers worldwide can join together as partners to focus their resources. What happens in this stage of the "rocket" of the Church?

*Pre-Evangelism.* Pre-evangelism—relief efforts, Christians winning favor in political, educational or business realms, medical work, etc., prepares the way, establishing the reputation of the character of God in Christ among an unreached people.

*Church-Planting.* Unbelievers come to faith in Christ and churches are planted. Those newborn congregations must be discipled to be strengthened, reaching out into their own people and crossing cultural barriers in their own history of being blessed to be a blessing to every people.

## An Integrated Vision

The whole Church, with its varying parts, functions, giftings and ministries working in unity, goes about the Father's business. We're not

# The Integrated, Overall Mission
## of the Church

Psalm 67; Acts 1:8

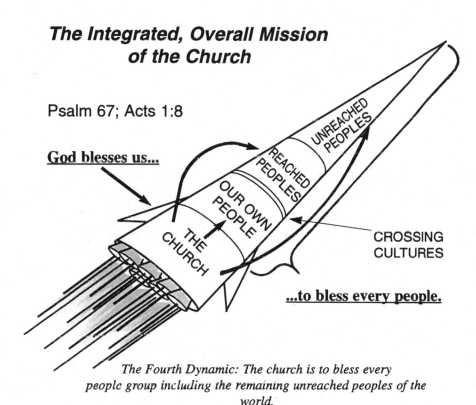

*The Fourth Dynamic: The church is to bless every
people group including the remaining unreached peoples of the
world.*

just a Family; we're a Family Business. God pours His blessing into us
to pass on His blessing in Jesus Christ to the whole world, people group
by people group.

Our job in the Family Business—our overall mission—is very specific:

> *We're heading toward an explicit goal.* It's a celestial city called Zion.
> Some from "every tribe and tongue and people and nation" will
> gather in the throne room of the Lamb (Revelation 5:9). Billions
> and billions of humans will enjoy a festival: "The Lord Almighty
> will prepare a feast of rich food for all peoples" (Isaiah 25:6, NIV).
> Looking back into time from that dazzling city, we'll see that the
> grace of God worked through His people in ministries from Je-
> rusalem to the uttermost parts to invite guests from every people
> to the party!

*The identity of these people groups is definable:* God has a "register of the peoples" (Psalm 87:6, NIV) listing the exact number of those yet to be reached. And we're getting close to a clear reading of that heavenly scroll.

*There is a timetable for the task.* The mission of your church is not a vague program of holding lots of meetings and trying to do everything until Jesus returns. The mission of the Church comprises a countdown of the discipling of the world's people groups: "And this gospel of the kingdom will be preached in the whole world as a testimony to all nations, and then the end will come" (Matthew 24:14, NIV).

Studying and praying through specifics like these can be tools God uses to help guide and lead you to your role in the global plan. God wants you to know the direction of your life-mission, and the mission of your church. It's your involvement in this cosmic plan that will bring you closer to Him as you trust Him in new ways and experience His power in greater dimensions.

An integrated vision in a fellowship is not only specific. It is also noncompetitive. Folks whose interests and ministries concentrate on the nose cone of seeing an unreached people discipled nevertheless affirm the other God-given ministries of the fellowship. These mission fanatics know that frontier mission efforts desperately need a strong power base. So the true mission visionary thinks through how the various home-front ministries fit into the overall mission of the Church. And good missions people become renowned for encouraging and promoting the women's aerobics group, a new building program, a second-grade boys' Sunday school class and fishing trip—and all the other God-given ministries in the church that on the surface seem to have nothing to do with reaching an unreached people.

An integrated vision in a fellowship is also liberating. An integrated, single vision in a local church also frees up the resources of a congregation. As a fellowship lists its assets in manpower, prayer power, finances, and talents (which we'll work through in Chapter 10), it invariably realizes its limitations. One church can't do it all.

Let's say a fellowship senses its origins, giftings, and interests seem to emphasize the second dynamic of the overall mission of the Church. They strengthen their own fellowship in all sorts of ministries so that they can unleash on their neighbors, their city, their own culture God's blessing.

Knowing that evangelism builds the Kingdom army, knowing that standing up for righteousness in our own culture is crucial to a credible message in other cultures, the church busses kids, holds training sessions for personal evangelism, prepares bag lunches for the homeless, visits children's homes, and more. And because this church knows that its ministries are merely a means toward an overall goal, in all they do they pass on a vision for the world.

So along with the familiar verses they teach kids bussed in from the neighborhood, they're also teaching them the song: "The B-I-B-L-E, it has one story you see, to reach all nations with God's love, the B-I-B-L-E." They know that these subtle yet powerful references to the nations lay seeds that in time will germinate, resulting in laborers for the nations 15–25 years down the road.

Now, shouldn't this fellowship also partner with another culture's church? Shouldn't they also focus on reaching an unreached people? Maybe not actively. Just as God graces individual believers with varying giftings, He usually gives a personality and an area of emphasis to a whole fellowship. As that fellowship submits to the authority of the Head of the Body, God aligns the giftings of that church into His overall plan.

A church needs to acknowledge, and especially in prayer be concerned with, each of the four dynamics of the Church. But every church need not feel pressured to do everything, to spread its limited resources too thin, to run ministries simply because "all the growing churches are doing this." As uncomfortable as it may sound to frontier mission zealots, not every church should commit itself to planting a church in an unreached people.

When a congregation knows what it's about, knows which areas of the mission of the church are its forte, the pressure is off. Pastors and elders and even mission committee members are guilt-free to say, "That's a great ministry idea but we don't have the resources for it, because this is where we're headed." And they do what all churches can do: trust God that their prayers for the nations are being heard and making an impact, and believe that some of our young people will someday be goers.

Meanwhile, this freedom to emphasize a church's strengths makes networking between churches all the more important. Let's say Church A, whose specialty is blessing its own people, launches a neighborhood ministry. Perhaps it encounters families who come from another culture. But because cross-cultural church-planting is known to be Church B's specialty, Church A blesses the efforts of Church B, while Church B benefits from the pre-evangelism done by Church A.

A unifying vision can be specific, noncompetitive, and liberating.

## Malfunctions in the Mission

How can this desire to be used by God among the nations backfire?

It can be divisive. Among all the competing interest groups in a church, the little "unreached peoples club" can whine for more bulletin space, more budget allotments, more volunteers. These frontier mission fanatics can point long, bony fingers in judgment at other believers in the fellowship and announce that if a Christian doesn't have a personal involvement in reaching an unreached people, he or she isn't in the will of God.

This "us-them" mentality can do more to destroy the unity in the church than anything else. In fact, focusing on an unreached people and touting oneself as one of those rare, noble disciples called World Christians can be one of the most obnoxious steps mission-minded believers can take in a local fellowship. They are rarely appreciated and hence are given little time or resources.

The image of the rocket representing the mission of the Church can, of course, be faulty for various reasons. Let's look at a few reasons that cause malfunctions in missions.

Sometimes we think that any attention paid to the uttermost parts of the earth has to wait until we've first perfected our Jerusalems, Judeas, and Samarias. Although it's true that Stage One, the blessing-strengthening of the local church, is foundational to ministry, it's not true that we can't concern ourselves with other cultures until our own is fully redeemed.

Remember, Jesus told us to be witnesses both—simultaneously—in Jerusalem, Judea, Samaria, and the uttermost parts of the earth (Acts 1:8).

Another malfunction in our mission can be getting stuck in Stage One. A fellowship that concentrates on strengthening itself for the sake of strengthening itself is like a body builder who pumps up his muscles until he can hardly move. There can be a fine line between seeking to grow internally and "he who seeks to save his own life will lose it."

A church that concentrates only on Stage One is like the powerful booster stage of a rocket with no place to go. The first stage blasts into action and careens in every direction like a deflating balloon. A church with no clear direction but lots of activity diffuses its resources; the people tire of activity and suffer burnout. Ministry activity—virtually all of it taking place within the fellowship—proceeds at a furious pace, but the fruit of ministry is sparse.

Without a clear understanding that their ministries are a means toward the overall goal of what God is doing, the people lose discipline.

Without a vision, the people lose focus. They, as the King James Version puts it, perish (Proverbs 29:18).

Another malfunction of our single-vision mission is neglect of Stage One. A fellowship might concentrate on blessing an unreached people but neglect strengthening its base. That congregation might be like a needle-nosed rocket nose cone drifting through space with no thrust.

Often mission activist groups feel a clear sense of purpose and direction but are frustrated by lack of prayer power, financial power, and people power. In frustration, these folks point fingers at the lack of vision of the pastor or elders, or at the rest of the congregation for their obvious selfishness.

If your overriding problem as a mission task force or mission mobilizer is the lack of resources, slow down somehow: You need to reconnect in new ways with the booster stage—with a strengthened church. You need to affirm and encourage the various ministries of the church, to work at integrating a vision of frontier mission within every God-given ministry in the church.

A mission-minded church might malfunction by failing to impact its own culture in Stage Two. What, then, gives it a right to tell an unreached people "blessed is the people whose God is the Lord"?

For example: You're sent from your hometown by a consortium of five churches to help reach the Buryat Mongolians, a people living in the Siberian stretches of Russia just north of Mongolia.

In the regional capital of Ulan Ude, you sit down with the elder political leaders of the city. They ask, "We do not worship your Christian God. Why should we allow you to stir up our citizens about Jesus Christ?"

You say, "In my hometown, the Christians have declared our city to be a 'hunger-free zone.' They're seeing to it that no one in our city goes hungry ever again. Would you like to see that happen here in Ulan Ude? In my neighborhood, Christians have developed a job training center for young people. Would you like several of these across your city? All the Christians in my town are helping solve problems of alcoholism and lack of child care for working mothers. They're helping people learn to read and are caring for the elderly.

"There are Christian businessmen and women in my home city who have been sharpening their skills for years as they have helped bless my town. Some have said they will come to Ulan Ude to teach seminars on starting new businesses. Others will help you receive grant funding from international foundations to create more jobs. Still others have volunteered to serve as consultants for your efforts to export your freshwater fish products and to develop energy sources."

You conclude: "Because Jesus Christ tells His followers to bless every people, we want to bless the Buryat people of Ulan Ude."

Imagine the city fathers still frowning at your offer: "And will you at the same time be telling them about Christianity? We are not Christians here; we are atheists and some are Buddhists."

You reply, "We could have an agreement: We will do our very best to bless the Buryat people. If anyone asks why we are doing these things, may we tell them about Jesus Christ?"

The elders turn to each other slowly, faces inscrutable. Finally one says—speaking English for the first time without translation—"Okay."

A church with a vision of its mission to reach the uttermost parts of the earth must have a strong Stage Two. Fulfilling your obligation to bless your own culture gives the credibility that missionary enterprises too often lack in offering God's blessing to an unreached people.

Besides, if a local fellowship isn't evangelizing its own community, it simply won't have enough prayer power and other resources to be effective in the big picture; no new believers in the church is a sure sign of a malfunction. A mission-minded church that isn't activating its local ministries is destined to talk big but accomplish little in God's great global enterprise.

## The Church With a Unifying Vision

What happens when a church catches a vision of God's heart for every people and works to integrate that direction into its overall mission?

One growing congregation focused for the month of October 1993 on praying for the unreached people of Bhutan during the AD2000 "Praying Through the 10/40 Window" emphasis. Not only was the entire congregation mobilized to spend hours in prayer for a spiritual breakthrough over this Lamaistic Buddhist territory, the church sent an intercessory team to Bhutan itself to pray down the strongholds holding the Bhutanese captive. Imagine the excitement of the entire church when, just three months later, a Bhutanese believer faxed:

> Good News! The king of Bhutan has officially allowed open preaching for Christians. Restriction has been lifted but the lamas [Buddhist priests] are strongly opposing the decision. Pray with us. Prayer changes even the mind of the kings!

Religious repression again threatens Bhutan. Still, be assured that this praying congregation is expanding its prayer skills and its vision.

Another fellowship found that involvement in the cross-cultural dynamics of the Church's overall mission prompted growth in the first stage of strengthening the Church:

"In fifteen years of pastoring and two major building projects, I have never seen such ownership of a project by our congregation than our Sandawe Project," says senior pastor Ron Mahurin of Cedar Crest Bible Fellowship Church in Allentown, Pennsylvania, in the United States. "We started in 1987 with a vision of reaching one people group, and since then we have had many families prepared and sent out. Our mission and building giving doubled, then tripled. Our congregation has grown, and our people have a heart for God's heart for all peoples!"

It began in 1987 when youth pastor Cliff Boone and pastor Ron read an article in an ACMC (Advancing Church Mission Commitment) newsletter about churches focusing on a particular unreached people group. Sensing the Lord was calling them to do this, Cliff contacted AIM (formerly Africa Inland Mission) with whom he had spent six months in Tanzania. The church and the mission agency decided to focus on the Sandawe people of Tanzania.

While this was being decided, the bishop of the Africa Inland Church of Tanzania was in the United States and met with the church leaders to discuss collaboration. A three-way partnership of local church, sending agency, and national church was forged based on the principle of Ecclesiastes 4:12, "A cord of three strands is not quickly broken" (NIV).

What happens when folks on the home front focus prayer on their people group? Former youth pastor Cliff Boone and his wife, Becky, now missionaries to the Sandawe, rave about their home church Wednesday night prayer meetings. "With all the many serious prayer concerns of that large church body, the people never fail to mention the Sandawe. There they are, old and young, from all walks of life, bowed before the Father, pleading on behalf of the Sandawe people—a people whom they have never seen but whom they committed themselves to reaching with the Gospel."

One hot Thursday morning in Kwamtoro, Tanzania—just a few hours after the Allentown church Wednesday night prayer-warriors had risen from their knees, a middle-aged Sandawe man called to the Boones from outside their shack. He pulled out three tattered Swahili tracts the Boones had given him months before.

"I have stayed with these little books for two months," he said. "I have read them and read them. I have talked with my wife about them. Now I have come here to be saved."

After serving the man refreshment, Cliff opened his Bible and carefully explained the Gospel message. After long discussion and lots of questions, the man said, "This is what I want. I want to believe in Jesus."

With the solid sending base of the Allentown church, the Boones say, "We have seen God do more than we could have imagined." Recently Cliff reported 20 believers among the 32–40,000 Sandawe. As well, the Africa Inland Church, mostly Swahili-speaking nationals from the majority tribe, had trained and sent their first missionary couple to the Sandawe!

But what has happened to the Cedar Crest Fellowship Bible Church with this focus on an unreached people? According to Pastor Ron, since 1987:

- The church has built and fully paid for a $600,000 addition to their building.

- They are almost at their goal of raising $800,000 to start work on a second $2 million building project.

- Their mission giving grew from $40,000 in 1987 to over $125,000 in 1992.

- The congregation has grown from about 275 members to its present size of 500 members, at a fast-paced average of 45 new persons each year (almost doubling in size!) Pastor Ron is quick to point out that these are new members; not just biological growth!

- Every financial area of the church has been strengthened—including special projects and the addition of two new, fully funded, staff persons.

Pastor Ron says they worried that this concentration on one people group would limit the mission focus of the congregation. What has happened, however, is an expansion of mission vision that seems to encompass all peoples. Thirteen family units have been sent out over a five-year period as new missionaries and ministers to many parts of the world. This focus on one unreached people has served to spearhead the entire mission program of the church.

When the decision to adopt the Sandawe was made, no one quite knew what to expect. But in the ensuing years, eight churches in the New York–Pennsylvania–New Jersey areas have linked up with each other, with African churches, and with Africa Inland Mission to reach the Sandawe. A Tanzanian pastor leads a church-planting team of missionaries including the Boones, the former youth leaders. The Sandawe are hearing the Gospel for the first time. Cliff reports, "Some are putting their faith in Christ, and a small church is started. The light is beginning to shine in a dark place!"

Pastor Ron and Cliff have written down their experiences in a workbook format for other fellowships and groups to study and adapt. To obtain their workbook, contact ACMC, PO Box ACMC, Wheaton IL 60187 USA. Also available from the church is a video produced in 1988 entitled "Our Bold New Missions Venture," which was used to introduce the Sandawe people to the congregation.

Whether your fellowship is in Allentown, USA or Nuremburg, Germany, you know what the Scripture says about being of one mind: "There is one body and one Spirit, just as also you were called in one hope of your calling; one Lord, one faith, one baptism, one God and Father" (Ephesians 4:4–6). It makes sense that we catch a clear vision of how our diverse ministries can be integrated into the overall mission of our church!

Now, what is your individual part in the overall mission of the Body of Christ? And how can you help others find their niche in God's plan of blessing His people to bless every people?

# Part II

Find Your Niche

You, the Twenty-First Century

World Christian

## CHAPTER SIX

# Your Strategic Role in the Kingdom

*Get ready to be globally significant*

NOVEMBER 1989, ST. PETERSBURG, RUSSIA — Use your imagination: You're an American third-grade Sunday school teacher from Claire- more First Baptist Church in eastern Oklahoma. You help wash the communion cups once each month. You were elected to the school board largely because of your local, notorious stand against pornog- raphy. Till this trip, you had never traveled much farther than Bull Shoals in Arkansas, Kansas City to the north, and Dallas to the south (when Oklahoma State beat SMU in the Cotton Bowl).

And now you're white-knuckled on the edge of a worn wooden pew in St. Petersburg, Russia. You're ice-cold, and it is strangely gloomy— as if the four electric bulbs dangling from the eighteen-foot-high ceiling are starved for electricity. You muse vaguely over the economic situa- tion in the former Soviet Union.

Last week you had leaned against the near-freezing wind in a city park. At the end of a long line of citizenry, you chatted with a sidewalk vendor selling light bulbs. "Where do you get the light bulbs?" you asked through your translator.

"From the government," replied the smiling merchant as he doled out bulbs and collected rubles. "They give me as many burned-out bulbs as I want every morning."

"Burned-out bulbs?" you asked. "You mean these people are paying you for burned-out light bulbs?"

"Of course," he happily replied. "They slip them in their coat pock- ets. Then they replace good bulbs with these burned-out ones at their places of work and take the good ones home. The government-paid janitors have plenty of work replacing bulbs, the citizens get cheap light bulbs for their homes, and I am running a very profitable capitalistic business!"

Now a week later, a gnarled old pastor next to you busily rips pages out of a Bible on his lap. Up at the podium one of your church members, Ralph Bethea, waves his arms in jerky frustration of preaching through a translator. Ralph expounds on a passage in Ephesians; his Russian interpreter, a gas meter reader during the week, translates for him. During his translation breaks it's obvious that Ralph is increasingly upset over the old man ripping pages out of the Bible.

Finally Ralph stops, jumps down from the podium and waves his hands in front of the pastor, saying "Nyet, nyet!" By the time the hubbub calms down, it becomes apparent that the pastor does this at every gathering of the congregation. Now in 1989 there are still so few Bibles to go around to the growing number of believers that a section of several pages is better than none; so the pastor rips the pages for distribution after each service. The translator says the old man has been doing this for nearly eleven years whenever he could get a Bible—ever since his own Bible, one that had belonged to his now-deceased mother, was confiscated by the KGB.

Suddenly a man in the back of the crowd calls out as Ralph steps back up to the platform to resume the message. The translator interprets: "This fellow says he is former KGB. He knows a warehouse where some Bibles are stored. He wants you to go with him."

An hour later you and Ralph stand in the near-darkness of a waterfront warehouse filled with, according to the suspiciously nervous KGB man—the *former* KGB man—more than 40,000 Bibles. "But," he emphasizes, wiping the sweat from his forehead in the icy air, "I cannot authorize you to *take* any of these. You must buy them. Policy says there must be an auction."

So near midnight you—the Oklahoma Sunday school teacher—stand awkwardly raising your hand now and again to "bid" for a warehouse full of Russian Bibles. In the end you let Ralph, the only other bidder, win the auction. And so for a few hundred dollars he buys 40,000 Bibles from the Soviets' dreaded secret police. The KGB man himself fires up a truck, helps you load the crates, and delivers you and the Bibles back to the little church where hundreds of believers still sit waiting for the end of the sermon.

The translator calls the entire congregation out to the street, where you and Ralph and the KGB man crack open the wooden crates and from the back of the truck hand out Bibles under a lone streetlight.

What, you ask yourself as you begin to work up a sweat in the frigid predawn night, does this have to do with teaching third-graders or fighting pornography in Oklahoma? There's more of a link in this crazy experience than the fact that I happen to be here. Maybe—

Suddenly in the gloomy street a group in the crowd bursts into cries and clapping, literally dancing in the cold light of the corner street-lamp. "What's going on?" you shout to the translator, irritated again by the language barrier. "It's the pastor," the translator yells back from the street. "He was handed his mother's Bible!"

## Your Specific Niche

You're qualified for a specific niche in ministry for now; either indirectly or directly, that ministry has to do with seeing that every people is represented before the throne of the Lamb. You have a significant role in this cosmic enterprise. It would be pathetic to miss your opportunity.

Your individual vision of your purpose on earth—as well as your fellowship's vision of its purpose—isn't a matter of picking a ministry out of a hat. It's a matter of seeing what God has already planned for you. And what He plans is discoverable as you continue to seek Him with an obedient heart. So let's think through how you and other believers can find your individual niches in God's global plan.

But before this book can help you locate your place in God's history, you need to be building on a good foundation necessary to any Christian ministry, formal or informal, paid or volunteer, at home or overseas, in your own culture or with people who leave you clueless. We'll look at those more general qualities before we go further in finding your possible place in reaching the unreached:

1. *Own the lordship of Jesus Christ.* To call Christ your Savior and Lord means to say to Him that you're willing to "go anywhere, do anything, say anything for His Kingdom."

Too many Christians get lost here, right at the start of their journey. They think that to arrive at this point you have to have read great theological books, shared your faith with multitudes and led many to the Lord, and spent countless nights in prayer. Only then do you finally reach a point called "spiritual maturity." Only then can you finally tell the Lord you're available for anything.

Don't *you* quit so easily! This isn't the "graduate" level of Christianity way over the heads and hearts of normal believers.

Here's why. Becoming a Christian is in its essence telling God that because He laid down His life for you, that you are giving your life over to Him, no strings attached. That's for all of us!

Make sure this is settled in your mind. Don't go any further unless you are willing to go wherever, do anything, say anything, even on the other side of the planet, understanding that attitude as a normal part of the Christian life.

God often looks for obedience before He reveals His will to you. As the old saying goes, "If you are willing to do God's will, He will reveal it to you." And as John 14:21 puts it, "Whoever has my commands and obeys them, he is the one who loves me. He who loves me will be loved by my Father, and I too will love him and *show myself to him*" (NIV, italics added).

*2. Acknowledge the "end goal."* The second foundation you need in discovering God's global place for you is to realize that no matter what He has you doing, somehow, some way your life is going to impact the nations.

This understanding of all-out commitment to obeying God's direction has prompted more than 30,000 Christians to sign "The Caleb Declaration":

> By the grace of God and for His glory, I commit my entire life to obeying His commission of Matthew 28:18–20 wherever and however He leads me, giving priority to the peoples currently beyond reach of the Gospel (Romans 15:20–21).
>
> Signed: _____
> Date: _____
> Witnesses: _____

These people have placed a higher priority on the unreached, yet they still have the "wherever and however He leads me" clause. Many of these Calebites have never left their home country, but they still impact the nations through prayer and by sending and mobilizing others.

Think and pray through that statement of commitment. The rest of our study together will be less than relevant if you still wrestle to accept God's desire to impact the nations through you, wherever He places you.

*3. Be committed to finish the race.* Here's a tough one. Living out a global perspective won't be easy. In fact, your greatest opposition may come from believers you love dearly—those close to you who love God (to varying degrees) but who have never caught a glimpse of this far-reaching plan of God. You may be the only one praying, the only one going, the only one excited. Don't let that stop you.

Greg Livingstone, in a manuscript on "Becoming Unstoppable," writes this:

Very little happens in God's work until God raises up a man or a woman who refuses to settle for less than what God has put on his or her heart. The world has long understood that motivation, determination, ambition, passion, vision, dreams, hunger, drive, guts, will to win, call it what you like, is by far a greater factor in who accomplishes something and who doesn't.

Did you ever run track? I was slow as a runner. So when our Aspen High School track team invited me to be the third entrant in a six-school meet to run the 440-yard dash, I was puzzled. They explained to me that each school had to enter three runners to be eligible and we only had two. If I would start the race, it wasn't important whether I could finish it or not; my running would enable our two fast men to perhaps win first and second place.

I was incensed. They didn't want me to run, they just wanted me for a body to satisfy the rule book. But, out of school loyalty, I showed up, dressed for the part. Insult was added to injury, however, when instead of lining up the runners in a staggered formation which would make the outside lanes the same distance as the inside ones, the track officials lined up all eighteen runners from six schools in a straight line. And there I was, number eighteen, clear out on the very outside edge of the pack! Well, I got mad, really mad; and just to show them all—the team and the coach and the track officials—I determined to win the race.

To this day, no one knows whether I jumped the gun or not, but I bolted out of the starting blocks and headed right for the inside of the track, and when the dust cleared halfway around the track, I was leading the entire pack! I was pushing my little legs like pistons on a runaway train at the pace one should run 40 yards, not 440! As I reached the halfway mark I could hear the coach exclaiming, "My God, what is Livingstone doing out in front?"

Well, almost needless to say, in running good training and better endowment usually prevail over sheer determination alone. Our two fastest runners soon overtook me, as did one other runner, but I came in fourth! I wore my yellow ribbon around school for the next two weeks just to prove it.

This determination is what the apostle Paul means by "run to win." Is that how you're running the Christian life? Are you an unstoppable? When the Goliaths of Islam, Buddhism, and Hinduism defy the supremacy of the One True God, as they do today, does all the determination of young David well up inside you, so that you determine in your heart, even if nobody else goes after this Goliath, for God's glory, you're going to go?

Anyone can get on the missions bandwagon when the Church

has seen a lot of success. Few can get excited about carrying the Gospel to the Muslim world in the face of one hundred years of apparent failure. God is looking for those who are filled with His courage and determination to face the impossible when it seems everyone else has lost their courage and determination.

We're here on earth to be blessed with God's goodness, including our adoption into His family through the blood of Christ; stewardship of our finances, health, and sanity in a reckless, unhealthy, and insane world; living out the love of God in growing relationships; and deepening in appreciation of the truths of God's Word and our worshipful response. We're blessed, however, to spread the blessing to every people group.

We're here to make sure that in our own way we contribute to more humans living eternally in heaven—humans from every people, tribe, tongue, and nation. Yet running the race may mean going counter-cultural—even counter-cultural to the church.

Aspirations and dreams you assimilate from the Christian culture around you may well trip you up. One major Christian university, for example, has the president's home high on a hill all by itself overlooking a lake. It's located right outside the dining area. It's magnificent. But what does it communicate? "You too can graduate from this university and get your own home with no one living around you, all the space you like—if you only work hard like this man does." This message is the exact opposite of Christ's command to be the salt of the earth, the light of the world.

A pastor in southern California bought a second home (half a million dollars worth) up in the mountains. What does that say? "Take care of yourself, you deserve a break." I'm sure many people in that church think, for all the wrong reasons, "You know, I could be a pastor too."

It is no wonder that when you announce you intend to go overseas to serve the king that you hear objections from Christians like "Is it safe over there?" "You're throwing your life away. Does God want you to do that?" "But there are so many needs right here . . ." Think through your responses. Then finish the race even if it means going against your culture.

Finishing the race may also mean holding up your shield of faith against the attacks of the evil one. To sideline you, Satan will throw at you everything he has.

Ken and Debra actively mobilized others, then prepared to leave for the field themselves. Before leaving, Debra gave birth to a healthy and vibrant son, Jonathan. In the process of getting ready for the field, they all needed shots—a standard procedure, yet one to be undertaken with certain precautions. However, through a doctor's neglect, Jonathan reacted severely to the shot. His brain was damaged and he is now behind developmentally. Yet Ken and Debra are still on the field giving their son (and now other children) the love and attention they need. It was an excellent attempt by the evil one to keep them from getting to the field, but it didn't work.

Another young man was preparing to go to the Muslim world as a missionary. While in training he met a man whose father had worked in Libya. During the course of our conversation he shared with me what the man's father had learned: If you get thrown into jail in some of these countries you face almost certain rape.

That shook him. He had told the Lord that he would die for Him, but never had the possibility of getting raped by another man as he carried out his commitment to God occurred to him. But by faith he overcame this dart.

Be prepared. The battle is tough. But persevere for God's glory and your integrity before Him. Prayerfully reckon with the highest price you might pay, continue to claim the sovereignty of God, and you will run hard to finish the race.

4. *Keep from clinging.* Another pitfall you might encounter on your way to understanding your place in the Father's global plan is clinging to a life direction you feel God gave you previously.

Let's say you came to know the Lord seven years ago. In the early years you were well grounded by being involved in Bible studies, evangelism, and worship. Your life was so changed that four years later you decided to serve the Lord full time.

At that time you knew only a few ways you could serve Him. You could be a youth pastor. Or a senior pastor. Maybe even a staff worker with a parachurch agency. Let's also assume that God spoke directly to you about how to serve, and as a result you have been a pastor for the past year.

Yet only recently you were exposed to a vision of God's heart for the world. At this point it would be easy to "cling" to God's original direction for your life. You're to be a pastor until the day you die, right?

But if your heart is set on up-to-the-minute obedience you can say, "OK, Lord, you led me into pastoral work back then, but now I have this new information about the needs of the Muslim world—the Buddhists, Hindus, Tribals. What fresh direction do you have for me now?"

In Luke 14:33, Jesus teaches about lordship. He sums it up: "In the same way, any of you who does not give up everything he has cannot be my disciple" (NIV).

Giving up all you have—possessions—might mean the physical possessions of this world, like cars, homes, and stereo systems, but it refers to much more. You also possess goals, dreams, desires, and probably a career. Jesus is saying that if you want to follow Him, even those less solid things are on the table, subject to change. Following Him might mean letting go of your own plans.

Sometimes the *hardest* possessions to swap for a new vision are the Christian goals and dreams God gave you at one time. Yet you must always be willing to change direction, lest the lordship of Jesus slip from your life. Even career missionaries have to follow close after Jesus, heeding His fresh direction. Most make many directional changes on the field, and almost all sooner or later head "back home," even if only for retirement. No one is exempt from needing fresh understanding of God's plans.

It's helpful to note that God can change His work for you even if you haven't finished what He's shown you to do. Remember Abraham? God told him, "Take your son, your only son, Isaac, whom you love, and go to the region of Moriah. Sacrifice him there as a burnt offering on one of the mountains I will tell you about." But before Abraham completed that God-given task, God stepped in and said through His angel, "Do not lay a hand on the boy. . . ." Then Abraham saw that God had provided a ram for the sacrifice.

Listen closely to God's voice so that when He gives you new insight, you can freshly evaluate what He desires you to do now. Then and only then will you be able to know your place in the global harvest.

5. *Acknowledge your role as a priest.* A priest? Yes, a priest!

God let the children of Israel know early on that they held a position of great privilege and also of great responsibility:

"If you will indeed obey My voice and keep My covenant, then you shall be My own possession among all the peoples. . . . And you shall be to Me a kingdom of priests and a holy nation" (Exodus 19:5–6).

What did the Old Testament priests do? Each year the priest would first confess any sins in his own life, then step through the veil of the Tabernacle or Temple into the Holy of Holies. In the very presence of God, he would intercede for the sins of the people, sprinkling the blood of sacrifices on the Mercy Seat. Then the priest would exit the veil and begin to serve the people, offering them the meat of the sacrificed animals.

Israel as a whole nation was to be a kingdom of priests for whom? For the other nations of the world.

God gives the same privileged position and the same responsibility to us as New Testament believers:

"You are a chosen race, a royal priesthood, a holy nation, a people for God's own possession, that you may proclaim the excellencies of Him who has called you out of darkness into His marvelous light" (1 Peter 2:9).

Most Christians assume that the "priesthood of the believer" only means that each of us can enter the very presence of God without going through an intermediary priest. That's good news. But that's certainly not all there is to this wonderful statement of our standing and calling before God. Christians are always blessed to be a blessing to every people. So it's easy to see that Christians are blessed as royal priests for two purposes:

(1) To intercede for the people of every nation of the world.

(2) To serve and to minister to them.

Knowing that God has called you to be a priest to the nations helps you sidestep the self-centered thinking that creeps into the mind-set of the contemporary church. Our thought isn't "What is God's will for MY life, how can I best serve God?"—overemphasizing *me* and *my* giftings, *my* desires, while underemphasizing God's global purpose. Our thought should be "Lord, I see what you are doing from Genesis to Revelation—you want your glory to be made known among the nations. What can I best do to help this goal be reached?" With this new question we are automatically seeking a global role, rather than settling for a narrow vision that is not completely pleasing to the Lord. Our abilities are targeted toward fulfilling God's purposes.

Being a priest even supplies a straightforward way to find your niche in God's plans: Think of ways to fulfill your twofold priestly role!

6. *Get to know yourself.* God meticulously designed you. You're one of a kind:

"For Thou didst form my inward parts;
Thou didst weave me in my mother's womb.
My frame was not hidden from Thee;
Thine eyes have seen my unformed substance;
And in thy book they were all written,
The days that were ordained for me,
When as yet there was not one of them" (Psalm 139:13–16).

Not only are you custom-designed, you have been custom-shaped by your life experiences. Not even other siblings in your family have endured, enjoyed, or experienced all that you have. You are unique. Your experiences in life have been lived by no other human being.

Think about how nature and nurture have worked together to shape you for a specific ministry. Could your ethnic background be a source of direction for you? Maybe your childhood in the home of alcoholic parents qualifies you for discipling others with the same problems and frame of reference. Could your adventures overseas as a young child (due to your parents' work there) have prepared you as a candidate for unreached peoples church planting?

God further sets you apart with the specific "measure of faith" that is yours, your growing ability to trust Him (Romans 12:3). What is it that you can trust God for? Do you believe He can get you in and among the Karalcalpocks of Uzbekistan? Can you trust Him to get you and a team of five others into Libya? If your faith is great, you could be one of the few God directs to work among the unreached peoples of the world.

7. *Determine what your spiritual gifting is.* God has added to your natural attributes, interests, abilities, and measure of faith at least one spiritual gifting. You are given a particular capacity to "manifest the Spirit"—a particular spiritual gifting (1 Corinthians 12:7).

There are scores of good studies available on spiritual gifts. If you're fuzzy on this crucial doctrine, study the biblical passages and check out several books on the topic at your local Christian bookshop. The following is a list of many of the recognized spiritual gifts which the Holy Spirit "distributes to each one individually just as He wills" (1 Corinthians 12:11). If you're comfortable with the Word's teaching on spiritual gifts, check off those that are your possible giftings from this list compiled from Romans 12, 1 Corinthians 12, and Ephesians 4:

apostleship
prophecy
teaching
evangelism
pastoring
serving
administration
wisdom
knowledge
faith
exhortation/encouragement
miracles
healing
tongues
interpretation of tongues
discerning of spirits
giving
mercy

The Spirit, of course, can give any kind of gifting "as He wills," so this isn't an exhaustive list. Some Bible scholars insist that celibacy is a spiritual gift (1 Corinthians 7:7). Peter Wagner suggests that even martyrdom might be added to a list of gifts! (1 Corinthians 13:3)[1]

Generally, determining which gift or gifts have been given to you by the Spirit can be clarified by

(1.) Personally studying the biblical doctrine of spiritual gifts.

(2.) Acknowledging that if it's a good thing for you to know your gifting, God will reveal it to you.

(3.) Taking a battery of tests that will help you determine your gifting.

(4.) Asking a mature Christian who knows you what they see as your gifts.

(5.) Trying out areas of gifts. See what works with those you serve.

8. *Practice your gifts in ministry.* The apostle Paul wrote: "There are varieties of gifts . . . and there are varieties of ministries" (1 Corinthians 12:4–5).

There are various ways to use spiritual gifts to serve others. Let's say, for example, that a believer has a spiritual gifting of exhortation or encouragement. The Greek term for this gift is serving as a *paracletos*— "one called alongside to help." Some refer to this gifting as a "counseling" gift.

Like all the other gifts, this one can serve in various ministries— from counseling non-Christian unwed mothers to counseling Christian married couples to counseling alcoholic men.

How can a believer determine which ministry or ministries best utilizes his or her spiritual gift? By practicing. If counseling non-Christian unwed mothers simply doesn't produce fruit, perhaps practicing that counseling gift on Christian married couples may "click."

A believer's role as an interceding, serving priest to others, *plus* that believer's unique personality, skills, interests and background, *plus* that believer's measure of faith and spiritual gifts can be acted out in millions of ways—in "varieties of ministries."

9. *Explore a variety of settings for your ministry.* This is the zeroing-in step. Here you are seeking to answer the question: "Where and among what people will I serve to accomplish the global task?"

There are varieties of gifts and varieties of ministries. There are also varieties of effects (1 Corinthians 12:5–6).

The effects of ministry are the practical results—what happens to whom. Which stage or dynamic of the overall mission of the church is affected by your ministry? An exhorter-encourager can minister effectively within a Christian fellowship in the first dynamic of the mission of the church. Or that counselor can minister effectively in the second dynamic of blessing non-Christians in his or her own people group. Or a counselor could serve a church in another culture. Or a counselor could actually minister among nonbelievers in an unreached people group.

How do you find exactly where and to whom your ministry fits? You explore! Don't settle for the noble-sounding but not necessarily biblical phrase "bloom where you are planted." If you know that you're to minister within your own fellowship, excellent! But if you limit God's use of you in His great plan by never exposing your giftings to other people, other locales, or other cultures, you're only serving where you are by default!

Going short-term overseas could help you in this area. Volunteering to various groups in the inner city could help as well. Whatever the case, don't be afraid to explore.

*10. Find your niche.* Having owned Christ's lordship and reckoned with its implications, and thoughtfully considered your role as a priest, your unique natural predispositions and life-shaping experiences, and factored in your particular spiritual gifts and ways and places to serve, you're zeroing in on God's personalized plan for you in His determination to reach the nations.

You may be facing the frustration you feel the first time you try to bake something from scratch. While *you* may find it hard to stir together all these ingredients and come up with anything resembling a picture-perfect cake, God doesn't. We're suggesting you undertake a thorough Spirit-led self-examination of who you are as a person and as a Christian. That takes time. But God has factored all this into His specific purpose for your life. The growth you experience in finding your place in His plan is part of His equipping you to do the work of His plan. So don't be frustrated by the process, and don't become so obsessed with the process that you forget where you're headed!

Regardless of your self-estimation, God's Word calls you a "masterpiece" of His divine planning. That's the literal definition of the term "workmanship" in this familiar verse: "For we are His workmanship, created in Christ Jesus for good works, which God prepared beforehand, that we should walk in them" (Ephesians 2:10).

The last phrase is sometimes translated: "good works which God has prepared beforehand for [you] to do." Not only are you unique; the route of your race to heaven is also unique. God knew before you were born the exact content of your every day on earth. And He "prepared beforehand" specific good works, a specific course of action for you to follow, a specific path. Note too how the context of this verse is in the midst of Paul's discussion of the Gentiles and God's desire to see all things (Ephesians 1:10) come together under Christ. Hear it again: God intends for you to be part of His global plan!

Paul was clear on his own customized course: "I do not consider my life of any account as dear to myself, in order that I may finish my course, and the ministry which I received from the Lord Jesus" (Acts 20:24).

Every believer needs to be reminded: God has a job for you to do in His Family business, a job you alone are designed for. And you have a choice. You can "present your body a living and holy sacrifice . . . which is your spiritual service of worship" (Romans 12:1). Or you can "set on fire the course of your life" (James 3:6). You can watch your uniqueness go up in smoke.

Every one of us can find our strategic niche in God's overarching purpose on earth. But perhaps a good addendum to this last entry is: Find your niche *for now*. God has a way of shifting His valuable harvesters from one corner of the field to another. If we cling to remaining permanently in our specific ministry in a specific setting, our niche may well become a rut!

## Finding Your Strategic Niche

Here's a review of the steps we've talked about:
1. Acknowledge the lordship of Christ in your life (1 Corinthians 6:19).
2. Make the end goal of all you do to impact the nations (Romans 1:5–6).
3. Run the race to win (1 Corinthians 9:24–27).
4. Don't unwisely cling to direction God gave you earlier (Luke 14:33).
5. Acknowledge your role as a priest (Exodus 19:5–6; 1 Peter 2:9).
6. Get to know yourself (Psalm 139:13–16).
7. Determine your spiritual gifting (Romans 12:4–8; 1 Corinthians 12:7–11).
8. Practice your gifts in a particular ministry (1 Corinthians 12:5).
9. Explore various settings for your ministry (1 Corinthians 12:6).
10. Find your niche (Ephesians 2:10).

Did you notice that Step 9—Explore various settings—was a key step in determining where a believer serves in the overall mission of the Church? But although this is the step that helps clarify the possibilities of being mission mobilizers, senders, goers, or welcomers, nothing was mentioned about a "call" to mission work. Why not? Glad you asked!

## Your Call

Many goers talk about being "called" into mission work. Most pastors speak of being "called to the ministry."

But when was the last time you heard your local church usher mention being "called" to be a servant? Or a sender being "called" to stay home?

Let's be candid: God can clearly call anyone He chooses for a particular task. And He can call in any way He wants—through obvious circumstances, through the direction of mature advisers, through Scripture. If He chooses He can call down through the clouds, speak through a donkey or from a burning bush to audibly clue a follower to his or her place of ministry. But nowhere in Scripture do we find that a dramatic "call" into ministry is a doctrine or a requirement to move out in ministry as one in a nation of priests.

The Bible mentions that individuals can be called to a particular life situation, such as being single or married (1 Corinthians 7:21). But most uses of the word "call" in the New Testament refer to our calling to become believers (see, for example, 2 Thessalonians 2:13–14 and Hebrews 3:1).

Moreover, most Christians aren't sure what they're looking for when it comes to being "called" into their role in God's global Cause. The idea is usually that as you come to a point of living an all-out commitment to Christ, you get some sort of supernatural "call" that tells you what to do. And that's where the call concept gets extra-biblical: God seldom calls people before they start ministering! As is often said, it's tough to steer a car while it's still parked. God's guidance to a particular ministry is more often a case of hearing His direction *while* we're moving on what we already know about His great plan: "Whether you turn to the right or to the left, your ears will hear a voice behind you, saying, 'This is the way; walk in it' " (Isaiah 30:21, NIV).

In fact, if God is not giving you light on His future role for you, it's dangerous to invent your own light—your own rationalizations of what He wants, pretending that a twist of circumstance is His call. Sometimes God simply allows you to step ahead in darkness by faith, relying on His faithful character. Darkness here isn't sin but simply a lack of knowledge. God says through Isaiah,

"Who among you fears the Lord and obeys the word of his servant? Let him who walks in the dark, who has no light, trust in the name of the Lord and rely on his God. But now, all you who light fires and provide yourselves with flaming torches, go, walk in the light of your fires and of the torches you have set ablaze. This is what you shall receive from my hand: You will lie down in torment (Isaiah 50:10–11, NIV).

In other words, don't push ahead of God regarding finding your course in His great plan. If it's a good thing for Him to reveal His niche for you well before you move ahead in ministering, He'll tell you (Psalm 84:11). If it's not a good thing, He won't. Don't agonize over not having a clear, supernatural call to ministry. Simply obey the first step He has already set before you. "Do whatever he tells you" (John 2:5, NIV).

## The Mission Call in Acts

Because of the elusiveness of this call idea, all kinds of potential cross-cultural workers are sidelined from effectively serving God. They're sitting and waiting for a personal edict from heaven—telling them what they'll be doing, where they'll go, and when they'll see their first convert. And although God wants them in full-time ministry, the edict they expect just might never come. So they wait. And feel restless. Frustrated. A little angry at God's silence, some may feel guilty—as if they're not spiritual enough to hear a call.

If we scan the book of Acts, we can note each person who was serving the Lord in cross-cultural ministry. A good question then to ask is: "How did he or she get there?"

It's sobering to note that 99% of the people serving God cross-culturally were there for one reason: persecution. That's right. The gospel spread like wildfire in Acts, chapters 2–7, but it never got outside of Jerusalem, in obedience to Acts 1:8: "Jerusalem, and in all Judea and Samaria, and even to the remotest part of the earth."

God allowed the stoning of Stephen, the beginning of great persecution of the church, in order to send all but the disciples to Judea and Samaria (Acts 8:1), ". . . those who had been scattered went about preaching the word" (Acts 8:4).

Notice the believers weren't jumping up and down saying, "The Great Commission—we're so excited! Let's go reach the world." Nor did they hear a voice out of heaven saying, "Go." They were simply running scared, but they accomplished what God wanted them to do—to spread the word. It has been said that if you don't practice Acts 1:8, you'll get Acts 8:1!

Well, what about the other 1% we find in the book of Acts? How did they get into cross-cultural ministry?

It's startling to find in Acts that about 74% of that 1% who were serving God cross-culturally were doing so because Paul challenged them to go.

Beyond that 74%, 18% were there because their church sent them. The clear example, of course, is when "news of this reached the ears of the church at Jerusalem, and they sent Barnabas to Antioch" (Acts 11:22, NIV). Now note that we don't know what it means when we read the words "they sent them." Barnabas could have been waving his hand screaming, "Me, me, me. Please, send me!" But he also could have been saying, "Me? Why me? I've got a good job, I'm dating this woman and things are going well. . . . Why me?"

The clear point is this: We don't know. But we do know that the church "sent" him because they saw a need.

It is a very biblical thing for the elders in your church to say, "Fernando, we really believe God has gifted you in working overseas and we want you to start praying about serving overseas on a team." If you respond, "What if I don't feel called?" they can easily respond, "That's okay. We've prayed about it and believe God could be directing you in this direction."

This is why it is so important to keep in close touch with your church. God may choose to use them—with no disrespect meant to you or your spiritual maturity—in discovering your global significance.

Finally, 7% of the Acts believers involved in cross-cultural ministry were there because of their own zeal. There seems to be no other obvious reason.

Four individuals recorded in Acts were clearly called—even short-term—to cross-cultural ministry: Philip, Peter, Paul, and Barnabas. Philip was ministering cross-culturally to the Samaritans when an angel miraculously spoke to him to go to the Gaza (Acts 8:26). If God does this to you, you'll probably get the message quickly! Peter, ministering away from home in Joppa, somewhat reluctantly obeyed God's vision to minister to the Italian centurion Cornelius in Caesarea (Acts 10). If you see a sheet coming out of heaven, pay attention!

But the most familiar passage about the missionary call speaks of Paul and Barnabas who were ministering cross-culturally in Antioch. Here, the Holy Spirit said to them, "Set apart for Me Barnabas and Saul for the work to which I have called them" (Acts 13:2). "Look," you might argue, "God clearly called them there!"

But remember, Paul and Barnabas were *already on the field ministering* when they got this clearer sense of direction. They didn't get this call in their hometowns in answer to "God, what do you want me to do?" It was the same with Philip and Peter. God can't steer a parked car.

It is more likely to be the exception than the rule to be "called" into a cross-cultural role of expanding God's Kingdom. God may want to get you overseas some other way.

Yet, there is a clear mandate found in His Word that can be rightfully appropriated as a guiding factor. The apostle Paul is the one clear biblical illustration of someone not already involved in global ministry who received a supernatural call to a cross-cultural ministry. God told him, "I am sending you to the Gentiles" (Acts 22:21; 26:17). It is estimated that at that time there were as many as 60,000 people groups on the face of the earth. God told Paul He was sending him to all the non-Jews—to 59,999 Gentile people groups! Hasn't every believer been called clearly throughout the Word to go to the Gentiles? From Abraham's mandate to be a blessing to every family to the psalmist's "Tell of his glory among the nations" (Psalm 96:3) to the Great Re-Commission (Matthew 28:19–20), all of God's people have already been called to "go to the Gentiles/peoples/nations of the earth"!

The great Martin Luther admitted that although he received great insight into God's will for his life from the Bible and from the counsel of friends, he never received a dramatic call to his lifework. Often, he said, circumstances simply propelled him into God's assignments.

Why, then, is it so often taught among believers that mission work demands a special call? Perhaps because so many missionaries refer to the idea. More than 80% of the Western missionaries now on the field say they sensed a "leading" or "call" by God to be a missionary when they were between ten and twelve years old.

Herbert Kane interviewed hundreds of missionaries and found that although most spoke of this definite call, upon careful evaluation most admitted that their call was actually a process. Sometimes the process covered several years, but in hindsight the missionary would say she or he was certainly, specifically called. Kane determined the "calling" process was:

*Curiosity:* What is this people group like?

*Interest:* I want to keep learning more.

*Understanding:* I'm beginning to get a heart for these people.

*Assurance:* I believe God could use me in this group.

*Conviction:* I'm virtually designed to minister among this people.

*Commitment:* As God leads, I will go!

*Action:* I'm being confirmed as one to go to this people group![2]

This experience-based insistence on a specific call—when God's

Word doesn't insist on it—often brings confusion about our individual roles in God's big picture. But God can even work through confusion. For example, a Frontiers mission agency team leader got so tired of waiting for "the Call" that one day he actually threw a dart at a world map. The dart ended up in the Middle East, which is where he happens to be ministering today!

Are you waiting for some kind of call before you move out to find your strategic niche in God's global plan? Wait no more. We as God's people have been very clearly commanded, commissioned, called. We are to align our lives with the objective of making follower/learners of every people—including our own. In Old Testament parlance, we're to bless every people group—gracing them with the privilege of joining God's family through redemption in Jesus Christ.

As the late musician Keith Green put it: "The call is already there; the problem is that our phones have been off the hook." Maybe we've just been too busy to listen to the very heart of God. And if we're training our children to expect that they will never do anything significant in the Kingdom unless they receive some zap of a special call, maybe we're misleading thousands or millions of potential goers, welcomers, senders, or mobilizers.

But let's pause and clarify for a minute. Listening for very specific guidance from God is definitely scriptural—once we're already moving in obedience. The follower who isn't following, the servant who isn't serving probably won't hear God's voice. But those who are already on the field of battle seem to be the ones biblically who receive specific fine-tuning direction from the throne room of God.

Now: Where do you fit?

## Do Not Sneer, Panic, or Faint

Some Christians insist that God has clearly called them to a specific role in His great plan. Some feel they're more spiritual than us run-of-the-mill Christians because they've heard specifically from God. Some feel they must be dumber than us run-of-the-mill Christians because God apparently had to spell it out, as if to a five-year-old.

But probably most believers don't hear a specific mandate from God to clue them in on where they fit in the Family business. Since most of us don't have that ethereal call, how can we determine where we fit?

Let's make a simple assumption. God wants to show you.

What does that mean? God has a specific will for your life. Maybe you believe that already and that's not the question you're asking. But to help you find what that specific will is, let's clarify one assumption you *should not* make.

Don't fall into the "default trap"—the trap of assuming that if you haven't gotten a specific "call" you must fall back to the default mode: God wants you to get a good job, get involved in a good church, and impact people right where you are. Haven't you ever been told you were in your own "Jerusalem"?

Unfortunately the "default theory" doesn't stack up for two reasons.

First, it's not biblical. Many people who tell you to minister where you are cite Acts 2, where the disciples first began ministering in Jerusalem in the power of the Holy Spirit. Surprise! The disciples weren't from Jerusalem. They were from the sticks, their accents so bad that the people in Jerusalem quickly said, "Are all these who are speaking Galileans?" (Acts 2:7). Those first disciples were in a foreign culture.

Although you are to minister right where you are (after all, if you can't do it where you are, why think you can do it over there?), don't assume automatically God wants you to minister there long-term.

The disciples began their ministry afresh in the power of the Holy Spirit in a cross-cultural ministry! Why? Because it was the most strategic place to start God's worldwide effort. There were people there from every tongue, tribe, and nation (Acts 2:5—"Now there were Jews living in Jerusalem, devout men, from every nation under heaven"). This was the best place to be because as those from other nations heard the gospel in their own language (Acts 2:6—"And when this sound occurred, the multitude came together, and were bewildered, because they were each one hearing them speak in his own language"), the seeds were planted for worldwide impact!

The question isn't "Should I start in my own Jerusalem?" but rather "Where can I best impact the nations with the gifts and talents God has given me?"

A second reason the "default mode" doesn't work is our natural tendency to default to secure areas, which usually causes us to trust in our surroundings rather than the Lord himself.

Remember those who were staying in Jerusalem in Acts 2–7? They were there because they knew nothing else. They had lived their whole lives there. Their jobs were there, their steady paychecks, their homes, their families and extended families. All of their security lay in that town. Why leave?

But God had another agenda. In a simple sense He was saying, "I have a higher priority than your security. I have a better plan for your life than staying comfortable. I want to use you to reach the nations, and if you're not going to go voluntarily, I'll send you." This is, as Dr.

Ralph Winter from the U.S. Center for World Mission states, the "Involuntary 'Go' mechanism."

God loves to put us in places where we have no choice but to trust Him, making His glory shine ever more brightly. Be sure it isn't the comforts of your own "Jerusalem" that keep you where you are. Settle it in your mind. You're not to stay where you are merely because of proximity or comfort. In fact, for the purpose of our study together, make an uncomfortable assumption: "Where I am right now is not where God will have me the rest of my life. I can expect God to release me to a new strategic role for His Kingdom. Change is a part of my future."

Whether your niche includes going, welcoming, sending, mobilizing, or whatever, let's again remind ourselves of the Caleb-Declaration-style commitment of the true disciple of Jesus Christ. A young pastor in Zimbabwe has the following tacked up on his wall:

> I am part of the fellowship of the unashamed. I have Holy Spirit power. The die has been cast. I have stepped over the line. The decision has been made. I am a disciple of His. I will not look back, let up, slow down, back away, or be still.
>
> My past is redeemed, my present makes sense, my future is secure. I am finished and done with low living, sight-walking, small planning, smooth knees, colorless dreams, tamed visions, worldly talking, cheap giving, and dwarfed goals.
>
> I no longer need preeminence, prosperity, position, promotion, or popularity. I do not have to be right, first, tops, recognized, praised, regarded, or rewarded. I now live by faith, lean on His presence, walk by patience, am uplifted by prayer, and labor by power.
>
> My face is set, my gait is fast, my goal is heaven. My road is narrow, my way rough, my Guide reliable, my mission clear. I cannot be bought, compromised, detoured, lured away, turned back, deluded, or delayed. I will not give up, shut up, or let up. I will go on until He comes, and work until He stops me.
>
> I am a disciple of Jesus.[3]

## CHAPTER SEVEN

# Goers Part 1: Deciding to Go

## Or "Please, don't send me to Africa!"

*"The approach of better times for Christianity may be compared to the grad-ual peeping out of green grass through the dissolving snow. The large wintry covering spread over all the nations is as a usurpation over immortal souls. At present [1740] the age of missions to the heathen and to the Jews is not fully arrived. But it appears a sin of omission on the part of Christian churches that they have not begun long ago to send missions to both. En-deavors of this kind would have been far more noble than the hitherto ex-cessive painstaking of Protestants to settle every subtle question in polemical divinity or rather to gain themselves only credit and celebrity in contro-versy."*

—*John Albert Bengel (1687–1752)*

KARACHI, PAKISTAN — You can hear the shouting before the wooden double doors burst open and an imposing bearded man dressed in white drags a beggar by the shirt collar into the police station. You're new in Karachi, here to model discipleship and train local churches in evangelism. You scoot over on your bench to leave plenty of space for the ragged old man, since you're already reeling with the smells of the city. Your hands constantly feel greasy, dirty; your feet sweat profusely in your shoes. You know you're feeling the first waves of culture shock as your stomach churns in the gloomy, green-painted police station. Dark ceiling fans circle overhead without effect in the stuffy room. Somehow even applying for a driver's license in this Muslim city be-comes a gruelling ordeal as an official, dressed in fatigues, squints over your personal documents on his desk for twenty minutes, looking up periodically to squint at you.

The rag-tag old man stumbles against you, and you fend him off—gently of course. You glance into his bloodshot eyes and perceive something mischievous. The man in white thumps on the official's table, turns to point at the ragged beggar, then at you, railing at the official in very loud Urdu.

You can't help but sneak another look at the man next to you, who smiles and says with a British lilt, "You speak English?"

"Why, yes," you say.

"Are you a Christian?"

You nod. "How did you know?"

His stubbled face is shattered into hundreds of wrinkles as he smiles. "I ask everyone if he is a Christian."

"What is the problem here?" you ask.

"The gentleman who brought me in here is an imam—a Muslim priest. I am part of a fellowship of disciples who love Muslims. We jump on buses and shout out our testimonies of the love of Jesus Christ. Then we give out Injils to whoever wants one. That is the Gospels of the New Testament. I do it all very quickly to surprise anyone who would react to the message with hostility. And then I jump off the bus." He nods toward the imam, who is still venting on the official. "This gentleman, however, was quicker than most. He made the bus driver stop immediately. He pulled me from the bus, waved a taxi, and threw me in." The beggar laughs with joy. "I said, 'Sir! I have been promoted! I am a poor man and have never ridden in a taxi before. Thank you!' But it only seemed to make him more furious."

You ask, "What will happen now?"

"I will probably be arrested again. I have been arrested many, many times. I carry this with me . . ." He paws through the deep pockets in his shirt and produces a grimy, folded packet of papers. "This is the section of our Pakistani constitution which grants the freedom to distribute literature," he smiles, winking bloodshot eyes.

And the beggar opens yet another window on your world—one in which radical, New Testament commitment invariably results in blood, sweat, and joy. You suddenly feel a bit inadequate as a missionary to Pakistan: What have you got to teach these committed believers?

"I and some missionaries," continues the old man, "were passing out Injils one morning, and a crowd of other Christians surrounded us, yelling and shaking their heads at us. 'Why are you giving our Book to these Muslims?' they were shouting. In that neighborhood, just days before, Muslims had gathered as much Christian literature as they could and burned it all in a large public bonfire. The Christians scolding us said that they had been insulted, and they were committed to fighting the Muslims, not sharing the Book with them! Some of these believers—"

The beggar shifts to look deep into your eyes. The imam has finished his tirade, and the official is churning through more papers on his desk. The old man says, "That crowd of Christians began to shout that they would burn us—the missionaries and me—if we continued to give Muslims in that neighborhood copies of the Injil! Can you believe it! We began to think —well, actually, I began to think, 'God, where are you in such a dishonorable situation?' And just then . . ." He scoots closer to you. "Just then, over the loudspeaker from the community mosque comes a loud announcement: 'There are people selling books. Find them. They are six foreigners and one local Christian.' Our hearts stopped. Then the loudspeaker continued: 'Buy these books. Act upon them. They are good books.'" The old man's eyes widen in joy. "Can you believe it! We never found out who or why the mosque was broadcasting this amazing message. But it was as if God were saying to us, 'Now you know where I am!'"

At this, the imam and the police official turn to glare at you and the old man. "You," says the policeman, waving papers. "You may take your driving license." He gestures toward the old man. "This beggar does not concern you."

"Yes," grins the imam.

The official continues, "He was simply distributing literature, which is, of course, allowed by our constitution."

"What?" shouts the imam.

The old man chimes in: "And, sir, I have free copies of the Injil for you and your policemen!"

"You." The official nods your way. "Come now."

You walk to the desk for your license, thank the policeman, and step toward the doors. You turn to the shouting between the imam and policeman and smile at the old man. He shouts over the din, "We will meet again, my friend. We will take a bus ride together!"

## Are You Qualified As a Goer?

Goers—missionaries—aren't going to save the world by themselves. They're not going to impress all those "national" Christians with their unheard-of spirituality. Actually, going is a pretty humbling endeavor.

More believers than we're led to expect are goers. With multitudes who haven't heard of God's love for them even for the first time, God must want more to go than are actually going. And virtually every believer can take on the challenges of a short-term cross-cultural ministry. But whether we cross cultures as a career or for a short period of time, we all need to understand the basics of "going." So stay with us as we look in detail at what it takes to become a goer.

First, let's go back to our rule of thumb for narrowing down your personal role in God's great global plan: Start from scratch and ask God for clear direction regarding what role He has for you in expanding His Kingdom—whether it is to go, stay, mobilize, or welcome. Assume what you are doing now is temporary until God shows you clearly His direction for you.

For most of us, it's easy to assume that we're not built to be missionaries. Beginning as kids in Sunday school, or as new adult Christians, we construct a mind-set that we aren't goers. (Much of this predisposition can be traced to the overblown notion that without a dramatic call one would be doomed to attempt missionary service!)

The belief that you're not a goer unless proven otherwise is much like the mind-set of a family in which it is presumed no one will go to college. Every kid in the clan is told from birth: "You're not college material. None of us is. Plan your life after high school accordingly." Would anyone in that family dare to take college-prep classes in high school? Would he or she even apply to a college? Of course not. Only by sheer determination or rebellion would a child of such a family break the mold, attend college, and earn a degree.

It's incredible how the enemy of human souls has convinced the Church that only a few hardy individuals are actually designed for missions. Is there any biblical precedent for training children in a Christian family that they're probably not mission material unless they have an earthshaking call to missions?

If that has been your training, you could begin to feel a bit uncomfortable: You may be a goer. The thought may have even crossed your mind at one time, but with conventional Christian wisdom insisting that only a few are "called," you probably had no trouble fending off the thought.

In fact, as you read this you may realize that as a youngster you sensed an urging toward global mission ministry, but have spent your life with a nagging guilt that you never obeyed that urging. Well, relax. You can still obey! Many mission agencies actively seek to recruit retired couples. Some work as church planters, others in home offices, others on the field facilitating—freeing up the evangelist-types to work with the target people by overseeing the day-to-day operations such as banking, shopping, and hospitality. Retired persons are an integral part of a church-planting team.

Perhaps you're still stuck on missionary stereotypes. If so, look over the following list of missionary openings published by just one medium-sized mission agency. Could you or a team of friends who have never dreamed of diving into a global role fill any of the following positions?

accounting
banking
art, illustration
avionics
business administration, management
business consulting
communications
computers
construction
dentistry
education—professors, teachers, ESL/EFL
electronics
engineering
hydraulics
industry
law
library science
linguistics
mechanics
media
medical specialists and generalists
quality control
science
secretarial, clerical
teaching English as a second language
tourism

The list is endless. Regardless of your skills, background, interests, and credentials or lack thereof, you could minister in hundreds of ways in other cultures.

That's an uncomfortable thought to most believers. In any time management, goal-setting, or personal-growth training, your "comfort zone" is a key issue. And Christians are especially susceptible to snuggling permanently into comfort zones. That is, the security of an eternal relationship with God can be lived out by simply resting in a lifestyle that is secure and comfortable while waiting for heaven. (That's where our "default call" mode often comes from.) That "Christian lifestyle," which is often determined by the consensus of your culture's Christians, can keep you from your life's Big Adventure.

Most of us came to Christ because of some discomfort. And coming to Him was in many ways very easy—like a ball rolling downhill. We responded to the comfort of the Comforter, of being accepted in the Beloved, of sensing peace with God, of looking forward to an eternity of bliss and blessing. With plenty of support from fellow Christians also firmly settled in such a wonderful comfort zone, a comfortable Christian lifestyle takes some—but not much—effort.

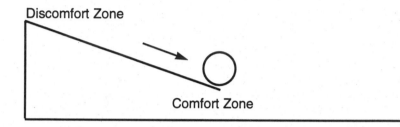

But then Jesus challenges us with discomforting sayings such as "If anyone wishes to come after Me, let him take up his cross" and "Anyone who does not give up all his own possessions cannot be My disciple." He calls us to a position of unpredictability, a lack of practical securities, a breaking from the herd—to a stance that is usually more uncomfortable than what we felt before we were believers. But now it's discomfort with a purpose: His Adventure!

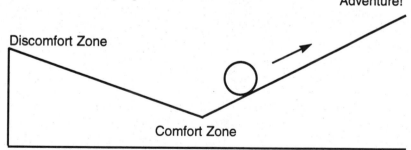

Throwing up your hands in absolute submission to a Master who could send you off to Inner Mongolia or even your nearest inner city is discomforting. But it's also what is meant by "living by faith." Living on the cutting edge of what God can do in you and through you is not comfortable in the sense of having lots of practical securities.

That's why it's often difficult for believers on the home front to imagine living in inconvenient circumstances as a minority in another culture. It's hard to see beyond the downside of a cross-cultural ministry, to see the rich personal rewards awaiting those who step out in faith. But being willing to leave your comfort zone is mandatory.

What would be your motivation for going? Your motivation for staying? If we stop to think about it, we realize that life can be full of hurts and disappointments wherever we are. The important question is whether or not we are willing to accept the role God gives us in reaching the nations.

Paul speaks to us from the fourth chapter of 1 Corinthians.

> So then, men ought to regard us as servants of Christ and as those entrusted with the secret things of God. Now it is required that those who have been given a trust must prove faithful. I care very little if I am judged by you or by any human court; indeed, I do not even judge myself. My conscience is clear, but that does not make me innocent. It is the LORD who judges me. Therefore judge nothing before the appointed time; wait till the LORD comes. He will bring to light what is hidden in darkness and will expose the motives of men's hearts. At that time each will receive his praise from God. (1 Corinthians 4:1–5, NIV)

If someone wants to stay in the United States because he knows that God needs Christian businessmen here and that he can make a million dollars and give half of it to missions, but his real excitement in staying is the enjoyment he'll gain living off the other half, his motivation isn't going to make it in God's eyes.

Beware of the pastor who wants to hold you back from the mission field because he wants you to help him fulfill his mission. Steve Manama of Tanzania shared at a conference, "My greatest enemy is he who would detract me from God's purpose for my life."

Be equally wary of the parent who pushes you into the mission field to appease his own conscience because he didn't go. Don't live out someone else's dream. It may not be God's will for you.

Another motivation that doesn't fly is going overseas because you want to escape American Christianity because of its "fatness in Christian teaching" and lethargic discipleship.

Stretch your willpower. Thinking big, living an adventure, demands some intense effort on your part. Climb out of your personal comfort zone and ask yourself, "What keeps me here?" and "What would it take for me to go?"

Pray for a clean mental slate when it comes to discerning your function in the Kingdom.

Presuming that you aren't going to remain in your own sending country merely by default and that God might actually direct you to be a goer, let's run through the academic basics of "What is a missionary?"

## Sent-Ones

Interestingly, the term missionary isn't found in the Bible. It comes from the Latin *missio*, which means "to send." The New Testament word "apostle" is about as close as the Bible comes to "missionary"; *apostolos* means "sent one," a "delegate."

In the most general sense we are all sent by the Master: "As the Father has sent me, I am sending you" (John 20:21, NIV). But the technical sense of being a "sent one" or an "apostle" is more specific. Only twelve held the office of an apostle—not bothering with questions about whether Matthias (Acts 1:26) or Paul (1 Corinthians 9:1) was the twelfth. The New Testament recognizes the one-of-a-kind significance of the original twelve. Peter stated the credentials of an apostle: "One of the men who have been with us the whole time the Lord Jesus went in and out among us beginning from John's baptism to the time when Jesus was taken up from us." He also states the purpose of the original twelve: "For one of these must become a witness with us of his resurrection" (Acts 1:21–22, NIV).

But the Bible also uses apostle—sent one—to describe others in the Church who did not hold the apostolic office. For example, Paul compliments Andronicas and Junias as "outstanding among the apostles" (Romans 16:7). Those sent by a church with a special message or mission were called apostles or messengers—such as Epaphroditus (Philippians 2:25).

And more strictly speaking, an apostle is one sent across cultural lines from one people group to another.

Paul rhetorically asked: "Are all apostles? Are all prophets? Are all teachers? Do all work miracles?" (1 Corinthians 12:29, NIV). His answer is clear in the New Testament Greek: No! Not everyone is an apostle, a sent one. We're all witnesses (Acts 1:8), but we're not all missionaries.

So the fact that a goer ministers in a culture other than his or her own is generally accepted in mission circles today. But there are other factors in the definition of a missionary that aren't so universally held. Missionary statesmen discuss heatedly the credentials of a true missionary. The discussions sometimes slip to the level of third-century debates about how many angels can fit on the head of a pin. But for

## Where Do Goers Go?

The question isn't so much *where* but *who* are the unreached nations—the *ethne?* God has a list, a "register of the peoples" (Psalm 87:6, NIV).

Regardless of how remote, resistant, forgotten, unknown, or bypassed by the Church a people group is, God has a "fullness of time" when He will "visit" each one with His offer of blessing, of redemption.

Most believers are very general about world evangelization. After all, it's a huge world, a huge task, and pinpointing specifics doesn't sound very spiritual. But it's just this vague generalizing of the Great Commission that keeps it orbiting on the fringes of many Christians' priorities. The pattern is specific (Matthew 28:19–20) and the peoples are specific. And just as Moses in his construction of the Tabernacle was to copy the exact design he had seen in heaven (Exodus 25:40; Hebrews 8:5), it makes sense that we pattern our world evangelization plans according to this realistic, distinctive "registry of the peoples" concept.

Which peoples still remain without a strong church movement? The following people groups are the unreached *ethne* of Afghanistan. (The list isn't taken directly from God's heavenly registry, so there may be errors. But you get the idea: Everybody living in Afghanistan isn't an *Afghan.*)

| | | | |
|---|---|---|---|
| Afshari | Jamshidi (Char Aimaq) | Narwizi | Shamushti |
| Amulah | Jati (Jatu) | Nishei | Share |
| Aret | Jew | Nuristani | Shina |
| Ashkui (Wamayi) | Judeo Persian | Nuristani, Waigeli | Shotuli |
| Balkh Arab | Kamdeshi | Ormuri | Shughni |
| Baloch (Baluchi) | Kamviri | Pahlavani | Sindhi |
| Bashgari (Kafari) | Kantwai | Parachi | Tadzhik |
| Bashkarik | Kara-Kalpak | Paruni | Tangshini |
| Barhui | Kazakh | Pashayi | Tatar |
| Chaghatai | Khowar | Pashayi, Southwestern | Teymur |
| Chilas | (Citrali, Qasqari) | Pathan | (Timuri, Hazara) |
| Dari | Kirghiz | (Pushton, Aghani) | Tirahi |
| Darrai | Kordari | Persian | Turkmen, Tekke |
| Darrai Nur | Kowli Gypsy | Persian (Parsiwan) | Uighur |
| Darwazi | Kurd | Prasuni | Urdu |
| Firozkohi | Kushani | Punjabi | Uzbek |
| (Char Aimaq) | Lahnda | Pushtun | Wadahu |
| Gawar-Bati (Narisati) | Laurowan | (Pathan, Pakhtun) | Wakhi |
| Ghorani (Gurani) | Malakhel | Qasqari | Wegal |
| Grangali | Mooluli | Qatari | Wolapuri-Katarqalai |
| Gujuri Rajasthani | Munji-Yidgha | Ramgali | Zargari |
| Gulbahar | Nangalami | Sanglechi (Eshkashimi) | |
| Hazara (Berberi) | Naroji | Sau | |

An actual listing of unreached peoples in every country is constantly being verified and is available from the Adopt-A-People Clearinghouse (see Resources).

the sake of educating ourselves in the discussions and arguments rumbling through the exhibitor aisles of international missions conferences, here are the basic schools of thought on what makes a true goer:

1. A true missionary is any believer who is sharing the Gospel.

2. A true missionary is any believer doing any kind of work or min-

istry in another culture—whether that people is considered reached or unreached.

3. A true missionary is any believer winning individuals to Christ in another culture, reached or unreached.

4. A true missionary is any believer planting churches in another culture, reached or unreached.

5. A true missionary is a frontier or pioneering missionary: any believer winning individuals to Christ in an unreached people group.

6. A true missionary is a frontier or pioneering missionary who is planting churches in an unreached people group.

Which is the correct definition? Who is a true missionary?

It is generally held that a true missionary is anyone ministering in a people group other than his or her own.

If a missionary is ministering among a reached people, the missionary's ministry should in some way enable the formation of that people's church. Stating that "true" missions is only "going where Christ is not named" to plant churches among unreached peoples is an arbitrary opinion.

Goers to unreached peoples are perhaps best described not as the only "true missionaries" but as "frontier" or "pioneer" missionaries. These may be involved in pre-evangelism ministry such as relief efforts or literacy training. A frontier missionary may concentrate on introducing individuals in an unreached people to Jesus Christ, or he may be planting a church—winning individuals to Christ and intently discipling them into an indigenous fellowship.

Regardless of giftings, ministry, work context, or whether or not a people is unreached, no mission role is above another. "The eye cannot say to the hand, 'I don't need you!' And the head cannot say to the feet, 'I don't need you!'" (1 Corinthians 12:21, NIV). The apostle Paul pointed out that "the Lord has assigned to each his task. . . . The man who plants and the man who waters have one purpose" (1 Corinthians 3:5–8, NIV). Every ministry in cross-cultural missions can work closely together in one purpose—to directly or indirectly offer every people, tribe, tongue, and nation the blessing of redemption in Christ. "From him the whole body, joined and held together by every supporting ligament, grows and builds itself up in love, as each part does its work" (Ephesians 4:16, NIV).

## Goers: Not One-Size-Fits-All

Serving in God's global enterprise as a sent one—an apostle, a goer—isn't a one-size-fits-all role. Missionaries aren't people who wear pith helmets, preach sermons under trees, and then come home and show slides. God has designed the role of a goer to be incredibly diverse.

Goers are gifts to the Church: "[Jesus Christ] gave some to be apostles"—sent ones (Ephesians 4:11, NIV). These gifts to the Church are in turn gifted; each goer has personal spiritual gifts—from administration to faith to teaching (1 Corinthians 12:7–11 and Romans 12:4–8).

It isn't location that determines whether a person is serving as a missionary but whether that ministry takes place in a people group other than that of the goer. A Dutch nurse teaching first aid among Khmer immigrants in Amsterdam is a missionary in every sense of the word.

There are self-tests to determine whether you're qualified to be a missionary (see ours in the Appendix beginning on page 253). But if we'd put them right here, you might quit before you start. You are your own worst critic. Let's look at it from another angle:

Before Jack came on staff with Frontiers, he was an engineer with Dravo, a corporation located right outside downtown Pittsburg, Pennsylvania, in the United States. When the thought of leaving his job and joining Frontiers first challenged him, he gave the answer that made him usable for God. If you can answer one question the way Jack did, you've got TMP (tremendous missionary potential).

The question: "Jack, how would you like to leave your job and come and join us in reaching the Muslim world?"

The answer: "No way. You want me to leave my job, leave my friends, leave all my security, raise support, and join you? I can't do that . . . but . . . I'll pray about it. . . ."

Because Jack was open to God changing his plans, God showed him the way.

Do you have TMP? Chances are you do. The God of the universe, the Creator of all things, He who said "Through me you can do all things" lives inside of you. And your availability is much more important than your ability. If you're willing to pray about it (and are truly willing to be obedient), He can and will use you.

After God spoke to Moses through the burning bush (Exodus 3), God informed Moses of His plan to redeem Israel. Notice in verses 7–10 how many times God refers to himself, and how few times He refers to Moses.

> The Lord said, "I have indeed seen the misery of my people in Egypt. I have heard them crying out because of their slave drivers, and I am concerned about their suffering. So I have come

down to rescue them from the hand of the Egyptians and to bring them up out of that land into a good and spacious land, a land flowing with milk and honey—the home of the Canaanites, Hittites, Amorites, Perizzites, Hivites and Jebusites. And now the cry of the Israelites has reached me, and I have seen the way the Egyptians are oppressing them. So now, go. I am sending you to Pharaoh to bring my people the Israelites out of Egypt" (Exodus 3:7–10, NIV).

Did you count them? God refers to himself nine times and to Moses once. But notice what Moses does in the next verse: "But Moses said to God, 'Who am I, that I should go to Pharaoh and bring the Israelites out of Egypt?' " (Exodus 3:11, NIV).

He's basically saying, "Excuse me, Lord. Didn't you just say that you saw their oppression, you heard their cries, you were concerned . . . How did *I* get involved in this?"

Moses focuses on his own inadequacies (the 10% reference to himself), completely forgetting God's enabling (God's 90% reference to God). Do you ever feel incompetent to be used by God cross-culturally? Be of good cheer—you're in great company!

God could have answered Moses' doubts about himself something like this:

Now look, Moses, you're not aware of what's been going on. Your tending sheep forty years hasn't been in vain. In fact, it's been my perfect will for you to break you, prepare you, make you totally dependent upon Me. You are now ready to be used by Me.

But God didn't answer Moses that way. In fact, God didn't refer to Moses' inadequacies at all. Instead, He used five simple words: "I will be with you."

And God said, "I will be with you. And this will be the sign to you that it is I who have sent you: When you have brought the people out of Egypt, you will worship God on this mountain" (Exodus 3:12, NIV). What was God doing? Putting Moses' focus back on the 90% and off the 10%!

Now there was a time when Moses thought he was capable of rescuing his people out of Egypt. This was back in Exodus 2, when he killed an Egyptian who was beating up a Hebrew. But when he thought he was able to be used by God to accomplish God's purpose, he wasn't. After forty years of tending sheep, he didn't think he was capable and God declared he was.

As God worked through Moses he was forced to trust God in ways he had never known before.

If you have unshakable confidence that you are qualified, you may not be dependent enough on God to be used. If you're fearful and feel inadequate, God may be declaring, "You're ready!"

## Hard Realities

Most of us are far more qualified to be goers than we think we are. But there are a few circumstances, character issues, or evidences of immaturity that indicate a person isn't ready to go. Let's shift gears and look at some factors that could keep a person off the mission field.

Bill Leick, personnel director for Frontiers in the United States, lists the following disqualifying factors for potential candidates at a given time. (Some of these issues can be worked through, making the candidate ready at a later date.)

No sending church
Deep-seated character issues (habitual sin, such as emotional abuse to spouse or children, chronic liar, pornographic or other addiction, homosexuality)
Mental illness
No experience whatsoever in sharing his or her faith, discipling someone, or leading a Bible study
Lack of practice of the basic disciplines of the Christian life

Other agencies, depending upon their philosophy, have other disqualifying factors:

Divorce
Remarriage after divorce
Single parents without custody of the children
Charismatics
Non-charismatics
Debt

Of course, during preparation training programs, mission agencies have a chance to observe candidates' behavior and character traits to determine further if one qualifies for foreign service.

Do you qualify? Remember that there are billions who don't know the glory of our Father in heaven—and He wants them to know it. It is His will, stated clearly from Genesis to Revelation, that His people go and spread the news. Why not take a step of faith and consider how you might get there from here?

## CHAPTER EIGHT

# Goers Part 2: Getting There

*Finding a way through the maze of missions*

1992, VIETNAM — Dhuc, Phrem, and Nih are itinerant evangelists ministering to Tribals in the mountain areas of central Vietnam. They are fairly new Christians themselves, and their entire training consisted of a three-week evangelism course offered by Tribes and Nations Outreach of Singapore.

One rainy afternoon in a highlands village, a medicine man who harassed and persecuted them returned to his house—which was at that split second blasted by a bolt of lightning! The man immediately ran back to Dhuc, Phrem, and Nih, knelt down, and began pleading for God's forgiveness. Soon the entire village was brought to faith in Christ. In less than five months, ten village chieftains and some 6,000 Tribals responded to the Gospel.

Down in Ho Chi Minh City, worried Communist Party cadres heard of these conversions and sent officers to mount a "re-education campaign." In one village meeting, an official gathered every man, woman, and child in the area in the village square. He then wrote two columns on a chalkboard: *For Christ* and *Against Christ*. "Now," he announced, "you are to write your name under the correct heading." The villagers— every one a new believer—sat motionless for twenty minutes. Then the eldest woman stood and said, "For twenty years I have tried to follow Marxism. Now I know that Jesus Christ offers a better way." She came up to the officer, took the chalk and signed her name under "For Christ." She then turned, and every one of the villagers signed the portable chalkboard under the same heading—all because of three dedicated Vietnamese evangelists who in all likelihood wouldn't meet even a few criteria of what many agencies think a goer should look like!

## Getting Ready for the Field

In the last chapter we said that, given the large numbers of people in the world who don't know Christ, God must want many more people to be goers than we think. And, we added, more of us are qualified to be goers than we can imagine. Greg Livingstone often starts Frontiers candidate schools with this challenging thought: "If you don't come from a dysfunctional background, we'll try to make room for you anyway. We don't look for perfect people because we've never met a man or woman being used by God who wasn't damaged emotionally by sin. God uses growing, available people who take His Word seriously."

Missionaries are normal, everyday people. Many have poor self-images. Many come from dysfunctional families (aren't all families dysfunctional to some degree?) The singles wonder if God will ever give them a mate. Married couples struggle to keep their marriage a priority. And parents all worry about their children growing up "normal" (whatever that may be!).

The key to a missionary's success is that he or she is hungry to learn.

God starts with you where you are, and little by little equips you. When you decide to go, the hunger to learn takes the form of willingness to wade into the sometimes complex process of getting ready for the field. As a goer you encounter questions about yourself, your faith, and your understanding of how to reach the unreached—all in the process of working through some very mundane tasks!

Are you hungry to learn? Let's look at some of the practicalities of getting there from here.

## Choosing an Agency

Many people feel open to be used by God overseas, but don't know where to go. They may have the idea that they have to be called to a specific people group. It doesn't have to be that way.

There are many ways that God could direct you to a particular country or people. Some ways include: friends to accompany you, use of your career, a particular agency's policies or theological issues.

It's okay to say, "I have a heart for all peoples. It doesn't matter to me what group I work with. I really would like to go with my friends." Going as a team of friends is not only a unique idea, it's a great idea!

You are better able to avoid the number one struggle that brings many missionaries home from the field: interpersonal relationship problems with other missionaries. Having already established strong friendships with others is a great asset! You then need to look for an agency that will take you as a team of friends.

Others of you may say, "My goal is to serve the King in my career. I've invested so much time and energy in it." That's okay! You just need to choose a field that can best use your career. Look for specific openings for your field and pursue them. (This can be done by writing InterCristo or Global Opportunities. See Organizations under Resources.) You will want to avoid agencies that ask you to be flexible in the area of career, if career is a priority for you.

Maybe what is most important to you is working with an agency with which you can truly be in harmony. God will honor that desire as well. Here are a few areas you'll want to look for as you consider an agency:

- What is the goal of the agency? Church planting? Translation work? Providing short-term opportunities? Discipleship? Evangelism?
- What is their statement of faith? Can you agree with it?
- What are the requirements for service? Bible school, seminary? Pre-field training?
- How long are you required to remain on the field (is there a minimum length of service)?
- Who makes the field policies—the field or the home office?
- Are you required to raise support? If so, how does their support policy work? Are funds pooled for the general use of all, or are monies that are indicated for you sent solely for your use?
- Does the agency help you raise support?
- Will they send a team of friends?
- Do they determine where you go or can you decide?
- Do they have training on the field? Language school?
- Are their fields bearing fruit?
- What is the role of the missionary wife?
- Is there adequate education available for your children? Who decides where they go to school?
- How are you provided for on the field? Housing—is it in community or private?
- Length of furloughs, and how often. Do they provide assistance or

housing on furlough? Are furloughs mandatory?
- Do they allow for retirement planning?
- Can you get answers to your questions easily?
- What do others say about the agency?

The doctrinal statement of an agency may be the determining factor for you. You may be flexible as to where you go, who you work with, or what you do, but you feel you need to be part of a group that allows you to express your God-given gifts and with whom you can fully agree doctrinally.

However you decide what agency to pursue, be sure you make your goals clear. Church planting is quite different from translation work, for example. And translation work is different from discipleship, discipleship from evangelism. Find out what you want to do and then go for an agency that lets you do it.

Once you have a goal in sight, hold lightly to everything else. Don't cling to anything that keeps you from your objective. Being flexible in everything, but your primary goal is the key to being an effective cross-cultural missionary.

And you will need to be flexible! You may go for weeks without heat in your house in the middle of winter. You may need to filter all your drinking water. Or build your own home in the middle of Mali. Or shower with a bucket of water—and only do that once a week.

A final crucial factor to remember in choosing an agency is this: Just as the key ingredient for getting to the mission field is availability, the key ingredient for being successful on the field is a hunger to learn—and to keep on learning!

Because of this, make sure the agency you choose to work with has ongoing on-the-field training. Pre-field training is like marriage counseling. You go to the pastor, hear half of what he has to say, nod your head thinking you understand. It's only after the honeymoon is over that you go back to the pastor and ask, "Now what did you say I should do when my spouse does this. . . ?" This is why on-the-field coaching is so important.

Being hungry to learn means being hungry for upgrading. Rick earned his doctorate on the field. Joseph is getting his degree while feeding the poor in Africa and translating Scripture into his target people's language. Many team leaders invite other team leaders to periodically give them an honest evaluation—a loving critique by their own peers.

Many come home from the field for Frontiers' M.B.A. program (Master Builder's Academy—1 Corinthians 3:10). There they learn what it means to be a team leader, with much of their study focusing on character building. No one is perfect when they go to the field, but after a time they get an idea of what they need to work on: How to become better equipped—not just in church-planting skills but in character development, and in life skills such as how to love your wife and family, how to get along with other missionaries.

## Preparing to Go

You may wonder if there is something you can do right now to train to go even if you don't know where you're going or what agency you will be going with.

One of the first things you need to do is *to develop a good relationship with the home church that will sponsor you or send you.* No one should attempt going to the field without a solid church behind them. You need a prayer base and all the encouragement you can get, not only to get to the field, but more importantly, to stay on the field.

Getting a home church behind you won't happen overnight. Most churches will want you to serve at least two years with them before they send you out. College students actively involved in a campus ministry, with little involvement in their local church, cannot expect to announce their decision to go overseas and be sponsored by that church. Get involved with your church and over time communicate your intentions with them so they know where you're headed.

Second, *learn to derive your joy from your relationship with Jesus rather than from serving Him.* Many people go to the field straight out of college, where they were actively involved in exciting ministries like Campus Crusade for Christ, the Navigators, Chi Alpha, or InterVarsity. Without realizing it, they have found joy in serving God—helping fellow students come into the Kingdom, leading Bible studies, and seeing lives changed. There's nothing wrong with that, but if service is your only source of joy, it's a setup for disaster.

The reason is that your first few years on the field will likely be spent in learning the language, adjusting to a new culture, and to mission procedure. In other words, there will not be much fruit. And if you have lost the joy of knowing and worshiping the Lord for who He is (and not for what He's doing through you), you could come back a "missionary casualty."

*Working toward a good self-image* is a third way to prepare. Myron Loss, in his excellent book *Culture Shock*, draws a direct relationship between culture shock and a poor self-image. Those who experience the most culture shock are the least secure in who they are as people and as believers.

One of the best ways to work on a good self-image is to find out who you are in Christ and learn to believe what God says about you. Neil Anderson's *Victory Over Darkness* would be a great book to start with.

A fourth area to work on is *learning how to resolve interpersonal relationship conflicts*. This is a critical area where many Americans fall short. We tend to avoid people we don't get along with, or if the problem is too acute we simply switch churches.

On the field, this is not an option. Your team is small, and you can't simply avoid people you don't get along with. If you've never learned how to apply Matthew 18:15–20; 5:23–24, and Galatians 6:1–2, you'll end up in trouble quickly.

You need to learn peacemaking not only to keep you on the field, but for church planting as well. A mission veteran says, "I used to think that peacemaking happened after the church was planted. I've now learned that peacemaking is a part of the church-planting process!"

And fifth, *spread your vision with others so that when you go you have a strong prayer base behind you*. You must have people ready to pray for you on the field before you can go.

What else can you begin doing right now? Or—if you aren't the goer—what can you suggest to someone in your fellowship who is planning on going? An Arab World Ministries field worker offers some other basic steps:

*Become equipped*. Frank and Gina Markow sensed God's leading to work with Jewish people in France. When they applied to Jews for Jesus, they found Frank's lack of a college degree would prohibit his working with the organization. So they are working hard on step one: Frank is getting his degree.

Mike and Miriam Cotton were struck with the needs of a Central Asian country when they visited there the summer of 1992. The urgency of breaking through to the spiritual hunger of these people haunted them constantly as they returned from their short-term trip. But what did God—through wise counselors—coach them toward first? Getting more training in a field Mike was already interested in: medical technology.

*Develop cross-cultural skills*. Frank and Gina don't have to wait to arrive in France to work with Jewish people—or with French people, for that matter. In their area they can seek out people from these backgrounds, learning what they talk about, their likes and dislikes.

Almost immediately upon their return from their short-term in

Central Asia, Mike and Miriam found in their own city a family from the people group they are targeting. The Cottons are finding that cross-cultural experience begins with simply being able to sit down and talk with people.

*Learn to work in small groups.* One of the most surprising side effects that hits many goers as they leave their own culture is the shock of having most of their outside Christian support stripped away. As an Arab World Ministries worker puts it, "It is important that you not become reliant on being part of a large group or a church with lots of social activities going on. Develop skills that will enable you to supplement your needs by teaching yourself. There will not be instant Bible studies, instant learning, or instant preparation for a Bible class. Be willing to start with nothing and build upon it. Doing things like this now and learning to be content with them will help you in a cross-cultural context."[1] Both Frank and Gina Markow and Mike and Miriam Cotton were members of large, active, mission-minded congregations. Both couples realized they needed to wean themselves from depending on that Christian context in preparation for the isolated rigors of missionary life.

*Get down to basics in your lifestyle.* The Arab World Ministries missionary states: "We have found that this is an issue that has sent many people home; they cannot adjust to living on a lower or a more basic level than they have been used to. Begin now by developing an attitude of flexibility, and recognize right away that life on the field will not be like home."[2] Both the Markows and the Cottons have already been practicing for years what's called a "wartime lifestyle." That is, they live as frugally as possible with not many frills, and appropriate money in whatever amount needed for crucial Kingdom purposes. In wartime, troops don't enjoy luxuries, but they do use very expensive weaponry. The Spec 5 who sits in the desert eating a tin of ration food leans against the tire of a multi-million dollar Patriot missile launcher. The Markows and Cottons travel extensively (to the envy of their well-heeled friends), buy the best in computer communication equipment to keep up on global happenings (to the envy of their computer-minded friends), buy the best of personal equipment and clothing so it will last (to the envy of their shopper friends), but they live extraordinarily simply. As all world Christians can, they gradually pared the expenses of their lifestyles to match the demands of their part in God's great battle plan. They live a simple life because "no soldier in active service entangles himself in the affairs of everyday life, so that he may please the one who enlisted him as a soldier" (2 Timothy 2:4).

## Pursuing Formal Education

Preparation for the field may or may not include formal education.

Before you disqualify yourself as a goer because you don't think you could ever go back to school, become informed. Many agencies aren't looking for Bible degrees before they take you on. They may be looking more for a strong track record of walking with God and good references.

There are a couple of reasons for this.

First, just as completing seminary doesn't make you a pastor (pastoring is a gift), getting a Bible degree doesn't make you a missionary. The apostle Paul knew it was through grace that he was saved (Ephesians 2:8–9), yet he also credited God's grace with getting and keeping him on the field. (Ephesians 3:8, NIV: "Although I am less than the least of all God's people, this grace was given me: to preach to the Gentiles the unsearchable riches of Christ. . . .") By God's grace you become an effective cross-cultural minister, just as by God's grace you will go to heaven.

Secondly, if you go overseas there is a great chance you will end up in the 10/40 window, where your secular skills are what get you into the country. Your resumé is in a sense your ticket in. A one- or two-year lapse in that resumé spent at a Bible school may not greatly encourage Islamic, Hindu, or Buddhist governmental officials.

Getting training on a secular college campus with Campus Crusade, InterVarsity, the Navigators, or some other excellent group may be just as effective in preparing you for the field. Many churches also have their own thorough training programs. So you see, it doesn't necessarily have to be formal training—depending on the agency you go with.

You could also reach a point where you overeducate yourself. Holly and Judy were two members on the same team. Judy, the team leader's wife, had her Master's degree in cross-cultural ministries from a seminary in southern California. Holly was a single woman, a very close friend of the family. She had never attained a degree but got into the country as a nanny for the team leader and his wife!

As the team began ministering, they found out that Holly, not Judy, was more comfortable ministering to their target people. That was because Holly loved to talk about the care of babies and the preparation of food, what she had occupied herself with most of her adult life. This is exactly what women in their target country did 95% of the time. On the other hand, Judy, who could also talk about babies and preparing food, really wanted more intellectually stimulating conversation. She found out that the women of their target people weren't at her level.

In some ways she was overtrained. Spending hours on end with the women was natural to Holly, but became arduous to Judy.

Today's college students have other issues to consider. It is increasingly difficult to pay for college. Many face the challenge of taking on thousands of dollars in debt in order to make it through school.

There is a simple rule regarding debt: Don't get into it! As much as possible, avoid debt. Most agencies won't take you unless you are completely debt-free. And if you've racked up a $30,000 debt (which is not uncommon even for nonmedical students these days) you're a long way from the field.

Avoiding this common problem will mean finding creative financial solutions. What can you do differently?

- Work your way through school. It may take you longer (six or seven years instead of four), but the work experience will be good for you. You will learn to be more effective in time management and use of your money.

- Switch schools. Unfortunately, Christian schools are expensive. Staying out of debt may mean switching to a less expensive secular school. Because there are so many Christian groups on state campuses, this won't necessarily have to be a "second-best" move.

- Go to your counselor and see if there are any scholarships you can apply for (as if you hadn't thought of that one already!).

- If you know you're heading to the mission field, and college is your tentmaking key to getting overseas, why not see if you can "raise support" to get you through school? See if people who know you well will help you out financially, knowing your desire to go to the field after school.

- Cut your expenses. Ask God for a couple near your school with an empty bedroom willing to give you free housing . . . possibly even free food (unless you're a rugby player at Canterbury of course).

If you're reading this and you're already in debt, you may ask, "What should I do?"

The agency you want to affiliate with will likely determine your next step. Some do not allow you to join as long as you carry any kind of a debt. In that case, you work until you're debt-free. But while you work off what you owe, make sure you're financially accountable to someone. It's easy to go from college to the working world and acquire more debt, not less. You buy things you can't afford, with an assumption that your new job will allow you to buy a nice car or new stereo.

Ask someone to look over your shoulder and ask the tough questions, such as, "Do you really need that?"

Some agencies do allow you to have debt when you go to the field. If you feel God's leading, check them out. These agencies believe that working overseas is the same as working in your own country, and that support can rightfully be directed to pay off debt. Many do stipulate that you inform your supporters that part of their money will pay your debts. If they have no objections, the agency won't either.

One creative solution to debt is to find someone gifted in giving who wants to see you go overseas. Talk to them about "incurring your debt." What does that mean? Find someone who believes in you so much that they will pay off your loan to allow you to go to the field. If you are fortunate to find someone willing to do this, you can go with just about any agency!

If you are in school to prepare to be used overseas, you will want to choose a degree that will be helpful on the field, but find something you like to do and something that is marketable in your home country as well, because there is no guarantee that God will keep you on the field all your life. You may need to come back for a time and work at a job in your particular area of study.

A degree that is unmarketable at home will likely be unmarketable on the field. If you need a higher degree to be employable at home, you probably need the higher degree on the field as well.

But avoid careers useful *only* in your own culture. Counseling and psychology may be adaptable. A law degree would be useful only if you specifically study International Law. And remember, a Bible degree alone won't get you into a closed country. They don't want Christian teachers.

Don't limit yourself to a standard list somewhere of "missionary jobs." God may give you a job in a highly specialized field. And He may have you go from one job to another as you minister in a closed country.

## Dealing With Singleness

Let's address the subject of going to the field as a single person.

One of the most common questions recruiters get as they travel around sending countries is this: "I'm a single woman. Can God use me on the mission field?" There's a simple answer to that, and it is a resounding YES. Half the unreached people in the world are women, and a rule of thumb is that only women can minister to women. For example, much of the lasting work done in the past decades in North Africa was done by single women.

But such a statement needs qualification. Many single women have been devastated on the field due to unwise planning and a lack of knowledge.

Mary, Susan, and Barb were three single women who committed to work together in a Middle Eastern country. They not only lived together, but worked together and studied the language together. They were an integral part of a team of three married couples and a couple of single men. Once a week the team gathered to discuss issues. The singles met later in their apartment to pray fervently for the people they were ministering to.

A few months into their ministry all three single women were walking down the street when one of them (who had a good understanding of Arabic) heard the words "There go the American whores." They were devastated. They were seeking to be holy and blameless, a light to the world, and they were seen as ladies of the evening!

The reason was because of what the nationals had seen: single men going into the three single women's apartment and staying there for several hours! Ministering in the Middle East as a single woman can be very difficult. In fact, some team leaders won't even accept single women because they see them as a liability.

Remember Holly and Judy? Judy and her husband, Tim, arrived on the field first and sought to bring Holly over to join them. But they knew there would be problems. If Holly lived with them, Holly would be seen as a second wife. If she lived outside the home, she would be seen as a mistress when she visited her friends.

How did they resolve this problem? Simple. Before they invited Holly over, Judy and Tim went to all of their neighbors and asked them what to do. The neighbors got together and discussed the pros and cons of where Holly should live. Once they resolved it, they went back to Judy and Tim and gave them the answer. When Holly did come over, she lived with the family. But no one ever thought that she was a second wife, because the neighbors knew all about the situation and were in on the decision.

The most difficult place for single women to minister is the Middle East. But there are many other places single women can go, even in the Muslim world. The Maningkabaugh of Indonesia are a matriarchal society; single women not only have no problem ministering there, they have lots of power! Much of Southeast Asia is wide open to single women. Pakistan has had a woman Prime Minister; they are beginning to think differently about women. The Commonwealth of Independent States (CIS) have seen many single women minister effectively. Single women have no problem in China, and Turkey and Eastern Europe are wide open to single women.

Now if you're single and desperately want to get married, remember this thought: "Make Satan pay for every day you are single." In other words, when you are single, you can do whatever you want for the Lord, whenever and wherever. Make use of your freedom to travel, because after you are married your freedom changes, and especially after you have children!

## Setting Realistic Expectations

Romantic notions of the exotica of missionary life are out. Realistic expectations are crucial to your survival as a cross-cultural worker—whether for the short term or the long haul.

If you prepare well, will you be a missionary success? Karen Dubert helps us rethink our understanding of success in ministry by citing four examples of missionaries extolled as successful:

- One spent half of her missionary years confined to her room.
- Another burned out his health by overwork within five years.
- One spent most of his time washing dishes, and considered picking up litter as important as preaching.
- Another buried three wives—one a lunatic—and neglected his family.

Who were these "rag-tag" missionaries?

- Amy Carmichael, a missionary with incredible impact, was painfully crippled for twenty years.
- Brilliant missionary surgeon David Brainerd was burned out by stress and decimated by tuberculosis.
- Medieval monk Brother Lawrence was a dishwasher extraordinaire his entire adult life and authored the book *Practicing the Presence of God*—a booklet still widely read after hundreds of years.
- William Carey, the "Father of Modern Missions," lost three wives on the field.

Perhaps the best advice for being a successful cross-cultural worker comes from Rollie Royalty, a Missionary Church worker in Spain: "Forget about being successful; just do God's will."[3]

If you have had a long string of successful accomplishments in your own culture, don't expect that you will save the world in another culture. Be prepared to serve. Examine any hint of patronization in how you're hoping to "help" in another culture. Especially when going to a reached culture, where your role will be less in leadership and more in serving and partnering. You will learn to admire the creative, bold ministries of local believers. Every people group's church has its courageous beggars willing to jump on buses to witness, as we learned in a previous chapter. Every culture's church has its developing Sauls and Pauls.

One stunning example is that of a young untrained believer in Nepal. In 1988 he was arrested for preaching in the name of Jesus Christ. Tossed into prison with 35 cell mates, the young man was able through God's grace to introduce every one of them to Jesus. When prison officials were appalled at his apostasy from Buddhism, they threw the young believer into another prison facility. And again, virtually the entire prison population found new life in Christ! Frustrated, the prison officials released the young man to keep him from influencing so many for Christianity. Once outside the prison walls—during a period in Nepal when Christian proclamation was completely illegal—the youth began openly preaching in the capital city of Kathmandu. City officials found they could do nothing against his brash witness because in Nepal a person cannot be arrested for the same crime twice. Growing in the grace and knowledge of Jesus Christ, the young man gathered a flock of believers about him and, just in time for the easing of religious restriction in Nepal, was able to build a 2,000-seat church building, where he still ministers today!

Never underestimate God's ability to incredibly bless the ministries of—by our standards—untrained or unlikely local believers. Never overestimate your role as an expatriate Christian.

If you're a Westerner don't expect, as in the colonial days of the mission enterprise, to be highly regarded as a respected foreigner. More often in today's nationalistic, sometimes anti-Western world, you'll be suspect, seen as a source of money—regardless of the talents you demonstrated back home. Even believers in other cultures will exploit your modern sense of vulnerability (as opposed to the old colonial "I'm-in-charge-here" demeanor). You'll often be treated as if you're an older sibling who picked on a younger one for years, only to find that the younger one is now your boss!

Don't expect to understand everything about another culture as it relates to yours. Some values, actions, language patterns, and worldviews can never be compared to yours. We're not all the same.

Expect practical problems in living conditions. Even if you're headed for a short term in a modern capital city, your day-to-day circumstances, whether married, single, or married with children will demand incredible tolerance. Living conditions and family problems are some of the most sensitive areas in which Satan can harass God's harvest workers.

## Raising Support

Another issue you may be wrestling with is raising support. You may need to be honest with yourself and simply say, "I don't want to raise support." If that's true, let's discuss a few things.

There are other options. Depending upon your training, the agency that sends you, and the location to which you go, you may be fully funded through your "tentmaking" skills. Not all agencies allow this. There are also pros and cons where it is allowed.

*Some of the pros:*

- Your status in that society may be so great, an agency will allow you to be supported by your work because you are so valuable to them.
- Your target people may be anxious to get to know you because you are so well known through your company.
- You may have a platform for developing good relations with people in high places that you wouldn't have if you were seen by the general public as a common visitor or tourist.

*Some of the cons:*

- Depending upon what company you work with, you may be expected to socialize with other foreigners, taking you away from your target people. (This could happen with any job.)
- You will probably work a 40-hour week, if not more, and could be too tired to learn a language or minister to your target people.
- Your salary may be such that you'll be more concerned about doing your job than ministering to the people.

Yet you may also need to grapple with an unwillingness to raise support as it is related to the lordship of Jesus Christ in your life. It could be a problem with pride. It could be a form of rebellion. Whatever the case, the Lord of your life has every right to say to you, "I want you to live on the field from the investments of others."

Living this way is actually biblical. Books that can help you with this concept are *Friend Raising* by Betty Barnett, published by YWAM, and *The Support-Raising Handbook: a Guide for Christian Workers* by

Brian Rust and Barry McLeish, published by InterVarsity Press.

One young man went to his parents and broke the news that he wanted to go on staff with an organization, and in so doing was going to need to raise support. His parents were so unhappy that they didn't allow him to raise support from any of their friends in or out of their church. Believing God wanted him to pursue joining this staff, he asked his parents to choose any city in the state. They chose one, he went there, and God provided all of his support through people who had never known him before!

## Preparing Parents

Some of you are no doubt young and are asking the question, "What do I do about my parents who don't want me to go?"

The Scriptures tell us to honor father and mother (Ephesians 6:2), whether or not they know the Lord in a personal way. What is the best way to do that?

Parents often won't be excited about you going overseas. The questions start out with "You're going to have to go beg for money? . . . not in our town" and progress to "There are so many needs right here in our own country—why do you have to go overseas?" to "You're going to raise my grandchildren where?"

In order to honor your parents in this, find out what drives them. For many parents their concern is for your happiness and security. When you find that out then you can answer them with a statement like "Mom and Dad, I won't be happy living out the American dream here. My greatest joy is going to be serving God where He wants me, and if that is overseas, I need to go there. Regarding safety, the best place I can be is in God's will. I'll be safer on the streets of Istanbul than I ever will be here in our hometown if I am out of God's will. . . ."

It will also encourage your parents to know that others in your church are wanting to send you. "Mom and Dad, I'm not making this decision on my own. The elders of our church are also behind me in this decision, and they believe it is God's will for me to go as well. . . ."

Let your parents know as much about the agency you would like to go with as you can. Do they have a retirement policy? Let them know. Is the agency audited each year? Let your parents know that too. Parents worry about those kind of things. Does your target country have phones, fax machines, allow e-mail? Tell your parents that; let them know how they can reach you at any time. Tell them about furloughs, vacations, anything that would make your venture look "normal" to them.

And if your parents aren't Christians or in Christian circles, be sure you use their terminology, not Christian jargon. It's vacation, not furlough. Tell them what kind of "job" you'll have, not ministry. You'll have people investing in you as partners, not donors just handing you money.

Whatever you do, communicate with your parents on every level of your preparation. If you're beginning to catch a vision of God's heart for the world, share that with them. Let them know what you're learning, bit by bit. Don't uncover God's will for your life after four years of college by giving them a phone call telling them you plan to serve God in Africa, when all along they thought you planned to come back and be part of the family business.

Although you never want to barter God's will with your parents, you may want to honor them by saying, "Mom and Dad, you've put me through four years of college, paying my way completely. Thank you for that. Would you feel comfortable if I worked at this career for two years and then went overseas?"

But what happens if after all your best efforts they simply say no? There are a couple of ways of looking at it.

Some say that if you're a single woman, you're under your parents' authority until you marry someone, who then becomes your new authority. Until that time, it is God's will for you to obey your parents. Only you can pray through that one and see if that's what God wants for you.

If you're considering a short summer project and you're in school, you probably want to heed your parents, especially if they're paying your way through college and want you to earn money that summer. While under your parents' financial wings, highly consider what they want for your life.

Don't limit God by thinking He would never show you His will for your life through what your parents want. God has every right to work through your parents and is quite able to use even non-Christian moms and dads.

If you simply can't shake the knowledge that God wants you to serve Him full time and everyone agrees with you, you then must obey God (Acts 5:28–29) and *lovingly* (honoring them) tell your parents what you must do before Him.

## Planning for Your Children

Many of you reading this book may be a bit older, with young children. You're thinking, "I could never raise my kids overseas." There's a very simple answer to that. You're right, you can't. But then again you can't raise your kids here without God's help.

If the Father of all creation beckons you to walk with Him overseas and to trust Him in all areas, He will provide for you there just as He does where you are right now.

One potential missionary couple was prayerfully thinking about leaving a comfortable home and lifestyle to join an agency in the heart of an unfriendly town with extremely high rent rates and a poor education system for their children. Their main concern: How would their children grow up in such an environment? When the mission director heard they were indecisive, he gave them a phone call.

"John, you do want to teach your son Graham to walk with God, don't you? What do you think you are teaching him if you are showing concern about his owning a home someday, being financially secure, and having a good education? How does that teach him about trusting God for his needs? What does it say about the war we're involved in?

"Wouldn't you like to teach him that we are in the business of saving eternal souls, that that is what is most important and we are going to do whatever it takes to get the job done?"

Strong words, but it made him think and reconsider.

You may be tempted to generalize from one or two stories of missionary kids you've heard about who haven't developed socially and emotionally, but have you looked around your local church lately? Where are the children of some of your church leaders? How about your own children? Are they free from problems because they grew up in North America? or Europe?

It is Josh McDowell who has told us that 50% of 17-year-olds have lost their virginity, and that in the Christian schools they only hold off one more year.

One of the biggest fears of furloughing missionaries is bringing their children home to the U.S. culture. They generally have an easier time of it in their country of service than in the United States!

Raising children on the field can certainly have benefits. They're not bombarded with materialism, they're sensitive to others' life situations, and most grow up bilingual and bicultural. And their education can be quality as well.

On many missionary teams, parents join together to home school, or have someone join their team to home school their children. Others use local international schools. There are creative ways to keep the family unit together on the field.

To those parents who may not be going to the mission field because of your children: What are you communicating to them? What are your priorities? If home and family should take first place, why did Christ give us the Great Commission? Was it a command or call to single people only?

Whatever you do, don't tell the Lord that you can't go to the field because you're worried about your kids! God loves your children far more than you do and He has a plan for them as well. It just may be that His plan includes their growing up overseas.

## Maybe It's Not Just Your Kids, Maybe It's You

Many adult men and women never make it to the field, not because of their children, but because of a deep-seated fear of failure.

This is especially true of men, and more specifically men in the West. Society does not give them the freedom to fail. They are traditionally the ones responsible before God. If things go wrong they are to blame—says Western culture.

Think a moment of the position these people place themselves in, and it is fairly easy to understand why they fear failure. They stand before churches saying, "This is what God is calling us to do." They lay their financial needs on the table and ask people, sometimes strangers, to invest their hard-earned money in an endeavor they themselves are unfamiliar with. They are not saying "I can produce" in so many words, but that is implied. Many are giving up their careers to go overseas.

The fear of failure on the part of men going to the field is especially great among those heading for the Muslim world. It is easy to think, "If they haven't seen a breakthrough for centuries, what makes me think I can effect one?"

Many think through the end result of actual failure on the field: "What if I go out and then don't see the fruit I have prayed for? Where does that leave me? What will my home church think of me, of my family? Will they help me get back into the mainstream in my home country if I fail on the field? If I'm out of the country for too long, will I be able to get back into my career again upon return? If not, what will I do? Flip hamburgers?"

Honestly, there is little room for failure.

How do you overcome this fear?

Realize that the wrong question is being asked. It is not so much a question of success or failure, but of obedience or disobedience.

Bill Bright's definition of successful witnessing is "sharing Christ in the power of the Holy Spirit and leaving the results to God." Results are not the key, even though unfortunately they are what many supporters look for in the missionary they are supporting. Obedience to God's direction is the key.

Jeremiah worked for fifty years without ever having people really believe what he was saying. Was he successful? Yes. He was obedient. This is the lesson many must learn. Obedience is success, not numbers of converts. Don't be caught not going overseas for fear of failure.

## Answering Objections

Many people ask if it's safe "over there." Again, there is a simple answer: "That's not a biblical question."

Where do we get the idea that serving the King is going to be safe?

Everyone wants a New Testament experience—they want to be filled with God. Well why not get thrown in jail? Being jailed is a very real New Testament experience. Weren't most of the Gospels written there?

Somehow many Christians (and pastors) have avoided the tough passages of suffering in the Scriptures. Wasn't Stephen stoned to death for his faith? (When was the last time you heard a sermon on that?) Don't the Scriptures tell us that through many trials and tribulations we must enter the kingdom of God? (Acts 14:22) Look at Paul's life:

> Three times I was beaten with rods, once I was stoned, three times I was shipwrecked, I spent a night and a day in the open sea, I have been constantly on the move. I have been in danger from rivers, in danger from bandits, in danger from my own countrymen, in danger from Gentiles; in danger in the city, in danger in the country, in danger at sea; and in danger from false brothers. I have labored and toiled and have often gone without sleep; I have known hunger and thirst and have often gone without food; I have been cold and naked (2 Corinthians 11:25–27, NIV).

Unfortunately, much of Western Christianity buys a doctrine that says "God wants you and your family to be safe." Quite honestly that isn't what the Scriptures tell us. The West needs to thoroughly investigate the Scriptures to understand that suffering is often a part of God's great Sanctification process to ready us to rule and reign with Him for all eternity. Don't run from the possibility of suffering.

Or many times, healthy global Christians hear a common question: "But there are so many needs right here, why go overseas?"

Often those who pose this question are missing a few things.

First, they've never seen the global heart of God. All they can see are the needs immediately around them. If you are up to the challenge, lovingly and patiently take them through the Scriptures and show them God's heart, from Genesis to Revelation. God wants the nations to worship Him.

Second, they've probably not experienced the glory God receives when you worship God from another culture! What joy they miss if they worship God only from their own culture, instead of seeing Him as the King of the nations. Praying with people from other nations expands our vision of God. What a joy to see the nations bring their splendor before the King!

> The nations will walk by its light, and the kings of the earth will bring their splendor into it. On no day will its gates ever be shut, for there will be no night there. The glory and honor of the nations will be brought into it (Revelation 21:24–26, NIV).

Third, share with those who doubt and question that while their primary part in God's global plan may be "local ministry," your part may be overseas. For all of us, it isn't a question of "What is God's will for MY life?" Rather it is "God, what are you doing in the world and how can I serve you?" God is working toward the goal of bringing people from every tongue, tribe, and nation (Revelation 5:9). And if He directs you to be a small part of that, you must fulfill that role, not worry about what it does to YOUR life. He is the King. He has paid the price. We are His.

Don't let other Christians slow you down by focusing solely on local needs. Help them act locally but keep expanding their thinking globally. Help them to see their ministry isn't to be an end in itself; it is a means toward the overall goal of world evangelization.

## Pressing On

If you still have nagging doubts, and you're thinking, "Maybe I'm supposed to be a goer, but I'm just not sure," do one of two things. First, apply with a few agencies, being totally open with them about what's going on in your mind. If one accepts you, a door has opened. Pray and make your decisions from there. If no one accepts you, the doors are shut . . . for now. (Remember, serving the King can come in "limited assignments.") Second, go short term and get a taste of the field. It may be that God isn't going to direct you until you "drive your car," taking a first step of faith by getting involved! Exploring a short-term cross-cultural ministry will also help you to be a sensitive welcomer, or to be an effective sender or mobilizer.

Whatever the case, don't get to the end of your life saying, "I wish I had at least tried."

## CHAPTER NINE

# Reaping the Harvest on Your Doorstep

*Welcomers ministering to international students*

TEHRAN — Stretch yourself: You're a fifteen-year-old Persian named Reza. And you're going to relive your tense, dry-throated journey of a real-life alien.

"Would you like another drink?" the flight attendant asks.

You don't hear her. You're too excited about arriving in the United States. You had been such an exceptional student in Tehran that your father has sent you to Seattle, Washington, to finish your education and live with your cousins, Ali and Hassan. What an honor Allah has given to you. How many other fifteen-year-old boys are able to leave their country and study abroad?

You're glad your father could send you out of the country at this time. There has been much political instability in your land and nobody knows what will happen. A certain religious leader, the Ayatollah Khomeini, has been making trouble for the Shah through a continual bombardment of his cassette tapes being sent into Iran. Having started in France, he is now in Iraq, mere miles from the border of Iran.

"Another drink, sir?" she repeats. You simply shake your head "no" to get rid of her.

The blue customs line is packed. In some ways, you're thankful you're not an American. It's already 10:00 P.M. and their line is going to be a long wait. So many have been leaving your country on Pan Am's direct eighteen-hour flight from Tehran. You are third in the yellow customs line for foreigners.

Finally it's your turn to open your luggage after breezing through security with your tourist visa. As you open your luggage you wonder why the man is looking so closely at the books you've packed.

"Can I see your visa?" the man asks. "Your visa." The customs officer's demand is louder the second time. He's tall, with a mustache and a dark complexion like your next-door neighbor back home, a man not known for friendly behavior. Not knowing what to do, you hand over your passport with all your papers.

"I see you're on a tourist visa," the man says in an unfriendly manner. "What are these books for?" You don't answer. "These books—why do you have them if you're going to be a tourist?" He seems agitated. "If you wanted to come over as a student, you should have gotten a student visa from Tehran. You're not allowed to get that visa here."

The next five minutes of questioning confirms what the customs officer suspected all along. You don't know a single word of English and. . . .

The hotel you stay in is fairly nice. You are treated well. But you feel sick to your stomach standing in line to board the same plane you deplaned just fifteen hours earlier. The eighteen hours back to Tehran is going to be the longest of your life. Your father will be furious. It took so much of the family's money to fly you over.

As the plane descends you awake from a nap. As you open your window to spot your home, you quickly realize something is wrong. What are those buildings? And what is that large body of water? That couldn't be the Caspian Sea—it's too close to the city.

Your mind races. Where is this plane landing? Had you gotten on the wrong plane? Did the customs people put you on the wrong flight? What country is this? How are you going to let your parents know what is going on?

If you were sick before, now you're really beginning to feel nauseated. You open the little white bag in the seat back in front of you. Your stomach erupts and your emotions numb.

Standing in the customs line you become more nervous. You are only two people away from being asked questions in another language you don't know. Where are the flight attendants with your passport? You pleaded with them to give it to you before they took off, but they insisted on keeping it for you.

"Can I see your passport?" the man asks in Turkish. You don't know what to do. "Your passport!" the man demands. He is irritated by passengers upset that the plane hadn't been allowed to land in Iran.

You don't know what to do. You speak in Farsi but that gets you nowhere. Tears well in your eyes, but you try not to let anyone see them.

Soon you are in an interrogation room. You know something is going very wrong. No passport, no papers, and you can't even communicate with them. . . .

Four grueling hours later your eyes are dry. You can't cry anymore. Your mind is numb. Whatever they're going to do with you is OK. You simply want to go and rest somewhere.

As you are put into a car a peaceful thought comes to mind. You think they're going to put you in a hotel like the Americans did and then send you back to Tehran. That's just fine with you. You recognized the flag under the picture of a man and you know Turkish delight isn't something you want to experience!

Your peace quickly disappears. This is not a hotel.

In jail, you become very bitter. Why didn't your cousins fly to New York to meet you? (They had said it was so easy.) Why did American customs not allow you in? How had your passport gotten lost? Why didn't the airline people take responsibility for you? Why did the Turkish police put you in jail? You are angry at many people.

But most of all you feel bitter and angry toward God. Why is Allah letting this happen? You have been a good Muslim all your life. You have been the best student in your school. God isn't supposed to let you down.

In the end you are becoming very weak. You have been in this cell for two months now with six men. Five speak Turkish; one speaks a language you don't even recognize. It's dark and dirty. You're not eating. You've lost your appetite.

But most of your sickness is prompted by your extreme loneliness. You haven't even been allowed to call your parents. They still think you are in Seattle enjoying the American life. Nobody knows where you are, nobody cares what you think.

A man with an AK–47 is motioning to you. The sign language is clear no matter what language you speak. You are to follow him.

Although it is poorly pronounced, you recognize it: Tehran! The plane is going to Tehran. Joy floods your sick and weak body. Talking with the Persian embassy representative not only made you aware of the takeover of Iran by the Ayatollah (resulting in the forced landing in Istanbul), but it also resulted in approval to allow you to go home. Soon you will be back in your parents' home, now that international flights have resumed.

As steps are rolled to the open door of the DC–10 that just arrived from Istanbul, everyone is told to remain seated. You are rushed by ambulance to the nearest hospital and your weak body is pumped with fluids to stabilize you. You are delirious. By some miracle, would your parents meet you at the hospital?

After four days your physical health is stronger, but emotionally you are a wreck. How could Turkish authorities not have known the Iranian border was still closed? Why are you now in an Indian hospital? Why can't you call your parents?

After a boring, lonely, two-week stay at a local hotel, PAN AM officials see the potential of a huge bill racking up. Iranian borders aren't going to open any time soon, and yet they have to put you somewhere. You're their responsibility.

Soon you find yourself living with an Indian family. Although at first you dreaded living with this family of six cramped into a small house, your fears are alleviated. These people are different. These people care.

It had been a long three months since anyone cared for you. On the first day, the family heard your story and insisted that you call your parents on their phone. You couldn't believe it. No official had ever offered anything like that.

Unable to go to Tehran, you are taken in by the family as one of their own, fed and loved. Though their surroundings are modest compared to your family's home, these people are happy, joyful. They have something you don't.

It is here in this small Indian home, packed in with a family of six that you first hear about the love of Jesus Christ. Through their love—and that of others—you now know the King! You've been *welcomed* into the Kingdom.

## Taking Care of the Fatherless, the Widow, and the Alien

God's rag-tag Christian army is made up of ordinary, everyday people. They live all over the world and have been given two great commands. They are to love the Lord their God with all their heart, soul, mind, and strength, and to love their neighbors as themselves.

But who is our neighbor?

When Jesus was asked that question in Luke 10:25–37, He told a parable about the man who was knocked out by robbers along the road. As a priest passed by, he did nothing to help the man. A Levite likewise did nothing. It was only a Samaritan (half Jew/half Gentile) who showed kindness to the man and ministered to him.

Now, in the days of Christ, the Samaritans were bad news to the average Jew. The animosity was so great that Jews avoided Samaritans at all cost when traveling between Galilee and Judea. Tensions ran high (Luke 9:52–54; 10:25–37; 17:11–19; John 8:48). But Jesus broke through those hostilities. What He was saying was this: "Your neighbors include people from other cultures, people you don't naturally like, those who are different, who don't dress like you do, who don't speak the same language as you. I want you to minister to them as well."

In the context of fearing and serving Him, God describes how He defends these "others" and tells us to do likewise:

> He defends the cause of the fatherless and the widow, and loves the alien, giving him food and clothing. And you are to love those who are aliens, for you yourselves were aliens in Egypt. Fear the LORD your God and serve him. Hold fast to him and take your oaths in his name (Deuteronomy 10:18–20, NIV).

> Cursed is the man who withholds justice from the alien, the fatherless or the widow. Then all the people shall say, "Amen!" (Deuteronomy 27:19, NIV).

Not only are we to love them and give them food and clothing, but God seems to indicate that we can even give our tithe to them:

> When you have finished setting aside a tenth of all your produce in the third year, the year of the tithe, you shall give it to the Levite, the alien, the fatherless and the widow, so that they may eat in your towns and be satisfied (Deuteronomy 26:12, NIV).

In fact, there are more than 40 references in the Old Testament alone to looking out for the foreigner in our midst. Why is God so concerned about them? Because He loves them just as much as He loves us. God's radical love extends to all peoples on the face of the earth equally.

And in His love, He often shifts peoples around the globe to locations where they are primed to meet Him. He moves thousands of Kurds to Berlin to form the first Kurdish churches. He moves Bawean Island workers from Indonesia to Singapore to meet Christians for the first time. He allows the government of the People's Republic of China to forcibly relocate Tibetan Buddhists to cities where Han Chinese Christians introduce them to Jesus Christ. He moves Mongolian students to Moscow to meet Nigerian believers who welcome them into the Kingdom.

Through the evil propagated by Satan, his emissaries, and even human beings, and through curiosity, illness, famine, business opportunities, tourism, family relationships, and hundreds of other means, God moves people who need Him to your doorstep.

This was to be one of the great lessons the Israelites were to have learned under Egyptian rule.

"The alien living with you must be treated as one of your native-born. Love him as yourself, for you were aliens in Egypt. I am the LORD your God" (Leviticus 19:34, NIV).

God says, "Remember how you were mistreated? Remember the pain you went through as a foreigner? Remember how you hated those different smells? How you despised the ways of those in control? So too, love the foreigners in your midst because you now can relate to them."

Unfortunately, much of the Church hasn't learned that lesson. Around 80% of all international students who study in America never make it into an American home. In New Zealand more than 80% of International Students never make it into a Kiwi home. What about your country?

## Welcomers and Special Graces

Making this command a priority immediately brings you, the world Christian, face-to-face with asking God, "Lord, if I'm not to be a goer, do you want me working with internationals here where I live?" If your heart goes out to the Rezas of the world, maybe God wants you to think of working with internationals in your area.

Working with internationals takes a normal everyday person—with special graces.

Pat Kershaw has worked with international students in the United States for more than 40 years. She claims anyone can work with them.

Pat has seen a chicken farmer in Goshen, Indiana, minister effectively to internationals, along with a 70-year-old scientist who helped develop the atomic bomb. Anyone can do it. Anyone.

Yet welcomers need to be strong in three areas to be able to minister effectively to internationals: in love, in their ability to demonstrate Christ through their lifestyle, and in wise use of time—bringing internationals alongside their already busy lifestyle.

International students go all over the world to better their education. And many, like Reza, are ripe and ready to receive the love and attention God wants them to have in His name. Many have been through hectic times coming to your country. All face some sort of culture shock; the sights, sounds, smells, and clothing are all different; all are homesick to some degree; all need a friend; all need love, sometimes in the simplest way.

One Libyan student went to study at Penn State University in the United States. Being fearful of eating pork, he daily went to a Kentucky Fried Chicken restaurant to eat. Each day he ate his food outside and deposited the trash in a container on the street corner. After five days of doing this, he was thoroughly scolded by another student for putting his trash in a U.S. mailbox!

Did he feel dumb? Did he need help? Did he want an American friend to help him learn the ways of this new country? Could he have used some love? Yes, Yes, Yes!

One way of manifesting the love of Christ to an international is in taking special notice of his everyday needs—needs you don't even think about, things you do for yourself without thinking.

*Envision yourself*

- Meeting a Malaysian at the airport and taking her to her apartment.
- Teaching a Tajik the difference between a penny, a nickel, a dime, and a quarter.
- Helping an Azeri from Iran set up a bank account.
- Driving a Khmer woman, from Cambodia, to the store and showing her how to grocery shop.
- Listening to a Jordanian Arab share about his poor grade in a basic engineering course.
- Hurting with a Mapeche girl from Chile as she tells you about her mother who has cancer.
- Having a Hausa couple from Nigeria over for tea and playing a board game with them.
- Sitting at a table and hearing all about the brothers and sisters of a Kazakh student.
- Taking an Aceh from Indonesia to see the tourist sights of your area.
- Having three Zhuang Chinese students over for Thanksgiving dinner.
- Listening to a Japanese student share about roommate problems.

Why is there such a need for this kind of help? Because the institutions who process immigrants and the educational institutions that invite students to your country are too busy to meet these personal needs. Schools, of course, help international students get courses set up and assign them an advisor—but after that they don't have time for anything else. They're too busy registering other students also studying at the same university. And once government agencies route immigrants through the official paperwork and entry requirements, they rarely take time to actually befriend internationals in any personal way.

It's in these areas, offering help above and beyond what official agencies and institutions can provide, that the love of Christ can be seen.

Not only does the love of Christ need to shine through what you do, but welcomers also need to reflect the character of Christ by living a lifestyle that demonstrates Christ.

Many internationals may come to your country with tremendous misconceptions about Christ and Christianity. For example, millions of Two-Thirds World immigrants come to Europe with an awareness of its Christian heritage. So, of course, they interpret all they see—drug addiction, prostitution, cold indifference—as the lifestyle of "Christianity." The global distribution of movies, television programming, pop music, scandal, and gossip usually reinforce the Two-Thirds' worldview that the "Christian" West is thoroughly corrupt and immoral.

It's no wonder that most Muslims throughout the world equate free sex, drugs, alcohol, rape, and divorce—all of the bad things of the West—with Christianity. And with one missionary for every one million Muslims overseas, no one has told them any different.

It is only when these internationals come in contact with revolutionary Kingdom Christians such as you that they see what Christ's character and love is really all about. This entails not just living out Christianity before them by being a good person (because many come in contact with good pagans), but also actively loving them with Christ's love.

One Pakistani Muslim tells his story:

> When I first came to New Zealand I thought this was a Western Christian nation and associated the immorality and violence and pornography with Christianity. However, I have come to understand that this is not a Christian nation, but it is secular with Christians living here. Christians are different; they really love and care and have a different lifestyle and are very easy to pick out from other people. . . . I have been going to look at different churches.

For this Muslim, the love and practical help he received from Christians opened the way for them to sow the seed of the Word of God. Different Christians have had input into his life by praying for his needs, testifying to the reality of Jesus in their lives, having long discussions about Christianity, and giving him a Bible and a *Jesus* video. One of his Christian friends was able to accompany him to Pakistan and stay with his family while the student was at home, and was able to share at length with some family members.

Welcoming international students to cookouts, taking them on family trips, having them into your homes during the holidays—all of this actively shows them the love of Christ. And what really ministers to them is to watch you as a believer trusting in the Lord when you go through hard times. This is when they see Christ's true character in you.

Doing these things requires a commitment on the part of the believer to be available and to make time.

But one word of clarification is needed. Reaching out to internationals doesn't mean you have to have lots of *free time*. It simply means *including* your international friend in your busy lifestyle. Robert and Theresa White of Austin, Texas, are an example of this type of commitment.

Robert is a busy executive working a more-than-full-time job. He also is an elder in his church. His wife, Theresa, is a full-time mom with four kids, three of whom are teenagers. (Does anything else need to be said about how busy she is?)

They worked with a staff member of ISI—International Students Incorporated—in their local area and through his ministry were linked with a Singaporean student, Anthony.

Anthony was their first international student. Their intent was to get to know him and make themselves available to him. But their time was limited. With four kids of their own, how were they going to fit Anthony into their busy lifestyle?

Upon hearing that his "adopted" family had four kids, Anthony started off with a somewhat pessimistic attitude. He had been an only child. Would he fit in? Would he be able to relate to the other children?

On their first meeting they all hit it off. The kids loved Anthony and Anthony loved them. And after one or two special evenings set aside to get to know Anthony, the family simply began to incorporate him into their busy lives. On his free weekends, he was invited to spend the weekend at the Whites' house, rooming with one of the boys, sleeping in the spare bunk bed. In many ways Anthony experienced a second childhood, playing hide-and-seek in the dark with the boys and playing all kinds of other games with them.

The relationship was solidified when Robert taught Anthony how to drive and helped him get a license. He simply became one of the family. He was soon called their "eldest son."

When family vacation time came around, they brought Anthony along. They took him to Sea World, Six Flags, Disneyland, and snow skiing. He celebrated all the major holidays at their home and even went to meet and visit with the grandparents.

The result?

The best evangelists weren't Robert or Theresa (although their active love for Christ spoke volumes to Anthony) but the children. On their first Christmas Eve together, one of the sons woke Robert at one in the morning. "Dad," he said, "I've been sharing with Anthony what Christmas is all about and he wants to invite Christ into his life. Could you help me?"

At the end of his education, Anthony had become competent and self-sufficient. His faith was growing, and he had gotten to know many other people. Though the family relationship was not as tight-knit as it was the first year, it remained strong. Robert and Theresa held a graduation party for Anthony, and many of his international friends who came left the party with the same thought: "I wish I could have had an American family like this adopt me."

Both Robert and Theresa hear others say they're too busy to work with international students. But the Whites know better. It's not a question of making free time for international students, but rather learning how to incorporate them into your busy lifestyle.

Although Anthony wasn't firm in any faith previous to his commitment to Christ, in many cases you will want special training to minister effectively to an international student in your area. Training might mean attending a seminar, or simply gleaning as much as possible from other international workers in order to grow in your understanding of cultural and religious differences. In this way you will be able to minister to those who already have strong religious convictions.

Don McCurry, who trains people all over the world to work with their Muslim neighbors, tells this story in his seminar:

> George Fanshaw worked in a large engineering firm which employed overseas nationals. In the course of time, George became good friends with Saleh Abdullah al-Fokra. George and his wife, Ann, invited Saleh home to a meal.
>
> During the meal, Saleh commented on how tasty the beef dish was. Ann remarked, "Oh, thank you! This is one of my new recipes for beef bourguignon. It has beef, lean bacon, carrots and onions, plus a little red wine." At this, Saleh became very upset and visibly ill. He asked to be taken outdoors as he felt he was going to be sick. George escorted him to the bathroom at which point Saleh threw up into the wash basin.
>
> George felt angry but did manage to assist Saleh to wash up. Saleh was both angry and embarrassed. He explained that he had never eaten pork or ever drunk any wine in his life, since both were forbidden to those who worshiped God. He didn't know whether to be angry at those who had betrayed him in this way or to apologize for creating such a bad impression on his host and

hostess. After a few minutes of awkward conversation, Saleh said he didn't feel well and asked permission to leave.

After Saleh had left, there were sharp words between Ann and George. "I don't ever want to see one of those foreign friends of yours again," she snapped. "What a stupid religion that is anyway! And who is going to clean up that mess in the bathroom?"

Learning the unique characteristics of other cultures and religions can save you time, energy, and sometimes embarrassment.

You will also want to learn what friendship means in other cultures. This is especially true for working with students from Muslim countries, where in many places a friend is someone who can drop in on you at any time, unannounced. Meals together are common. Friends share finances freely. With this definition, they have friendship—what we regard as close friendship—with a few people.

In many Western cultures friendships have less commitment and are shared among more people. Given these two opposing definitions you can see how conflicts could arise. Many times you'll need to "earn" the friendship of an international through your loving actions.

Jack and Joy had learned to go beyond their own definition of friendship to be used by God to reach out to internationals. It ended up "costing" them six months' use of their second car, which they loaned to a Jordanian couple in dire need of transportation. Because of this they earned the right to be heard (what all international workers need to earn). They had demonstrated true friendship, were able to share Christ freely, and now have Jordanian friends who will open the door to them anytime they ask.

Being available and giving up your time could mean a change in lifestyle. Mike and Janet have an international live with them and charge nothing. John spends many weekends taking internationals to a national tourist spot. The Goldmans have many internationals over for dinner and spend hours talking to them about their country. The Smiths have internationals into their home on most major holidays.

You will need to learn patience as well. "Not everyone is going to respond favorably," Pat Kershaw says, "when an international student shows up two hours late for dinner or doesn't show up at all because he got a better offer and didn't call to let you know!"

You also need time to learn to be "street wise." Jean Heibert has spent many years learning lessons no one taught her. One of the most important lessons was learning how to deal with international students who became Christians and wanted to serve Him full time.

"Depending upon their culture," says Jean, "many come with only one experience: obedience to their parents. They are thinking that someday they'll go back, take over the family business, and be the 'social security' and 'retirement' for their parents. Once they come to know Him and want to serve Him full time, tremendous conflicts arise between them and their parents when they deviate from that plan. Most parents are adamantly against their children raising support. Some students are disowned."

Many workers encourage internationals too quickly to go into full-time Christian work. Jean Heibert likes to wait and be patient, encouraging students in that discipline as well. Although she doesn't make it a 100% rule, there are times she has seen students not only get their parents' permission by waiting, but many have led their parents to the Lord in the process. Had it been rushed, they could have been cut off forever. Learning this lesson in patience took years.

A commitment to loving an international student, incorporating them into your lifestyle, giving of your time and availability to be a friend—could that be you? Keeping an eye out for those who look different or dress differently than you may lead you into a ministry God has for you.

Why can this type of ministry be so key? Because today's international students may be tomorrow's leaders back in their home country.

International Students Incorporated, a ministry dedicated to reaching out to international students in the United States, reports that 100,000 international students go to the United States annually to study. There are more than 800,000 there at any one time. All communities have internationals among them. Many of them will become national leaders.

Top leaders in nations around the world today were schooled in the United States. Below is a list of some of these people.

> The King of Bahrain—Sheikh Isa bin Sulman al-Khalifa
> The Governor General of Barbados—Dame Ruth Nita Barrow
> The Prime Minister of Belize—George C. Price
> The President of Cyprus—George Vasiliou
> The President of Ecuador—Sixto Duran
> The President of El Salvador—Alfredo Cristiani
> The President of Honduras—Rafael Leonardo Callejas
> The Governor of Hong Kong—Sir David Wilson
> The President of Ireland—Mary Robinson
> The Prime Minister of the Ivory Coast—Alassone Ouattara
> The Prime Minister of Jordan—Tahir a Masri
> The President of Malawi—Hastins Kamuzu Banda, M.D.

The President of Mexico—Carlos Salina
The King of Nepal—Bir Bikram Shah Dev Birendra
The President of Nicaragua—Violeta Barrious de Chamorro
The President of Nigeria—Major General Ibrahim Badamosi
    Babangida
The Prime Minister of Norway—Gro Harlem Brundtland,
    M.D.
The President of the Philippines—General Fidel Ramos
The Prime Minister of Singapore—Goh Chok Tong
The Prime Minister of Sweden—Ingvar Carlsson
The President of Tunisia—Aine El Abidine Ben Ali

Could tomorrow's leaders be living right in your neighborhood?

Maybe you would like to do something, but you're still a little fearful. "The university itself has its own subculture," you might be thinking, "but international students are a subculture within a subculture. I wouldn't know where to begin." There's hope.

ISI has a kit available to show you everything from the first steps in reaching out to internationals all the way to learning how to get your church involved. Interested? See the Resources section for an address and write to the "Coordinator of Volunteers."

Of course, welcoming doesn't just mean ministering cross-culturally to students. There are tourists, refugees, business people, and other immigrants of other cultures living or visiting in your country. For example, the pastor of a six-hundred-member Evangelical Free Church was burdened for the Iranian community living in his city. As a result, he invited a guest speaker to teach a ten-week course about Islam to a Sunday school class for those interested in learning about Muslims. During the class, attendees were challenged to reach out to the Iranians in their area and plant a church. Today a team is working to plant an Iranian church.

Ministering to internationals could be a full-time job or simply something you do in your free time. Whatever the case, don't forget the fatherless, widows, and aliens!

But maybe welcoming isn't your niche. Maybe God wants you to focus on being an effective sender. You could be a believer who specializes in sending others to the nations—whether those nations (peoples) live in other countries or in your own!

## CHAPTER TEN

# Serve As a Sender

*How shall they go unless they are sent?*

*"I spent twenty years of my life trying to recruit people out of local churches and into mission structures so that they could be involved in fulfilling God's global mission. Now I have another idea. Let's take God's global mission and put it right in the middle of the local church!"*

—*George Miley*

GUINEA-BISSAU, WEST AFRICA — Sharp strands of grass slice at your legs at every step. You're walking in the second grouping, just behind Brazilian missionaries João and Solange Oliveira, who in turn walk slowly behind a Fulani man carrying the baby Rebecca's casket. Behind you, winding out from the village, are twenty of the area's Muslim leaders, other members of the Brazilian mission team and then hundreds of Fulani villagers.

You arrived on the coast of this dank, humid country just in time to hear that out in Gabu, the small village (*tabanca*) that was your destination, Solange finally delivered her baby. But by the time you bounced into the tabanca in late afternoon, staggering off the infernally hot, sour-smelling bus, the news was a slap to your faith: The difficult labor had lasted the entire night, and six hours after her birth, baby Rebecca died.

The Oliveiras had sacrificed everything to be here. One of the thousands of new missionary units Brazilian churches had sent in the past few years, they and their team often lived for weeks at a time on rice. They couldn't obtain medical care. They couldn't easily communicate with home, and their support funds only arrived infrequently. *Is this any way to treat your sacrificing servants?* you think. *By allowing their first child to die?*

The processional finally reaches a clump of trees around the Muslim cemetery outside Gabu. João had immediately gone to the chief, the Bigman, to ask his permission to bury the baby. The Bigman answered in the Fulani language: "You are not like other foreigners who have come here. You live among us, not in the city. Yes, you may bury your baby in our Muslim cemetery. And you may do it in your Christian way. I will send runners to the other villages so all the Muslim leaders of the region may attend."

Now the little casket is lowered into the dirt of the flat African savannah, and you sway in the heat, in the disorienting fatigue of your travel, in the tragedy of the moment. The Brazilian mission team leader's funeral message is that sometimes God allows a precious seed to die and be buried, that new life may spring forth. That God redeems.

Two days later Clarice, the twenty-three-year-old co-leader of the Brazilian team, invites you to accompany her to a neighboring tabanca called Casambe. "It will take your mind off things," she says. "And it's good exercise—about an hour and a half of hiking."

You arrive while it is still relatively cool in the morning; still you mop the perspiration dripping from your chin. You're fascinated by Clarice's presence as this young Brazilian negotiates with the two imposing Bigmen of Casambe. Speaking through an interpreter who knows the Fulani language as well as Portuguese, they finally grant permission for Clarice to tell the people about Isa, Jesus the Messiah. "We know who you are," they say. "You are the foreigners who have lived among us. You have buried your baby in our Muslim cemetery. You are one with us now. Let us first send out runners to gather all the people from the fields."

The 150 villagers settle into squats around Clarice as she begins in Crioulo, a Portuguese creole, to tell about Isa. Her translator is a young high-school-age boy. You understand neither Crioulo nor the Fulani language as you sit on a mound of grass off to the side. But you sense what Clarice is saying as she challenges the villagers to respond to the call of Jesus Christ. You know the background of this people group— that they proudly ruled much of West Africa hundreds of years ago, that branches of the Fulani are called by varying names in several countries, that their dialects differ greatly. Yet they as a people have resisted the message of Christ. In Guinea-Bissau particularly, very few Fulani have come to Christ, and those few have been severely persecuted. Now Clarice asks who will follow Isa. Fifty-four Fulani stand, including the two Bigmen.

Clarice widens her eyes at you and motions for everyone to sit down again. A second time she explains the Gospel and the cost of following Jesus as Lord and Savior. And again, fifty-four Fulani stand to receive Christ.

Neither Clarice nor you can believe the response. Perhaps the young interpreter is misquoting Clarice's challenge. So a third time, the young Brazilian woman presents the Good News and the persecution that invariably follows conversion in an Islamic society. Fifty-four of this most-resistant people group stand to commit their lives to Jesus Christ. And new life springs forth in Guinea-Bissau.

How could such a tragedy turn into an unprecedented break-through for the Kingdom? Three months later you find out. On the island of Kona, Hawaii, just before the time of your visit to Guinea-Bissau, a Christian schoolteacher named Asher Motola realized he had done very little to urge his students to an understanding of unreached peoples. So he gave them an assignment: Research an unreached people. One team of eleven- to fourteen-year-olds studied the Fulani.

Gripped by the fact that very few missionaries were ministering to the Fulani, and amazed that virtually no one was praying for the Fulani, the team of students made up a flyer urging awareness about this people group. They recruited thirty-five adults who committed themselves in writing to pray for the Fulani of Guinea-Bissau during a specific period of time. Of course, that period of time was when baby Rebecca died, and when for the first time in Guinea-Bissau history fifty-four Fulani were brought to faith in Jesus Christ!

## Senders—Part of the Team

Although the praying youngsters and adults in Hawaii didn't know it, although they were thousands of miles from the front lines in Guinea-Bissau, they were part of the multinational force that God used to break through to the Fulani of Guinea-Bissau. They apparently made the difference in prayer—one of the crucial tactics of the harvest force teams known as senders.

In a war, for every frontline soldier in combat there are fifteen to twenty support personnel. Without that support, the soldier would never be able to mount an effective attack on an enemy. In the same way, every frontline missionary needs a competent, efficient sending team.

It's often said in mission circles that believers are either goers or senders. Generally the idea matches the classic scriptural passage on the essential role of sending: "How then shall they call upon him in whom they have not believed? And how shall they believe in him whom they have not heard? And how shall they hear without a preacher?" (Romans 10:14).

Those whose ministry is teaching ten-year-olds in the church are, in this general sense, senders. They prepare potential goers for the future. Those who serve in hospitality in the church help strengthen the church, which contributes to a strong base for sending. So again they are part of the general sending team of the Body.

But for our purposes—as we discuss the practicalities of mission work—let's think of senders as those whose home front ministry is directly involved in mission action.

## Specialists in Sending

God seems to be raising up a whole new army of home front believers whose lives are saturated with a passion for His global cause.

Senders might team up to form the support base for a specific missionary—that is, they could provide every individual, couple, or family serving cross-culturally with "behind the lines" backup comprising at least six trained specialists:

> Logistics specialist
> Prayer coordinator
> Communications specialist
> Researcher
> Financial manager
> Re-entry coordinator

Or sending specialists may serve the Body at large, serving several missionaries and even several agencies as

> Missionary trainer
> Missionary pastor/counselor
> Administrative worker
> Researcher
> Mobilizer

Many of the roles of a missionary's sending team are carefully described in Neal Pirolo's excellent study book *Serving As Senders* (see Materials and Courses in the Resources section). The point of the *Serving As Senders* study is simply that these sender-specialists are involved in mission work as passionately as is a frontline missionary—although the home front senders most often are involved on a part-time, volunteer basis.

What do senders do?

*A logistics specialist facilitates practical arrangements. He or she (or a team functioning as one) can*

- Pack a missionary's goods as she or he heads for the field.
- Arrange a missionary's travel to, from, and within the target area, including planning and handling contingency plans for emergencies.
- Locate, get specs and costs of needed equipment and supplies, pack and ship items.
- Arrange travel for visitors or short-term groups to the target area.
- Train a substitute to take on these jobs whenever necessary.
- Train other churches' sending teams to handle logistics.

*A prayer coordinator can*

- Pinpoint spiritual targets for intercession from information provided by the team researchers, mission societies, and the missionary.
- Inform prayer groups of these prayer points regarding the people group.
- Enlist specific prayer warriors to intercede for the personal needs of the missionary.
- Offer global-scale prayer training.
- Promote regular prayer for the missionary and the people group through announcements, take-home items, family devotional reminders.
- Set an example of consistent prayer for the missionaries.
- Promote periodic prayer events on behalf of the people group and the missionary.
- Train a substitute to take on these jobs whenever necessary.
- Train other churches' sending teams to coordinate prayer.

*The sending team communications specialist(s) can*

- Establish lines of communication with the missionary on the field—via letter, fax, phone, amateur radio, e-mail, courier.
- Work with the prayer coordinator to communicate to prayer groups

and the entire fellowship the essentials of prayer requests, praise, and the missionary's concerns.

- Regularly produce and distribute a news-prayer letter on behalf of the missionary.
- Promote regular and special opportunities for various ages of church members to communicate with their missionaries.
- Communicate with other churches, mission societies, and missionaries who are working among that same people group.
- Submit articles, news releases, and prayer publicity to local, regional, or widespread Christian media to promote awareness of the targeted people group.
- Train a substitute to take on these jobs whenever necessary.
- Train other churches' sending teams to communicate.

*The sending team's financial expert(s) can*

- Work with missionaries before they go, to determine realistic personal and ministry budgets, finance management methods, transfers of money, financial expectations for reentry from the field.
- Help plan the details of support-raising, or present financial plans to the proper church bodies if the missionary is to be fully supported by the local church.
- Monitor or initiate plans for appropriate insurances—medical, life, property, etc.—and taxes as well as retirement or reentry finances.
- Handle any of the missionary's financial matters while he, she, or they are on the field.
- Evaluate personal and ministry expense patterns, and advise on wise financial action.
- Raise funds for the mission effort—pursuing grant funding, exploring secular financial sources, mounting an ongoing support appeal to the church.
- Keep contributors accountable for regular giving and regularly, genuinely thank them for their support.
- Train a substitute to take on these jobs whenever necessary.
- Train other churches' sending teams to handle missionaries' finances.

*A sending team's reentry coordinator(s) can*

- Discuss with missionaries before they go the expected dates and events of the missionaries' return—for visits, rests, and permanently.

- Regularly update the missionaries on the field as to developments in the home front's popular culture—including what teenagers are wearing, what issues are in vogue, what's happening in Christian circles.

- Work with the missionary to carefully plan the personal aspects of any homecomings, and implementing and/or coordinating the work of such homecomings.

- Plan and arrange events at which returning missionaries can, in a reasonable schedule, share what God has been doing in and through them, and arrange for furlough housing as they travel.

- Keep updated, and inform the missionary of schooling, employment, and ministry opportunities that are possible when the missionary returns to his or her home culture.

- Plan and arrange for the ongoing roles of returned missionaries within the fellowship.

- Arrange for any necessary counseling for returning missionaries and family members.

- Train a substitute to take on these jobs whenever necessary.

- Train other churches' sending teams to handle missionaries' reentry challenges.

Every missionary moving into cross-cultural ministry should have such a team on the home front. After all, how shall they preach unless they are sent?

But don't let the term "specialist" throw you off. Serving as a sender may mean you are only one step ahead of the missionary you are working for, calling others up and asking, "Hey—my friend is coming home and I want to help. What do I do?" Senders learn on the job, just as do most people in their work!

Neal Pirolo's *Serving As Senders* study cites some of these and many other sensible jobs for each member of a missionary's sending team. In addition to Neal's great insights, there is another specialist needed: the team researcher.

What does a sender specializing in research do?

## Research: Looking to the Fields

If a fellowship or the Church at large knows nothing about a particular corner of the harvest field, there won't be much prayer to thrust forth laborers into that area and its people group. Knowing little or nothing is the starting point for one of the most crucial and yet unnoticed roles in mission work: research.

Often the missionary on the field is immersed in the language, local customs, and personalities of local contacts in a people group. But he or she may have difficulty gaining accurate information about demographics, about the actual history of a people (sometimes contrasted with the local legendary versions), about the overall culture itself, as well as current news. A home front researcher can often glean this valuable information and provide it to the missionary.

Research gives direction to the harvest force. Let's see how. In the mid–80s the DAWN (Discipling A Whole Nation) approach of researching an area was implemented in the Silicon Valley—Santa Clara County in California. DAWN director Jim Montgomery says the pastors of this area—with its dozens of megachurches, its 24-hour-a-day Christian TV and radio broadcasting—were shocked to find what was really happening in their valley.

First, research showed that only 6.8% of the population on any given Sunday would be in any kind of Protestant church. That percentage included just 4% of the ethnic population. A full 40% of the population at that time—undoubtedly increased now—was non-Anglo. Of these, 300,000 Hispanics had only 45 churches with 3,475 members—only 1.2% of the Hispanic population. There were no churches at all for nearly a thousand Afghan Pashtu, nearly 9,000 Native Americans, over 2,300 Ethiopians of various ethnic peoples, 6,000 peoples from India, 566 East Europeans, 4,000 Persians, and more than 600 Arabs from Iraq.

Just as Nehemiah's "research" of his homeland's sad condition prompted him to prayer, fasting, and action (Nehemiah 1; 2:11–18), the research on Silicon Valley provoked the Christian leadership of the area. At a session reporting the findings, one San Jose pastor simply exclaimed, "Shocking!" Another said, "I was crushed. I fell on my face in prayer." Another responded to the information: "I had no idea of the size of the mission field right here." After sifting through the details of the research, the leaders of much of the Body of Christ in Santa Clara County gathered to commit themselves collectively to grow the Church of the valley from its average 85,000 to 300,000 by the year 2000—with a church for every people![1]

Many believers think that since the Gospel fits every human condition, we simply take a one-size-fits-all approach in communicating that Gospel. For example, a mission-minded Korean congregation in the Los Angeles area sent their pastor on a short-term evangelism trip to Mongolia in 1991. His experience in evangelism involved on-the-street witnessing. He had led hundreds of Koreans to Christ simply by stopping them on the sidewalk and sharing the Gospel, so what he planned to do during his time in Mongolia was to stand on the street corners of Ulaanbaator and, with memorized phrases in Halkh Mongolian, tell passersby about Jesus. He was ready. His message was prepared.

What he failed to take into account, however, were the recipients of his message. Mongolians are not Koreans. And his street-evangelism short-term trip ended largely in disappointment.

All this points to the rather obvious necessity in cross-cultural ministry of understanding the people you and your missionary are reaching out to for Christ. If the Korean pastor had taken the time to study, to talk to others who know the Halkh Mongol culture, to pray for God's heart for this people, he would have known that street-corner evangelism isn't necessarily the most effective way to reach Mongolians.

## How to Find Information About a People Group

Imagine yourself talking by phone, faxing back and forth, sitting down to tea with missionaries, tourists, and business travelers who have some firsthand knowledge of a particular people group. Imagine the planetary list you'd compile of videos you track down in Hong Kong, monographs in the University of Moscow, books now out-of-print but sold in a London antique book shop, experts from Cincinnati or Singapore, CIA or People's Republic of China governmental studies on a people.

Imagine yourself praying with others who have a heart for that people that God would reveal His wisdom about them.

Well, imagine no more. It's probably a good time to start rolling up your sleeves: Let's overview how you can get to the core of God's heart for a particular people group.

First, contact the Adopt-A-People Clearinghouse (see address under Organizations in the Resources) to see if any agencies are actively working among your people group. If the Clearinghouse doesn't have the information, check in the MARC Mission Handbook (again, see the Resources) to see which mission agencies are at least working near your people group. Unfortunately, most of the Handbook's "work among" information is still listed only according to political country. But at least you can get a ballpark idea of which agencies are around your people.

Next, send your name and address to those agencies and request that you be placed on their mailing list for any magazines, newsletters, or updates they publish. Include a large self-addressed, stamped envelope and request any information they might have about your people group. Mission agencies are in the business of bringing the Good News of Christ to the world, not answering every uninformed believer's questions. So make sure your request is clear and polite, be patient for a response, and make sure you plan to use this information, not just get heady with global trivia.

The agency-generated information is just the beginning, and may not even be your best source. It may be slow in coming, and your regular perusal of agency publications may only sporadically pinpoint work among your particular people group. But while you're slowly piecing together this work among information, you can get very, very busy tracking down the rest of the world's information on your people. One of the most helpful research articles for novice researchers is "How to Find Hidden People in Your Library," by Allen Starling, a researcher with Gospel Recordings ministries. An adapted version can be found in the appendix of *Catch the Vision 2000*.

More often than not, libraries are where the information is that you want. For hundreds of years, anthropologists, sociologists, and explorers have amassed incredible amounts of information about the world's cultures. Many of these professionals have been agnostics or even anti-Christian, thinking they were pursuing these cultural studies for the sake of their careers or for the cause of science or curiosity. Wrong! God is using this information for the Kingdom. Most university libraries are packed with key insights into the cultures of even unreached peoples—insights just waiting for a home front researcher to unearth and pass on to frontline mission teams.

For example, a South African missionary to a particular people in a Muslim country lived among the people for years. He diligently studied the language, developed relationships, and compiled a notebook as he searched for keys to understanding the people group. Yet in one quick visit to the University of California at Los Angeles library, the missionary discovered an entire roomful of vital information about every aspect of that people group's culture!

You may be a sender whose design, gifting, ministry, and arena of service is research. You love to learn library computer search systems. You enjoy digging for vital information about a culture, information that just might provide a key breakthrough for a mission team. Maybe you're a sender with a specialty in research!

And perhaps you can expand that role into being a researcher for the overall cause. Once you get good at researching information on a particular people group, city, or area for one missionary, it makes sense that you broaden into new areas of research and share information with other mission teams.

## What Are You Looking For?

Just what information do you want about your particular people group? All that there is, of course. But realistically, you need to dig up information in about twenty-four categories.

# Culture Wheel

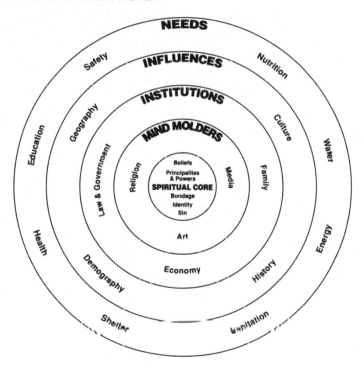

Frank Kaleb Jansen, executive director of the Adopt-A-People Clearinghouse, has developed a holistic "culture wheel" that provides a framework for gathering information on a people group. Originally devised to quantify the effects of prayer on an entire people, the Holistic Perspectives Model when used by us nonprofessional researchers

---

Culture Wheel adapted from the Holistic Perspectives Model developed by Frank Kaleb Jansen. For more information and an actual model, see Resources for the Adopt-A-People Clearinghouse address.

can simply help us zero in on the core of God's heart for a particular people.

Keeping in mind the following overview is only that—an overview—plan to focus your research according to these categories of information. Brainstorm more questions than are listed below to give you even more direction in researching a people group.

Let's look at specific questions to answer in each of these areas.

## Basic Needs:

*Safety:* Is this a threatened people? By what forces, and by whom? What is the crime factor? Are there practical dangers—such as weather extremes or poisonous animals—that are part of their everyday lives? How are these concerns handled?

*Nutrition:* What is the basic diet, and how nutritious is it? What is needed or wanted but not generally available for a healthy diet?

*Water:* Is clean water available? In what locations? Is water treatment widely practiced?

*Energy:* What forms of energy—hydroelectric, wind power, coal, fuel-burning—are already harnessed? Is this energy available to all? What energy-producing or energy-conserving projects might be attractive to this society?

*Shelter:* What is their shelter like? Is ownership of shelter or property important? How many and what relationships live together? Is providing more suitable/less-expensive housing a priority of families? Of the governing body? Are the people open to other forms of shelter and other construction materials?

*Sanitation:* Is pollution in any form present? Is it accommodated or resisted? How does sanitation affect health?

*Health:* What health problems are evident—including alcoholism and other substance abuse? Which are preventable, and how can they be prevented? What is the ratio of population to number of doctors, nurses, hospital beds, clinics, etc.? Are medicines available?

*Education:* What percentage of the people are literate? What age groupings are literate? If there is formal schooling, what ages attend? What is the basic education curriculum? How many are now involved in higher education? Studying in what fields?

## Major Influences:

*Demography:* How many are there? What ages? What percentage of men and women? What number of widows, orphans, households? What is their life expectancy? What are the percentages and numbers of various religions and belief systems, including true and nominal Christians?

*History:* Where and why did this people form as a culture? What are the major events of their past? What patterns emerge in this people's history—from earliest records to the present? Is local, oral history significantly different from the official historical facts? If Christianity had historic contact with this people, how and when and through whom did the Gospel come? What were the positive and negative results of these entrances of the Good News?

*Geography:* Where do these people live—including pockets of refugees or emigrants around the world—and where are the population densities? How has the geography of their homeland affected who they are? What geographical features could prove to be obstacles to the natural spread of the Gospel?

*Culture:* What do the following tell you about this people: their stories, songs, sayings and riddles, holidays, habits, schedules, leisure pursuits, national temperament, conversation styles, values, humor? What are the usual habits, concerns, lifestyles, and expectations of children? Of teenagers? Of the middle-aged and the elderly?

## Basic Institutions:

*Family:* How prevalent and what are the attitudes toward divorce, single parenting, sexual promiscuity, marriage as an institution? Who's in charge in a family? What is the role and perceived "value" of men, women, the elderly, boys, girls? Who fulfills what functions? How large are families? How does a family spend its time at home?

*Law & Government:* How does government affect these people's lives? What laws are perceived as obstacles to the Gospel? Why? Is politics important? Who is now in power and what does that mean?

*The Economy:* On what is the economy based? How does the standard of living compare to other similar cultures? What is the economic history? What about the future?

## Mind Molders:

*Media:* What are the most effective communication channels among this people? What are the most popular media formats? How friendly or financially interested are the media to work with Christians? What is media's next step in this culture? What misinformation is propagated among the people through media?

*Art:* What art forms are valued? What is the tone of the various art forms? What does traditional art tell you about this people? What does contemporary art suggest, and why any change from traditional forms?

*Religion:* What forms of religion are present? Has Christianity made any inroads in this society? If so, has it been a true or a counterfeit form of Christianity? Are true Christians a force in this society? Are Christian missionaries, churches, institutions, or formational Bible studies present—and if so, who are these Christians? Regardless of what the people really believe, how do the predominant religious institutions affect people's lives? What teachings contrary to scriptural truth are propagated by religious institutions? What is the specific history of the religious institutions in this culture? What's happening now?

## Spiritual Core:

*Beliefs:* Either including or apart from institutional religious teachings, what does this people really believe on a heart level? What are their fears that you could attribute to spiritual reasons?

*Identity:* What does this people think of themselves? What do other peoples surrounding them think of them? What does God think of them; what facet of His character could they—in their redeemed state—most brightly reflect? Who are they?

*Sin:* What are the sins of their past and present?

*Bondages:* What consequences of these sins keep this people shackled in further sin and spiritual darkness?

*Principalities and Powers:* As the evidence at a crime scene reveals key characteristics of the criminal, so the painful marks on this people will reveal the character of the spiritual entities assigned to keep this people in darkness. The name or names of these spiritual powers is not essential, but understanding the characteristics of the "principalities, powers, and rulers of darkness" whom we are to struggle against is crucial. What lies are they telling the people? Who are these powers?

A late-night project for you sometime might be running your *own* people group information through this grid of questions, adding your own questions as well. As a representative of your culture, you probably have all the information you need without resorting to your library or profound research. And the exercise might reveal more than you would imagine about God's heart for your culture, about how your personal Christianity is padded with your people group's character. It might suggest key areas for prayer, new approaches to ministering among your own people, or even the key characteristics in your people group that God would love to redeem to reflect His glory!

Although this has been only a cursory prompting to learn about a culture, the point should be clear: Look unto the fields, not just at the handles of your plow. You might be absolutely amazed at how an important tidbit of information you uncover can help an entire team get into a closed country or unlock a whole people group to the message of redemption in Jesus Christ!

Growing proficient as a sender may lead you into full-time ministry, and specializing in research is only one of the sending roles that will pull you beyond the scope of supporting your own local churches' missionaries. Senders are also desperately needed to fulfill critical positions in mission societies as administrators, trainers, and other behind-the-lines roles. If your dream is to fulfill the functions of a sender full time as a ministry, consider contacting your favorite mission society and inquiring about position openings. In the U.S., you can easily find such opportunities through InterCristo, a ministry-position clearinghouse that can be accessed via a toll-free phone call (800/426–1342). In many other countries, Centers for World Mission (see Organizations under Resources) can keep you updated on positions open with sending agencies.

Or maybe your fellowship is considering the leap that forces teams of senders to fully prove their mettle: Perhaps your church is thinking of sending its own mission teams.

## The Local Church As a Sender

Can a local fellowship fulfill all the roles necessary to put and keep missionaries on the field? Can churches act as their own mission agency?

Although the question invariably chills many veteran mission agency executives and experienced missionaries alike, it's a question that is increasingly being answered with a hearty "Yes we can!" from churches around the world.

Does the local church sending its own mission teams work? Sometimes. Yet the dangers are legion: The church loses its financial base when large contributors move away, and missionaries on the field suffer. Or missionaries are endangered on the field, involved in serious political chaos, become critically ill, or even die—and the home church has no experience in handling such contingencies. The fellowship acting as its own mission sending agency feels reluctant to ask for advice from established mission societies, and so is left to learn every lesson of mission activity the hard way—by trial and error, and error, and error.

But more and more churches are facing the obstacles and determining that by God's grace they can serve as a missionary's entire sending team. One of the advocates of such a venture is George Miley.

George was a missionary with Operation Mobilization for about twenty years. Today he is president of the Antioch Network, a fellowship of local churches sending church-planting teams to unreached peoples. And he's convinced that local churches can do the job of developing, sending, and supporting competent mission teams to the unreached.

George's vision of churches sending teams was spurred by the realization that at most church mission conferences, we hear about countries rather than people groups. And the countries we hear about are the countries where our current missionaries are serving. So most prayer, finances, and manpower naturally flow toward where we already have a mission force. No wonder, George thought, that we still send roughly 90% of our new missionaries to fields where there are already well-established missionary populations.

He also felt that established, traditional mission agencies can be difficult to turn in new directions—like battleships that take miles to turn. George says, "It strikes me that it could be much easier to get a local church to target one unreached people than it would be to get a missionary agency to start sending missionaries to Turkey rather than Brazil; Nepal rather than the Philippines."

Further, when missionaries are being supported by dozens of churches, they can hardly claim to have a home church that guides and nurtures them. Every trip home means being spread thin among dozens of congregations.

And finally, George is excited about local churches sending their own church-planting teams because the laypeople in practically any local church make great church planters! Professionally trained missionaries often enter a restricted country to serve an unreached people by taking on another identity—working uncomfortably as a businessperson, a teacher, or health worker. George says, "Rather than making people into missionaries and then trying to make them business people or teachers, let's just take business people or teachers and send them! They can enter these countries in their true vocational capacity, relate to people honestly, as they are, and still work to see them come to Jesus."

But isn't world evangelization such a massive task that only large, organized institutions can handle the demands? George points out that large, well-resourced corporations are only now realizing that small groups of highly autonomous workers can be more effective in innovative production than can large masses of workers managed on a larger, more impersonal scale. "The most powerful church-planting movement in history," George says, "such as the spread of the Church in China, came out of smallness. There were no great organizations or nationwide television networks, or computerized donor lists, or consolidated financial resources. It was just people sharing with people, and the explosion of small groups, most of which could fit into homes." These small-group teams, sent in the full sense by their local churches, can piece by piece do much of the remaining task of world evangelization.

But what about the local churches who send poorly trained teams or make colossal mistakes that established mission agencies long ago learned to avoid? Several years ago one large church sent a team into a tightly restricted country to bless a particular unreached people. In a rush of volatile political events, the team was kidnapped by terrorists. Feeling solely responsible for their missionaries, the local church wrung its hands and mandated its mission committee to throw together a plan for this unexpected twist in their mission program. They actually began hiring a commando team of mercenary soldiers to infiltrate the restricted country and attempt a rescue of the missionaries! Fortunately, news got around to proper authorities in the church's home country, and the illegal, disaster-prone plan was aborted before this well-meaning mission committee started a war!

Local churches are often thoroughly ignorant of the nuts and bolts, the contingencies, the cautions and political protocols of international mission work. Mission agencies exist to handle just such problems—and new ones are forming all the time that don't have to struggle against old traditions. It seems obvious that an interworking of these two "models" of the Body of Christ can bring the most efficient synergy to the sending process. Churches can become more practically involved in the sending of their own mission teams. And mission agencies can partner one-to-one with local churches to ensure the safety and on-the-field effectiveness of those teams.

Regardless of the options—agencies alone sending missionaries, a local church sending missionaries, or a realistic partnership in sending—involvement on the field is crucial to a local church's vision of God's heart for the whole world.

(You may contact the Antioch Network at 7854 Nichols St., Lemon Grove, CA 91945 USA.)

## A Sender's Lifestyle

The term "World Christian" has been bounced around pop-Christian circles for nearly twenty years. The phrase is, of course, much older. It now seems to describe a believer who is conscious that his or her lifestyle doesn't need to reflect the unredeemed values of society. What is a World Christian? Simply a disciple who realizes that whatever ministry or activities God has given him, it is to be done wholeheartedly as a means toward the overall goal of reaching the nations. It is a person who balances the Great Commission with the Greatest Commandment, loving God with all your heart, soul, mind, and strength and loving others as yourself.

How different are World Christians from other Christians? In some ways, very little. They still spend much of their time doing day-to-day chores, filling their role in life (being a parent, spouse, friend), fulfilling the requirements of a job, fixing things around the house. They too work on character issues in their own life, study the Scriptures, read Christian books, seek to be broken and humble before God. Both seek to keep the greatest commandment, loving God and loving others. But in other ways, they are very different.

The World Christian uses his free time differently, keeping in mind a global perspective. He prays more for the nations and helps others catch the vision for God's glory throughout the world. He spends his finances wisely, freeing up more money for the global expansion of the Kingdom. He always envisions how his ministries and activities can somehow result in eventually having an impact in the nations.

Living a World Christian lifestyle as a sender doesn't mean taking a vow of poverty—since poverty isn't necessarily spiritual and wealth isn't necessarily unspiritual. But being good stewards of money as we seek first the Kingdom of heaven is definitely a mark of a World Christian sender.

Putting money into a $7,000 computer setup may be entirely appropriate in a World Christian's ministry. Putting that same amount into a solid gold golf club as a Christmas present for Uncle Harry may not be appropriate. But the lifestyle of a globally significant sender isn't mostly about money. It's about character.

Serious sending means living a lifestyle with characteristics such as

- Noting how culturized my Christianity may be.
- Seeking to understand how we've been blessed and how we can use that to bless other nations.
- Maintaining personal purity for the sake of His name and for the sake of demonstrating His grace to the principalities in the heavenlies (Ephesians 3:10–11).
- Going out of my way to learn about and meet people of other cultures.

- Affirming all the God-given ministries of the church as part of what He is doing in the big picture.
- Diligently mounting my part in the spiritual battles in the heavenlies as I intercede in disciplined prayer.
- Fellowshiping with believers to encourage and be encouraged.
- Sharing the great news of what God is doing.
- Constantly submitting to the supervision of God as to where I go and what I do in ministry—with no reservations.
- Serving the church.
- Becoming more and more of a student of the Word.
- Passing on a world vision to those around us we are allowed to influence.
- Developing all the other qualities of a true disciple of Jesus Christ!

You don't have to be a missionary to live a holy, focused, streamlined, effective life that impacts whole people groups for Jesus Christ! You can rejoice as a sender.

And maybe you're one of those strange sender specialists known as a mobilizer.

## Chapter Eleven

# Mobilizing the New Harvest Force–Part 1

## Can you wake a hundred sleeping firemen?

*"Boy, I got vision. And the whole world's wearing bifocals."*

—Butch Cassidy
(character in the movie Butch
Cassidy and the Sundance Kid)

**Moscow** — You're leaning against a grimy post in the Intourist section of Domodedyevo, the Moscow airport many Westerners call "The Temple of Doom." You've been waiting all afternoon to rendezvous with us as we fly in from Novosibirsk. Probably 2,000 Russians and a few groupings of Asians stand crushed in this building made for half that number. There are no seats. Beggar Gypsy children circle through the crowd, pulling at your sleeve and sing songing their pleas with deep, fine eyes. The ceiling is a dark brown. There are no lights on anywhere in the building. There is none of the expected airport background music; announcements crackle over loudspeakers only sporadically as these domestic flights are delayed, canceled for lack of benzine or, miraculously, arrive and depart. Otherwise the airport is silent, the clumps of black- and brown-coated passengers waiting patiently, laden with their ubiquitous plastic bags.

You stare out at the overcast runway. You can't shake the mental image you've drawn of Russia: a woman in her fifties—not old, but resigned—who has been for decades battered by some vodka-swilling husband, who thinks she's fat and stupid. She's the hapless spouse of communism.

You've just returned from the Intourist desk where you again asked

about our flight, again spelling our names: "Stearns. Sjogren." The
kind, young blonde still could not confirm whether we were on the
expected Aeroflot flight. "Spacebo," you said, (literally "God our Savior"), which is the way every atheist in the communist era also said
thank you throughout the Soviet empire.

Now we come stumbling through the streaked double-glass doors.
We hug you and ask, "Any banana street vendors outside? We're starved
for fruit!"

"Da, da, da," you say. "All over the sidewalk. Bananas from Ecuador,
babushkas selling old sweaters and shoes, cigarettes, vodka, old light
bulbs . . ."

"Any news on any more CoMission teams getting booted out of
schools?"

You nod. "Two more teams were told to leave their school districts
this week. Lots of folks are feeling uneasy."

We all wait for our bags, knowing it sometimes takes hours for luggage to be transported from an arrived plane to the baggage area. "Ever
hear how the CoMission effort was first mobilized into action?"

"No," you say. Your knowledge of the CoMission is that more than
70 Western ministries cooperated to get thousands of Christian educational consultants into the former Soviet Union. These then trained
school administrators and teachers to teach courses on biblical ethics,
morals, and the life of Jesus Christ. The impact—to say nothing of the
strategy itself—has been nothing short of brilliant. Now the enemy was
beginning his backlash campaign to again get the Truth out of the
schools of Russia. And now you're amazed at how all this effort was
mobilized because of one person's step of obedience. We stand eating
bananas in the Temple of Doom and tell you the story:

> On the other side of the world, in 1989, a California pastor's
> wife was agonizing over what thousands of ministry families ex-
> perience—a church split. In her despair, she attended a Sunday
> evening service to view an Underground Evangelism film on the
> plight of the suffering churches of Romania. Struck with their
> commitment in the face of persecution, she wept openly during
> the service and was bothered all the following week with the
> thought that perhaps she should do something—such as go to
> Romania. As unlikely as that was before the Romanian revolution
> of '89, she told God, "Help me lift up my eyes from my personal
> pain; and I'll go if you want me to."
>
> The following spring she attended an Association of Christian
> Schools International (ACSI) conference where she was asked, of
> course, to go to Romania. ACSI mission consultant Phil Renicks

had just received a fax from a pastor in Timisoara, Romania, asking for someone to come help set up a Christian school.

On her drive home from the conference, she again vowed, "Lord, I'll go if you want me to go. But I'm so inadequate. I have to know it's you pulling me to Romania."

That next Sunday morning, she was singing in the struggling church's choir when she noticed two visitors slip in late. After the service, not particularly wanting to talk politics with church members, she rushed to the rear of the auditorium to welcome the visiting couple. "My name is Margaret," she said.

"So sorry we were late," the man said. "We drove up and down this street, asking the Lord which church we should attend this morning. God told us to come here."

Margaret noticed an accent. "You're not from California?"

"No. We are from Romania. My father is a pastor in Romania. In Timisoara."

The next summer in Timisoara, Romania, Margaret helped evangelicals open a Christian school. Swiss and French churches provided desks and other materials, Romanians the manpower. As her visit ended, the Romanian believers beseiged her with a special request. "The only Bible cassette tape we have is a radio broadcast of an American named Bruce Wilkinson. Tell him when you return to America that he must come. Do not let him say a word until you tell him to come to Romania." Margaret smiled, unable to explain the distances in America, the impossibility of her meeting Bruce Wilkinson.

Early in 1991, Margaret attended an ACSI conference in the Northwest. As she settled to listen to a seminar speaker, she received a note: "Margaret, the person who was to give the appeal for a missions offering at the next plenary session has suddenly become ill. You've been somewhere on a mission trip, right? Could you say something?"

At the appointed time, Margaret walked to the platform, looked out over the faces of thousands of Christian schoolteachers, and poured out her heart for the people of Romania. She began to weep as she spoke, and closed with a challenge to go as well as give. Her tears had smeared up her glasses, and she stumbled as she stepped away from the podium. Suddenly a strong hand guided her to a seat on the platform so she could recover while the offering was taken. "Thank you," she said, wiping her eyes and her glasses.

"That was a remarkable challenge," said the man who had seated her. "My name is Bruce Wilkinson."

In her shock, Margaret remembered. "Don't say another word.

I have a message for you from the believers in Romania."

"Oh no," he said:

"You must come to Romania."

"Oh no."

"And now," the session leader was announcing, "let's hear from Bruce Wilkinson, president of Walk Through the Bible Ministries headquartered on the East Coast in Atlanta."

Bruce stood, swayed toward the podium. His topic? Brokenness before the Lord. But he was so choked up he couldn't speak for a full minute. God was going to take him to Romania.

During his visit in the summer of '91, one of his final meetings was attended by a visitor who sat at the back of the group and openly wept in response to Bruce's challenge that the schoolchildren of Romania needed to know the love of Jesus. As the meeting closed, the man lamented in a language no one initially recognized. Finally a Romanian who understood German, and a German who knew some Russian translated the diplomat's plea. He introduced himself as Evgeniy Kurkin, a Russian educator. He said to Bruce, "We closed God out of our country. And it caused so many problems in our society we cannot count them. We must put God back into our country. And we must begin with our children."[1]

Bruce immediately counseled with others in ministries impacting the former Soviet Union, such as Paul Eshelman of the *Jesus* Film Project, who told him the time was now to move into the schools of these formerly communist countries. But it would take an unprecedented cooperative effort on the part of scores of ministries to meet the challenge. And so the CoMission coalition was born.

Margaret Bridges insists this is God's story—not hers, not Bruce Wilkinson's, not the CoMission's. Margaret simply obeyed the step-by-step challenges God placed before her in her small, seemingly insignificant niche in His great plan. And since August 1992, thousands of Christians, tens of thousands of prayer hours, and hundreds of thousands of dollars have been focused on giving the millions of schoolchildren of the former Soviet Union the truth about Jesus Christ. All because one pastor's wife in Walnut, California chose to take her eyes off her own painful circumstances and look to the harvest fields.

We finish our bananas and our story. "So what about you?"

"Me?" you say. The luggage has finally arrived, and the hundreds of patient Russians from the Aeroflot flight suddenly become a rugby team mob, pushing and shoving as if they're certain someone will steal their bags. And they're probably right.

"Yes, you," we say. "Just wait till you see what God might mobilize through your obedience. Far beyond anything He's done so far through your ministry. Maybe you'll get a clue in Aqtau."

"Where?" You frown, shoved roughly by a wide, old babushka.

"Aqtau. It's somewhere just west of Saturn. Or Pluto."

"What?"

But before we take you off to Aqtau to hear what happened in South Africa, let's think carefully through this new ministry area that's being called mobilization.

## Desperate for a Vision

Something's going on in churches. Maybe especially in Western churches we're realizing it's time to do or die. In fact, George Gallup estimates that in the United States alone, the next ten years will see the demise of about 100,000 churches.[2] And they'll die not from lack of funding or programming—but from lack of vision: "Where there is no vision, the people perish" (Proverbs 29:18, KJV).

That is, without a revelation of what God is doing the people lose constraint. They become unfocused, lacking discipline.

Whole denominations these days are realizing their need to focus on a vision of their part in God's big-picture plan. Few put it so candidly as the Lutheran Church-Missouri Synod:

> According to new research, we're making some colossal mistakes—all of our Lord's churches on earth—in our approach to world mission work. And there is colossal ignorance among us of what world mission work is all about. Everybody thinks he knows what it is, just as we're all "experts" in sports and politics and religion in general. But as the studies show, practically none of us really knows much about the science and theology of mission work.
>
> And there is amazing inactivity and inattention devoted to world missions, not only in congregations but also in seminaries and denominational programs of church bodies and the various parts of them. Are we short-changing our members? Are our congregations actually guilty of malpractice?
>
> Now then, how does *our* church body stack up—and our colleges and seminaries and congregations? With most of us, no doubt, there is a "great gulf" between what Jesus asked us to do

and what we're getting done with our hearts and heads and hands.[3]

But in every church fellowship, God desires to show clearly to the heirs of the promise the unchangeableness of His purpose (Hebrews 6:13–18). Did you catch those words? His purpose is unchangeable. It was the same when Abraham walked the earth. It was the same when David led Israel. It was the same when Jesus was here on earth. It is the same today. Mark it down and memorize it. God wants to bless you and your church so you can reach those around you and reach the nations! This is the direction in which all churches need to be heading.

Yet in order for this to happen, a paradigm shift needs to take place, especially in the Western church—a shift away from the "cultural worldview" to the biblical worldview.

It takes time and considerable input to shift a person's worldview. So helping a whole fellowship focus and rev up for new outward-looking vision requires the patience of a counselor, the acumen of a teacher, and the enthusiasm of a cheerleader—all facets of that increasingly important role of the mobilizer.

## Mobilizing As a Ministry

If your heart's cry is for the whole world, if you can't seem to hear God directing you to go to one specific people or area, if you're gifted naturally and spiritually in communicating and encouraging, perhaps your strategic niche is that of a mobilizer. You can encourage, exhort, prod, lure, hand-hold, cajole, and pray whole churches into a sharper vision of their part in God's global purpose.

Jesus gives two parables regarding stewardship. One is found in Matthew 19:14–30; the second is found in Luke 19:12–27. These are not redundant. Each lesson contains something unique.

Although few see it, there is a big difference in how the servants start out. In Matthew, one servant is given five talents, another two, and another one. In Luke, there are ten servants and they equally divide ten minas.

In Matthew, the servant with five made five more. The one with two made two more. The one with only one talent hid it. God scolded the latter for not using his talent and gave it to the one who had ten. The lesson: God rewards *faithfulness* with what we've been given. "To whom much has been given, much is required."

The Luke passage talks about three of the ten servants. One has earned ten minas more, one five, and one none. Remember, they all started out equally with one. God then takes the one and gives it to the one with ten. Because they all started out equally, we learn God not only wants us faithful with the talents we've been given, but He also rewards the maximum use of those talents. God wants us to *maximize* the use of our talents.

In the past, anyone with much of a passion for cross-cultural ministry was usually expected to go—to be a missionary. But today we recognize the possibility that a burden for missions might mean staying within one's own culture to mobilize senders and goers alike—maximizing the impact a person can have on the world. Veteran missionary-author Don Richardson and missiologist Ralph Winter often use an apt analogy:

> Imagine yourself seeing a huge, raging fire in the distance. You could run to get a bucket, fill it with water, run to the blaze, and dump water. Then you could run again and dump more water on the fire. And again, and again. But perhaps, on first seeing the danger of the fire, you could run and wake up one hundred sleeping firemen—who would do at least a hundred times what you could have done yourself.

The presumption that a burden for a people or city or region of the world means you individually must go is perhaps one of the greatest obstacles to the efficient completion of the Great Commission.

The job of some of you reading this book is to wake up the sleeping firemen. God has gifted you in upfront communication skills and networking abilities. You fit and work well in your culture. For you, going overseas would have a far less impact. Sure, you might go and plant three, maybe four churches in your lifetime, by God's grace. But if you stay and mobilize, you might recruit one hundred other people equally gifted for church planting overseas who may plant four churches each! Maximizing the use of your gifts means staying (at least for some time until you are freed up by God to go).

Your talents can raise up not only laborers, but pray-ers as well.

For example, the four million Kanoori people of Nigeria, Chad, and Niger are still a thoroughly unreached group even though mission efforts have persisted among them for more than 60 years! Lone missionaries or sometimes small mission teams from various societies have chipped away at the enemy's strongholds around this people decade after decade with virtually no effect. The cry of many of these societies has been faithful: "Come and help us among the Kanoori." But few have gone, and the inroads of the Gospel are still meager.

But who is praying against the strongholds of the enemy over the

Kanoori? Seriously, take a poll of as many devout believers as you can and ask: "Are you praying for the Kanoori? Are you saving any funds for Kanoori outreach? Are you discipling any believers with a view toward their spending some time researching the Kanoori—or going short or long term?" You know what the answer will be: "Never heard of them."

Perhaps the reason so few breakthroughs have been seen among the Kanoori is that no one has mobilized the prayers of thousands of serious intercessors. No one has pressed for funds for Kanoori outreach—regardless of which mission society you send the money to. No one has mounted a dedicated campaign on the home fronts in England, Norway, Russia, Korea, The Philippines, Chile, or elsewhere to coach hundreds of believers toward ministering among the Kanoori. Their cause hasn't been advocated among the broader Body of Christ. There hasn't been a mobilizer to stand in the gap for the Kanoori.

Ralph Winter has recently insisted that the number one priority in global mission is mobilization. A second priority is a renewed emphasis on the part of missionaries in reached fields to train and mobilize those mostly two-thirds world believers as frontier missionaries. And, lastly, a third priority is to send frontier missionaries. Why is sending frontier missionaries only a third priority? Because if the first two priorities were met, we wouldn't need to concern ourselves that there aren't enough frontier missionaries going to unreached peoples! Mobilization is crucial!

## Mobilization Basics

### What is a mobilizer?

A normal everyday Christian who walks with God yet has a global perspective and who stays on the home front to rouse others to action.

### What is mobilization?

When a country goes to war, it isn't just the frontline soldiers whose lives are affected. An entire line of support personnel must stand behind them, supplying whatever the combat troops need to do battle. And back on the home front, massive mobilization is required to keep people aware of their part in the war. Posters and radio programs, small-town parades and publicity campaigns urge people to pray for their troops, to write to them to keep up their battle-fatigued morale, to sacrifice luxuries for the sake of the war effort, to give up the use of items that are more desperately needed on the front lines, to volunteer for support positions from medical assistants to entertainers, to put their personal money into special accounts such as "war bonds" so the proceeds can be used for the war effort, to go to work at new jobs in order to produce materials needed in the conflict.

Think back over the items of this analogy and ask how you might motivate, train, and activate people in your culture to such vital responses to a national crisis. Those ideas are probably exactly how you can motivate, train, and activate believers to their part in the global spiritual warfare against Satan's false kingdom of darkness. To mobilize is to get them moving.

### What are the characteristics of a mobilizer? Consider a sample listing:

- Needs to be able to be a servant.
- Desires to see laborers raised up to finish the task of world evangelization.
- Possibly has the gift of encouragement and exhortation.
- Is "apt to teach"—but may be more effective in recruiting others to teach.
- Speaks in front of groups without (too much) fear.
- Leads others well—although he or she may not know it.
- Has a general heart for the world, possibly focusing in on one people group.
- Sees the priority of waiting and mobilizing others as well as going.
- Is part visionary—seeing what can happen as God matches empowered believers with key opportunities of ministry.
- Is part implementer—driven to see visions become realities.

The first characteristic listed—having a servant heart—is critical. Mobilizers must first win the right to be heard before being allowed to speak. One mobilizer moved to a new town and joined a church because he felt it was God's will. But he soon found that the pastor had a reputation of not allowing individuals like himself to have significant opportunities for mobilizing. Realizing this, the mobilizer went to the pastor with this question: "Pastor, how can I serve you in this church?" Within a year, he had won the pastor's heart and was free to mobilize in any way he saw fit.

Many mission zealots unintentionally squelch mission interest with guilt-riddled diatribes, or more and more impassioned pleas for money for a broken, dying world. This can be dangerous. And the most dangerous zealot of all is "the mobilizer with an attitude." This is a sincere believer who thinks he or she will motivate churches into broader vision by shaming them into action. In fact, Larry Walker of ACMC has listed some characteristics of the mobilizer with an attitude.

A note to fanatic mission mobilizers: Notice that we're not saying that anyone with a low commitment level to mission vision has no commitment or a low commitment to Jesus Christ. Many solid believers who are, in their understanding of Scripture, thoroughly committed to Christ may evidence very little mission commitment. It's often a matter of not receiving clear teaching on God's heart for every people group that results in low mission commitment. It's not that non-mission-minded believers don't love Jesus as devoutly as mission fanatics. *Selah.*

## Mobilizers With an Attitude

If a mobilizer is cursed with pride, he or she quickly becomes a major pain in the neck of a local church body because of such attitudes as

- *Real mobilizers don't eat steak.* Ethnic foods alone please this palate. Of course, this key tenet has been recently facilitated by the success of Tandoori Take-Away and Egg Roll Express.

- *Real mobilizers don't have fun.* They do not go to movies . . . unless the film is a documentary on foreign cultures, of course. Even then, popcorn is never allowed, since it would be a frivolous waste of mission funds. They do not go to the beach or the lake; the task of world evangelization is too urgent to waste time in exercise, relaxation, or fellowship. They do not like sports, games, or television. *Especially television!* They don't go to parties because they know there are millions across the globe who are suffering. (Besides, they weren't invited.)

- *Single mobilizers don't date.* Instead, they form "strategic partnerships" with members of the opposite sex. (After all, where could they go on a date?)

- *Real mobilizers don't like church.* A local church is so teeming with ignorant, anemic Christians that it is difficult to commit to any real local ministry. The final frontiers of unreached peoples is the only justifiable ministry area; all other interests in the church are immature.

(The mobilizer with an attitude is adapted from a concept by Larry Walker of ACMC in the U.S. in his *Seven Dynamics* seminar. See Training Helps in Resources section.)    The pastor never has enough vision, and there's not a single layperson with any vision at all—except, of course, for the mobilizer with an attitude! Why fellowship intimately with self-focused pea-brains? (Which is precisely the question the rest of the church asks itself about the mobilizer with an attitude!)

As a mission mobilizer, don't even use the word "help" to describe your heart to serve the church in its vision-building: "I want to *help* you, pastor, to get this church moving"—as if the pastor can't do that. A true mobilizer has a servant heart that rejoices in facilitating others in their ministry dreams and visions. The mobilizer with an attitude doggedly tries to pester others toward his or her own personal agenda, his or her own vision of what the fellowship should be and do. And the cause of God's team as a whole suffers.

But that's certainly not your intention. You've got a true, servant heart, right? You're more than willing to study the history of a fellowship, to see why God called it into being in the first place. That's often an exciting clue to that fellowship's role in the dynamics of the overall mission of the church. And you're more than willing to acknowledge that Peter Wagner is correct when he insists, "The vision for where God wants the church to go usually is channeled through the pastor."[4]

Do many of the positive characteristics of a mobilizer match your personality and skills? If so, maybe you need to focus your ministry on mobilization.

## What does a mobilizer need to know?

Many things are listed below, but realize that you will learn most of this as you mobilize, not before—and that you'll probably never master any one of them. You will constantly be upgrading your knowledge as the years go by.

1 *Know God's Word*. An overview of the Bible; basic Bible doctrine; the mission theme of the Bible.

2. *Know God's World*. Geography; the basics of world religions; as many areas and cultures as possible: political, economic, social, spiritual trends, current events and issues; Christian and secular sources for concise global information.

3. *Know God's Work*. Global and regional histories of the expansion of the Church; general knowledge of the task remaining; mission strategies—prayer points and entry strategies for as many peoples as possible, which ministries are doing what, and among what peoples; sources for concise global information about the harvest force.

### How do you become a mobilizer?

Great question. Actually, there's no precise answer. In the States, ACMC and the A.D.2000 and Beyond Mobilization Network suggest certain standards for being recognized as a professional mobilizer. Yet a firm, "official" list of requirements, and steps toward becoming a mobilizer is still arbitrary. Here are some suggestions:

1. *Study* carefully a basic mission course such as *Start, Catch the Vision 2000*, or *Unveiled at Last/Destination 2000*. (See Materials and Courses in Resources section; both are available through your local Christian bookstore.) Make this a serious study, not just another perusal.

2. *Take* the *Perspectives on the World Christian Movement* course. (See Resources for contact numbers of the Perspectives Study Office to ask about correspondence, extension, and residential Perspectives courses.)

3. *Initiate* or enlist an existing prayer team to pray for your mobilization ministry.

4. *Link up* on the Genesys computer network, where much of the information referred to in this book is constantly available in updated form in the World Christian Net conference area. If you don't have a computer and modem, conscript a computer whiz to be your connection. You'll then naturally move into electronic mail exchanges with other mobilizers like yourself around the world.

5. *Ask* your church leadership's permission to encourage mission vision in your fellowship. If there is a missions committee, ask to join it; it can help keep you accountable. If there isn't a missions committee, enlist an accountability structure. A small group that includes some church leaders will keep you humble and wise in your ministry efforts.

6. *Study!* Make a specific list of action steps to keep up on the items under D. *What does a mobilizer need to know?* (God's Word, His World, and His Work), and work at it. Perhaps enroll in Bible courses at a Bible college, seminary, or correspondence school. A mobilizer with a great heart but no useful, biblical information is, frankly, useless! Find out what God is doing where, how, and through what kind of mission organizations and individuals. Devise a system for keeping facts and contacts updated and easily accessible. Get on everyone's mailing list!

7. *Contact* several mission societies, denominations, or fellowships of churches. Ask them what they need in terms of prayer, manpower, and finances. (Don't make promises about being able to provide such resources, simply promise to publicize the needs.)

8. *Train* a mobilization team in your area. Do it yourself as a group,

using the basics of this book to fill at least 24 hours of instruction and interaction, or call in a World Christian team for a "Run With the Vision" mobilizer's training workshop (see For Mobilizers in Resources section). The synergy of several mobilizers working together is crucial to your personal impact in rousing all the saints to new vision.

9. *Take* local college or training seminar courses on networking and on personal and media-based communications. Even the skills taught in many sales courses can add to your ability to communicate the challenges of God's global plan.

10. *Keep* tabs on all of your contacts. Get a good system for keeping names, addresses, phone numbers.

11. *Learn* the basic skits presented in this book and then perform them at small Bible studies first, getting the basics down. Then do some at various Sunday schools, really learning the material. Then advance to entire churches (Contact Caleb Project, address under Organizations in the Resources section, for skit scripts.)

12. *Find* out when local churches are having their mission conferences and ask if you can do your presentation. Use *A Sunday for the World* or *View from on High* as a guideline (see Resources).

13. *Lead* studies in your home on *Destination 2000* or *Catch the Vision* and seek to mobilize a few mobilizers to join you.

14. *Consider* becoming a *Perspectives* coordinator. For more information on this, contact the U.S. Center for World Mission (see Organizations in Resources section).

15. *Pray.* Set aside a specific weekend or longer to pray for God's anointing on your vital ministry.

Mobilize!

## Can mobilizers specifically target a people?

The Caleb project in Colorado has helped mobilizers see that they can zero in on a specific people group. They've done this by defining what are called "People Specific Advocate" (PSA). A PSA is a person (or couple) committed to mobilizing prayer, finances, and new laborers to a specific people group. Their work varies with the people group targeted.

John and Ann are two of those targeting the Uzbeks of Uzbekistan. They work in partnership with others (always sharing information) to inform the church locally and globally as to what needs to happen in order to reach out to the Uzbeks.

They spend their time creating and sending out newsletters and prayer letters, visiting churches, traveling to Uzbekistan to get a firsthand look at what is going on there, and doing research for the missionaries there.

One of their greatest mobilization tools is taking laypeople on prayer journeys in Uzbekistan. Pastors are also mobilized through "leadership trips," which help them to not only have vision beyond their church, but also see how they can personally get themselves and their church involved (through teaching, and through encouraging missionaries).

It is very possible to mobilize specifically for a distinct people group. To find out more, contact the Caleb Project (see Material and Courses in Resources section) for more information.

## Does mobilization have to be full time?

Some of the best mobilizers mobilize part time. Bob Hall, who has led the way in getting New Zealand mobilized with a vision for the world, is a full-time sociology professor and does his mobilization at night and on vacation time. Wendy Wenklejohn has a part-time job and goes to school as well, but has been effective in getting many people to take the *Perspectives* course in the cities of Detroit, Ann Arbor, and East Lansing in Michigan, U.S.A. Randy works four days a week so he can spend three-day weekends traveling around his area of the world mobilizing the church through skits with his family! In short—no, you don't have to be a full-time mobilizer. Many fit it in when they can.

## What's the point of mobilization?

Let's think through what we mobilize the saints toward and how to do it.

First, what's the point? To release prayer and resources for the Kingdom.

*Mobilizing Prayer:* One of the exciting signs of our times is the springing up of a fresh compulsion for prayer. In Norway, villages are focusing their prayers on their own "Bible-less people group." In Australia, all-night prayer vigils precede every "Reclaiming Easter" march. In Albania, groups of hundreds of children converge each day at a policeman's doorstep to pray before going off to school. In Bristol, England, zealous prayer gatherings grew so large they had to be divided into postal-code groupings—a strategy that is sweeping across the entire country. In Uruguay, believers lobby for a national day of prayer to be observed annually on October 31—Halloween—and thousands participated in the first 1993 observance by gathering on Parliament steps to pray.

But remember, as a mobilizer don't be let down by small numbers.

Larna had a heart for mobilizing those in her church in Christchurch, New Zealand, to reach out to internationals. For a long time she and a friend were the only ones who faithfully prayed that God would move not only in their church, but in their nation. After a year and a half of their faithful praying, God began to move. Today not only is God moving in her church, but Larna (a mom of three children and a part-time veterinarian) is known nationally as a person to talk to to discover how to reach out to internationals.

Not only does a fresh power of prayer—either by yourself or with others—batter against the gates of hell surrounding unreached people groups, it is also the key to "thrusting [the literal wording] forth laborers into the harvest." Jack McAlister of World Prayer 2000, a ministry that urges leaders to tithe their day in prayer, suggests that not Matthew 28:18–20 but Luke 10:2 should be called "The Great Commission":

> The harvest is plentiful, but the laborers are few; therefore beseech the Lord of the harvest to send out laborers into His harvest.

Jack points out that the passage presents two problems: the vastness of the harvest and the scarcity of workers. And it gives the solution: Pray to the Lord of the harvest. He thrusts forth the laborers. After all, it's His harvest!

And when God says "beseech," or "beg," it implies an ongoing action. The Greek verb here is used when a man with leprosy fell on his face before Jesus, begging him ". . . make me clean." You also find this verb when a father runs up to Jesus and begs him to deliver his son from a demon. The implication: Don't stop asking God for this (don't stop praying) until He gives you what you want. Commit yourself to pray until you see it completed.

The growing reawakening to the power of serious prayer is a worldwide phenomenon in the Body of Christ. Prayer leader David Bryant says of the prayer movement in the U.S.:

> Is it possible that God could kindle the fires of spiritual revival in our nation at this critical point in our history? In my travels around the country in recent months, I've witnessed an unprecedented grass-roots prayer movement that I'm convinced will prove to be the precursor of a sweeping moral and spiritual rebirth in America. Something extraordinary is taking place. It may be the most hopeful sign of our times.[5]

There are many examples of these "extraordinary" signs. As many as two million high-schoolers gather annually in the fall at their school flagpoles to pray on a day designated "See You at the Pole." About 10,000 regularly meet in Minneapolis, Minnesota to pray. In that same city, 300 congregations have committed themselves to pray for revival for seven years—just "to see what God will do." About 13,000 attended a recent prayer gathering in Portland, Oregon. In the Raleigh-Durham area of North Carolina about 8,000–10,000 join in area-wide prayer meetings.

Hundreds of thousands of believers gather at municipal buildings to pray for America on the National Day of Prayer. Groups of about 70 pastors each gathered in four different cities (Spokane, Minneapolis, Cleveland, and Colorado Springs) in late 1993 to pray for nationwide revival. One group met for half a day; another spent four full days in prayer and fasting. No one in any of the groups knew that similar meetings had been planned at the same time. Southern Baptist leaders are uniting their congregations across the country in what they call "solemn assemblies." Based on the book of Joel, the meetings essentially are calls for repentance and denomination-wide renewal.

Meanwhile, the Church of God (Cleveland, Tennessee) has set out to recruit retired pastors to pray for spiritual revival. The original goal of the strategy was to enroll 1,000 clergy. Today the number of participants in the program, "The PrayerBorne," has climbed to nearly 5,000. At Stanford University, 300 to 500 students from all campus ministry organizations meet regularly to pray for revival and evangelism. In Whittier, California, about 300 high-schoolers gather monthly to spend three hours in prayer—no program, no adults, just prayer. In Los Angeles, between 300 and 1,000 pastors gather every quarter to spend half a day in prayer for their city and country.

Bryant goes on to compare the current trends in the prayer movement to the beginnings of the first and second Great Awakenings that brought revival to America during the mid–1700s and early 1800s. He holds that this movement is "unprecedented," because of the numbers it involves, the breadth of the movement, its scope, the strategy employed, and the leadership that has emerged.[6]

But, in all honesty, it would be naive to think that all this prayer is focused with God's *whole* purpose in mind. This is the challenge of the mobilizer: to help the praying believers to see that their prayer (for fellow students at schools, for members in their churches, for their families) is only an initial step, a means toward what God wants to do in reaching the nations. Without that overall vision, we could lose out again.

It has happened before. In the 1880s American and English church leaders such as D. L. Moody, A. T. Pierson, Hudson Taylor, Royal Wilder, and others tirelessly challenged the Church to catch a vision of the possibility of finishing the task of the Great Commission by the year 1900. Pierson wrote in 1881: "These are the days of giant enterprises in the interests of commerce, science, art, and literature. Why not carry the spirit of sanctified enterprise into our religious life and work? I set forth a proposition that by the year 1900 the Gospel shall be preached to every soul on earth!" Wilder said, "If we consecrate life and property, world evangelization becomes practical and easy by 1900."[7] These influential leaders moved the Western church to new levels of giving financially and sending out thousands of new missionaries.

At that time the Student Volunteer Movement, with its watchword "The Evangelization of the World in This Generation," swept through colleges in the U.S. and Canada. The movement was propelled to national awareness by the missionary commitments declared at an 1886 month-long student evangelism conference hosted by D. L. Moody at Mount Hermon in Massachusetts. One hundred, or about 40% of the students present, signed the statement: "We the undersigned declare ourselves willing and desirous, God-permitting, to go to the unevangelized portions of the world." The Mount Hermon call to mission service was simple: "Show if you can why you should not obey the last command of Jesus Christ." And thousands responded to lifetime commitments as goers and senders.

But in 1895, A. T. Pierson wrote: "We are compelled to abandon hope because we have failed to mobilize prevailing prayer"—prayer, that is, that went beyond themselves and sought closure to God's glory to go out to all nations.

Now, a hundred years later, we need to remind ourselves that we'll get nowhere if we don't mobilize global-scale prayer. Fortunately, efforts to pray for the nations are mounting. The October 1993, 1995, and 1997 efforts of praying for the 10/40 Window is involving tens of millions of believers worldwide. The challenge to pray for breakthroughs in the Muslim world during the Islamic month of Ramadan is likewise joining hundreds of thousands of believers in intercessory prayer.

One of the frustrations of the worldwide prayer movement is that the pray-ers get little direction on what to pray for. That's where mobilizers must be filling the information gap, providing to formal and nonformal prayer groups a constant stream of vision-expanding prayer requests and praises from God's global campaign. Otherwise these prayer movements tend to fizzle, with the focus remaining on the group's own needs and culture. Salvation Army founder General Booth, pleased with fires of revival in his day, nevertheless warned that "it is the nature of a fire to go out." Mobilization of prayer means that mobilizers provide prayer fuel about the overall mission of the church.

*Mobilizing Resources:* Again, what's the point in mobilization? First, to encourage the release of global-scale prayer. Second, to facilitate the release of resources. This entails not only finances, but people as well. Let's talk about finances first.

In North America, an ACMC poll of several mission agency executives recently found that the time required for a family to raise support is getting longer all the time. Currently, a missionary candidate can expect to spend at least a year and a half on deputation. Of course, that timing depends greatly on the charm of the candidates' personalities, whether they're heading to a "popular" field, their past track record, and what kind of ministry they'll be engaged in.

Dick McClain, director of missionary personnel for the Mission Society of United Methodists, says that churches tend "to respond in an emotional rather than a strategic way in deciding whom to support. When times are tough, missions is the first to go. In most churches, missions is just another program that doesn't get first billing and certainly not first dollars."[8]

Whole books have been written about the need for finances and peoplepower for the tasks of the Kingdom. Articles and sermons make the point eminently clear that Christians spend more on pet food than on the Great Commission. It's no secret that frontline workers always need more funding, more equipment, more co-workers. But let's not join the ranks of those who simply point long, bony fingers of recrimination at the Church for hanging on to its blessings so tightly. Instead, let's mobilize.

One of the greatest fights the mobilizer has is with "the Joneses." Too many Christians try to keep up with the lifestyles of those around them. The challenge for the mobilizer is to get Christians to figure out what it costs to live in their culture, and then cap their salary at that level. So when God blesses them with raises, they can "survive the blessing" and pass *all* of that money on to world evangelization, rather than buying bigger and better things. Can you imagine having people make $120,000 in the United States and give $60,000 of that away! Oh, how the finances could be released!

Mobilizing others to give also happens when you inform them. Many don't give because of a lack of knowledge both of what God is doing throughout the world and of what His Word says. Hal and Bev live in Jackson, Mississippi, close to the heart of the southern United States. They were abruptly introduced to reading the Bible correctly—

as one book, with one main story—during a weekend missions conference. Riding home with the speaker, Hal said, "I've been going to church all of my life and I've never heard this before." Today, Hal and Bev are intricately involved in giving to world evangelization on a monthly basis.

Janet, a mom and businesswoman, decided all on her own to free up $200 a month of her tithe for world evangelization after reading *Destination 2000*. Now she and her husband support a couple working in Morocco. They see their finances as a means toward the overall goal of what God is doing in the world.

Many Christians are creating their own ways to meet the need to free up more resources. Mark and Kenny, businessmen on the East Coast of America with a heart for the world, caught a vision for manufacturing and selling stands to hold a TV on top and a VCR underneath—perfect for college dorms, for example. Mark and Kenny not only manufactured them in their own business, but began to market them and direct 100% of the profit to world evangelization.

Wise mobilizers challenge others to specific opportunities.

John was a young engineer in Houston, Texas. When a mobilizer went through his church, John not only caught a vision but was given a unique challenge to a specific need. "John, how would you like to get other engineers together to support a team in the middle of an island off the coast of India working in a totally Muslim area?" Because John was given the specifics on this team, he not only started supporting them with $50 a month, but he got others to do so, and together their funds totalled $200 a month. With their finances came their prayers, and then they themselves as they visited the team a few years later.

Freeing up resources isn't just about finances. It's also about raising up new laborers.

Today the people are available like never before. Only 1% of the North American Christians ages 18–35 would be enough laborers to do the job. Just tithing 10% of our regular 10% would do it! Worldwide, only one-tenth of 1% of that same age group would provide enough laborers. The potential is there. That is why God calls us to "beg" Him "to thrust out laborers."

Jesus used a particular Greek verb when referring to "thrusting out" laborers into the field. That particular verb, *ekballo*, is only used in a few places. It is used most frequently to refer to casting a demon out of a person. It's used when Jesus tossed the money changers out of the temple, and it's found in the parable where evildoers cast the prophet out of the vineyard and killed him. Finally, it's also used to describe the crowds leading Jesus to the hill to throw Him over. Do you see something common in all of those instances? In these references, it was always against the will of the person.

Get the picture? What Jesus is saying is "Beg God to kick Christians out into the mission field—even against their will!" Why against their will? Probably because too many Christians have gotten caught up in being blessed by God and missed their responsibility to be a blessing to the nations. God is looking for those who can survive the blessings. The mobilizer helps people become aware of that.

How will they get "kicked out"?

It could be a global economic turmoil that sends Christians all over the world (against their will) looking for work. As they go, they'll share their faith.

More likely it may be Christians getting their lives totally upended through a visit by a mobilizer, a weekend conference, or a short-term trip, causing them to totally change their goals, plans, and dreams for their future. Somehow, within a small period of time, their lives are rearranged.

One mobilizer puts it this way: "I love to challenge people to go into full-time Christian work. The worst they can say is no, but it's challenged them to rethink why they are where they are and why they do what they do."

Making Christians aware of opportunities (and challenging them to those) can be a mobilizer's greatest asset. Many Christians love challenges, and challenging them to become involved in meeting a specific need on the field may be just what they are looking for!

Specific needs on the field range from doctors, relief and development workers, engineers, teachers of English as a second language, and more.

John was an electrical engineer floundering in his efforts to get to the field. He finally met a mission director who gave him a slot to fill. "Can you fix video machines?" John was asked. "No, but I can find out how, why?" "They've got them all over the Middle East, but no one can fix them." Today John is in the Middle East because he was shown a specific need and he ran with it.

In Pakistan and Afghanistan, many war victims have lost legs and arms. One man caught a vision for ministering to them, but didn't know how. Although a mechanical engineer, he learned about prosthetics (fitting artificial limbs to victims) and began to recruit a team. It was amazing how many people in that field responded to help this team leader once they saw the strategic need for their field of expertise.

Jim Moats, President of Issachar (a nondenominational Christian organization committed to establishing the indigenous Church among the unreached Muslim people groups of Central Asia) and a business entrepreneur, challenges other Christian business and professional people to use their planning and networking skills to escalate the work to establish indigenous churches in Central Asia. He always finds these people amazed to realize that their skills are needed for establishing the Kingdom globally. With Issachar and its field partners, these lay-people "learn and earn" their way to supporting and initiating critical field projects.

And this isn't only for needs on the field, but needs at home as well.

Brooke was a ninth grader who caught a vision for the world simply by watching the video series *Destination 2000* in her small Christian high school. Living in Colorado at the time, she wanted to use her sum-mer for the King. Hearing of Frontiers' need for summer workers, Brooke got her mom to drive her out to Arizona, where she earned room and board in exchange for her faithful summer service. It was a blessing to Frontiers as well as to Brooke!

As a mobilizer, a small act like publicizing a need in a church bul-letin insert can link someone up. Carolynne volunteers for a mission agency near her home because of an announcement stating a need for a part-time accountant. She loves it so much that she turned down a paying part-time job simply to serve the King, while saving the mission agency the salary of a part-time accountant.

Mobilizers also keep an eye out for retired couples. Dick and Joyce were a retired couple who came to a point in their lives where they were tired of playing golf and tennis all day long. After having been exposed to a correct understanding of the Scriptures, they gave six months of their life serving as full-time assistants to the general director of a mission agency!

Jim and Donna had their first "retirement trip" already planned, with tickets in hand, when they got a call from a mobilizer a week before retiring. After hearing about a specific need for a couple to run a hospitality home in London as well as to help out in the International Headquarters, they got a refund on their tickets, sold their brand-new car, rented their house to their daughter, and embarked on the journey of their lives—and loved every minute of it.

Many times the most effective mobilizer is one who stays put to nurture the contacts he or she has made over the years. Troy worked for a chemical company in his area very successfully. Repeatedly he was given awards for being the most successful salesman. Repeatedly he was given promotions. Repeatedly he turned them down.

Why? He and his wife, Judy, were committed mobilizers. His pri-ority was to mobilize those in his area. Promotions would have taken him away from those he was the most effective with because of the relationships he had built over the years. His priority was not to make money. His job was merely a means to meet his family's needs so he could mobilize others to God's glorious task of reaching the nations—the task to which God directed him.

So the answer to "What's the point of mobilization?" is to release millions of hours of prayer and finances and workers into the harvest force. To see churches planted, discipled, and reaching out into their own cultures—and then on into other cultures. All in order to glorify Him together for eternity!

## Planning for the Future

One last word. Any serious mobilizer keeps in mind the greatest long-term resource of all: children. Today's children are tomorrow's missionaries.

It is reported that 85% of those missionaries who go overseas for the long haul made a decision for Jesus Christ and/or missions before the age of sixteen. The largest percentage of these made the decision between the ages of ten and twelve. Mobilizing children with a vision for the world is crucial!

Unfortunately, for years mobilizing children was unheard of. Only in the past decade has the Church gotten serious about making mission-minded material available for children. Today, more and more material is being created by pioneers like Jan Bell, Geri Templeton, Gerry Dueck, Debby Sjogren, Jill Harris, and Ruth Finley. And they are putting quality materials into young hands.

Although most disciplers of children don't realize it, teaching children about God's Word without an integrated vision for the world is doing the children a tremendous injustice. It's like giving a little girl a new doll that can talk without giving her any batteries, or giving a young boy a model airplane but no glue to put it together. Something vital is missing.

But now groups of concerned people are holding entire expos for the sole purpose of training teachers in how to teach missions to kids. The first known was held in a sunny hot corner of the United States in June 1994. Jill Harris, the dreamer of this meeting in Phoenix, Arizona, had one key idea: God's heart for the world needs to be integrated into every lesson children learn. Missions is not to be a compartment of the Christian life, it is to be the end goal of all we do.

Today, excellent resources for teaching children exist, such as the *Destination 2000* Teacher's Training Video Curriculum, Jan Bell's "P-

Words" and "Kidscan Network Catalog." Great children's mission books exist from Monarch Publishing, Crossroads Publication, Wycliffe, and others! See the Children's Resources section in the back of this book to find out how you can get more information.

Whatever you do, give the children you influence a vision for the world so that they can become tomorrow's laborers.

Now, how can you as a big-picture mobilizer serve your congregation as it begins to run with the vision?

## CHAPTER TWELVE

# Mobilizing the New Harvest Force—Part 2

## Challenge your church to its global destiny

*"Congregations that intentionally affect their times have a sense of purpose and a plan; they have a vision of what God is calling them to be and to do. The person who articulates the appropriate vision for the church is both the cause and result of a mobilized church; both the church and the leaders are mutually empowered in the process."*

—Carl S. Dudley

KAZAKHSTAN — "This is it?" Gritty-cold, wild wind whips your hair as you stand on the bleak runway. A faded yellow truck with a cattle-car-style body roars out of the little block building that is the Aqtau, Kazakhstan airport terminal. It's our shuttle, coming to rescue us from the gale-force maelstrom blasting in from the steppes.

The desert here is dirt. And the Five Gusts, the five-day mistral of spring is throwing dust high into the yellow air. You can't tell if it's overcast or just dusty. When a gust suddenly subsides, you see forever in every direction: no shrubs, no trees, no hills. Flat, foreign-planet desert. "I thought Aqtau was on the Caspian Sea." You try not to sound like a whiner. "I see what you mean about being just beyond Saturn."

The entire planeload—including Kazakhs carrying small trees and Russians with immense plastic bag-boxes—mash into the shuttle that's designed for a third of our number. "Aqtau is one of the Soviet planned cities," we explain through the tangle of arms hanging on to the overhead bars. "The world's first accelerated breeder reactor was built here, and a construction crew from St. Petersburg came down and built the entire city in about 1964. It has about 300,000 people, but you can walk across it in about 40 minutes because it's all concrete high-rise flats. Gray concrete. No paint. No color."

"Where is it?" you shout over the roar of the shuttle truck.

"About 30 kilometers away," we yell back. "Over there. No street names, just numbers: numbered roads, numbered apartment buildings, numbered schools."

You see nothing but dust.

But later, in a missionary's flat overlooking the turquoise Caspian, you begin to see that this gray, concrete settlement is teeming with spiritually starved people and is one of several key hotspots in what God is doing in Central Asia. Your steaming hot shower has refreshed you. You just hope you're not glowing; the water is heated compliments of the huge nuclear reactor nearby. After days of grueling travel, you're finally comfortable with a sharp cup of Turkish coffee among a multinational gaggle of believers, missionaries who represent four societies working together. And it is here as the sun sets red over the Caspian that your head begins to swim with the amazing mix of events, people, and places in God's planetary enterprise.

A Korean shares the rigors of her team's train trip across Kazakhstan. An American outlines the exciting invitation he's received to teach in the local teachers' institute and praises the fine, happy hospitality of the Aqtau citizenry. Just then a fax comes in from a Swiss worker in Krasnodar, Russia. On a lap-top computer, electronic mail messages ask questions and share breakthroughs from Auckland to Oslo. And a veteran missionary tells what God did behind the scenes in the April 1994 South African elections that marked the end of apartheid. He settles back with coffee and a chunk of wafer-like cake, an Aqtau specialty, to tell the story:

For months before the South African elections of '94, the world dreaded the day for the balloting. The Inkatha freedom Party of KwaZulu was boycotting the election, and everyone expected a bloodbath. It was such a volatile situation anyway, with all the races in South Africa voting together for the first time. Of course, the media made Zulu chief minister Mangosuthu Buthelezi out to be some kind of thug, but there were good reasons for the boycott. The situation was a powder keg. Michael Cassidy, head of African Enterprise, said—well, here's the fax I got at the time: Cassidy called on leaders to find a constitution everyone could support; otherwise there would be "indefinite conflict by which we bequeath to our children and grandchildren a pile of ashes." He told these leaders that, let's see: "While your relationships are wounded and bleeding, your followers pay the price in real blood." The boycott promised violence at the polls and the bloodshed would be horrific. Remember? We all waited in despair.

Days before the election, the international negotiating team that had been called in gave up and went home. Except for one man. Washington Okumu, a believer from Kenya. Professor of economics. One believer.

On Friday, April 15, Buthelezi also had given up. He left Johannesburg for Lanseria airport to return to Ulundi, to report to Zulu King Goodwill Zwelithini that his nation and South Africa should prepare for the worst. But at this point, well past "zero hour" for South Africa, Professor Okumu decided to make one last attempt at negotiating an agreement. He drew up a rough draft of a new proposal and shot out to the airport for one last appeal to Buthelezi. But the Zulu minister's plane had just taken off.

Heartsick, Okumu phoned the headquarters of African Enterprises to share this last incident of bad news. The AE offices told him, "Stay where you are. Pray, and we'll pray!" So the Kenyan professor of economics fell into a chair in the airport waiting room and prayed.

And Buthelezi's plane strangely developed mechanical problems. This fax I got in those days says Buthelezi gave a statement later: "We were hardly airborne when I was told there was a problem and we had to turn back. It was as though God had prevented me from leaving, and, like Jonah, I was brought back. I told Professor Okumu my forced return was a Godsend."

Okumu leapt to present his new plan to Buthelezi, who agreed to meet one more time with a representative of the African National Congress and the RSA home affairs ministry. So where do they get together? At a prayer meeting, of course!

Twenty-five thousand believers gathered that Sunday for a Jesus Peace Rally in Kings Park Stadium in Durban. In all the weeping and praying, the crowd was totally unaware—as was the rest of the world—that the three officials were meeting at that very time in an upper-level VIP suite in that stadium!

The result? The final proposal was miraculously agreed upon. And a few days later, as we all saw, the elections passed peacefully in a festival atmosphere. Warmth and goodwill prevailed as voters of every race lined up patiently to launch the new South Africa. The world was astonished. Amazing what God can do through just one or two alert, full-on disciples, eh?"

Somehow that one additional story really hits you. "I want to be part of this," you say.

"Why, sure," says one of the missionaries. "You can help God's team here in Aqtau to recruit English teachers, business instructors—"

"No." You try to find the words. "I don't mean just here in Kazakhstan. I mean part of this whole thing—this worldwide network going on, these sovereign moves of God, this . . . this . . ."

"This vision?" They smile knowingly.

"Yes."

## Running With the Vision

This isn't a book about nice missionary ideas. It's not about urging you to join someone's program. But it is about a vision—a global vision that encompasses an incredible mass of individuals and ideas and energy and miracles. And it is blatantly calling you to pick it up and run with it.

Why did God tell Habakkuk to write the vision plainly? So that he who reads it may run with it (Habakkuk 2:2). Who is reading and running with it? A messenger, of course. A messenger like you who can bring an urgent, new vision to churches—a fresh vision of our part in the history of God's global plan.

When you mobilize a campus fellowship, church, or any group of believers, you bring a clear message of vision—vision that can be implemented. But how exactly does that happen?

The basics in mobilizing a campus group, a church, or any fellowship toward new mission vision include

1. Developing a prayer core to pray for the vision of that group.

2. Determining where a fellowship is in its level of mission vision, who the key "movers and shakers" in that fellowship are, and what makes the hearts of those leaders pound wildly.

3. Selecting the best resources to encourage individuals in their growth as World Christians.

4. Implementing a three-step plan to serve that fellowship as it catches, builds, and finally acts on a vision of its mission in the harvest field.

To maximize your efforts in this task, remember that you already have a heart for the world and are probably already doing quite a few things. And as a zealous mobilizer, you will often try the shortcut of starting a project personally while simultaneously starting another project, and another—with a view, of course, to "handing the task off" as soon as possible.

Your goal is to work smarter, not harder. Try to bring as many people into this Kingdom-expanding business right from the beginning. Don't try to do it all yourself. If you do, you simply become a tired, burned-out, worn-out mobilizer, critical of those who lack vision. Soon you will be trying to motivate others into action through guilt.

Let's look more closely at the steps of how you as a mobilizer can serve your local church:

## Step 1: Develop a prayer core.

Nothing happens without prayer. Don't read quickly over those words, thinking, "Yeah, right, now let's get on with it." Prayer is your first foundational step as well as your second, third, and fourth. Prayer cannot be overemphasized. Why? Without it, you can't change a single person's perspective. It's the Holy Spirit who does the work. You must work not only in partnership with Him but in dependence upon Him.

If anything is seriously going to happen in the lives of those in your fellowship, you know the enemy—whose false kingdom will be threatened—will try to squelch any vision in its infancy. Just as forays into Satan's territory prompt defensive barrages from his diabolical hosts, you can be sure that attempts to stir up believers' vision for the world will meet with serious spiritual counterattacks. This is why this first step is so crucial: Get solid prayer warriors praying for your fellowship's vision and against the enemy's interference and attacks—which usually strike relationships, finances, and health.

What will this prayer group look like? Well, quite honestly (depending upon where you are beginning) it could be a prayer group of one—you praying faithfully by yourself for a fellowship. Yes, that's right. Remember Larna from New Zealand? She did it for a year and a half, and God honored her steadfastness.

In these times of prayer, you ask God to move not only in the fellowship as a whole, but specifically in the lives of individuals ready for the vision. You'll also need to ask God for others to join you in the real battle of prayer.

Write it in soap on your bathroom mirror: Step One (two, three, and four): Pray.

## Step 2: Choose resources appropriate to your fellowship.

To energize a new mission vision that points toward a church for every people, each step of mobilizing a church or campus fellowship must be guided by user-friendly, clear resources. People need to have something in their hands to work through new ideas.

Throughout Church history, most of the 788 major global plans to evangelize the world haven't caught on in the Body of Christ as a whole.[1] Among all sorts of reasons for failure, a common one was that they were simply great schemes based on ideas. Ideas are powerful, but ideas alone won't impact a whole fellowship, a community of fellowships, or a whole people with new insight. Hands-on tools are crucial in mobilizing Christians to catch, build, and act on a new vision of their role in God's unchangeable purpose.

Choose appropriate resources for your group. Categories of recommended materials are listed in the Resources section. As you come up with your own custom-designed resources for these various stages, and have tested them, share them with other mobilizers in other churches and areas.

To help guide you through the maze, consider calling someone who has already been mobilizing. (Some of these mobilizing mentors may even be available by e-mail.) They will be able to help you think through what resources are the finest and how to best use them. Checking with them first could save you hours of time. (We the authors can help you connect with key mentors. Contact us through Frontiers or World Christian—See Resources.)

## Step 3: Serve your fellowship as they catch, build, and act on a vision of God's heart for every people.

By God's grace the men and women, children and adults of your fellowship will start to catch the vision of God's desire to build a people comprising citizens from every tribe, people, and nation on the planet. You're no longer just analyzing your fellowship and feeding them persuasive information, they're coming back and asking for more—or at least they're *beginning* to respond!

What do you do then? Think of your work of imparting ongoing vision as having three stages. First the vision catches. Then it builds. Finally it takes action. Part of mobilizing is leading your fellowship through each step, as it becomes ready.

## Step 4: Determine the vision of the group—of individuals and of the pastor.

In mobilizing a fellowship, remember a few key things.

First, no matter how big or small a fellowship may be, it is made up of individuals. And just as you eat an elephant one bite at a time, so too will you need to look toward mobilizing your fellowship one person at a time. Some will be more ready than others. And just as others catch the vision, you'll find new people joining your fellowship who are clueless regarding what you are talking about.

Secondly, in mobilizing individuals the 20/80 rule applies. That is, 20% of the church gives 80% of the money and does 80% of the work. Because of this you want to start by focusing on that 20%, the key people of that fellowship.

Akin to that, you don't locate leaders by looking for titles. Leaders are those who lead. There can be many true leaders in your church who have no title. Look for those influencers. These may be the ones God wants you to focus on.

Find out how decisions are made in the fellowship. Does your fellowship have a committee of two or three that makes decisions in this area? Bear in mind: A church does not adopt a people group. Individuals within the church make that decision for those in the church. Whether the church owns it or not remains to be seen.

In all of this, your biggest battle may be in mobilizing the top leader or pastor of that fellowship. If the entire fellowship isn't getting a steady diet of God's heart for the world through the teaching up front, you may run into a brick wall. Much loving prayer will need to focus here if that's the situation you find yourself in.

So where do you start? By realizing that there are "steps" that you take them through.

Communicator James Engles uses a commitment scale to determine the best methods of evangelism. If a non-Christian is at a basic level one in his understanding of Jesus Christ, challenging that person to a level-seven commitment to the eternal lordship of Christ probably isn't going to work.

In the same way, if the mission vision of a person or fellowship is at level one, you'll be beating your head against the wall to implement any vision that requires an all-out, level-seven commitment to God's heart for every people. You can't push believers into a higher commitment than they're ready for. Remember the Comfort-Discomfort Zone chart? Most believers don't find it comfortable to be challenged to a vision beyond themselves!

Therefore, find out where your fellowship is. That will show you what "levels" or "steps" to start on. Following, are seven levels, from level one: "Hey, I just became a believer," to level seven, "Here I am, send me."

To mobilize for results, list the assets of your church. What is it you're trying to do as you serve a campus group or church whose vision is growing? You're going for greater awareness and knowledge, yes. But you're more specifically going for a Spirit-powered release of resources—an exciting flood of prayer power, finances, and manpower. What resources are in your fellowship? Actually take inventory:

*Prayer Power.* How many of our fellowship spend specific time in prayer daily? What do they pray for? How many "man-hours" of prayer are available if every member would spend at least fifteen minutes in informed prayer daily? Are we open to quarterly prayer "events"?

A Mobilizer's Message | Mission Commitment Level

**How can I serve you as you act on a vision of God's heart for every people?**

(A solid commitment is expected.)

Level 7: We'll do anything, go anywhere for His great global Cause.

Level 6: We're working to integrate a vision of God's heart for every people into our lifestyles and into our fellowship.

Key question indicating a mission commitment is ready to be challenged to act on the vision: "What do we do now?"

**How can I serve you as you build that vision of God's heart for every people?**

(Some commitment is expected—a commitment to learn more.)

Level 5: We'd like to be more active in cross-cultural ministry.

Level 4: We're getting a new perspective on Scripture, and are burdened now to pray for other peoples.

Key question indicating a mission commitment is ready to be challenged to build the vision: "How can we find out more about this?"

**How can I serve you as you catch a vision of God's heart for every people?**

(Virtually no commitment is expected.)

Level 3: We're understanding more the value of cross-cultural ministry.

Level 2: I'm starting to become aware of the fact that there is a world out there and God is concerned about it.

Level 1: I'm a believer, committed to Jesus Christ.

*People.* What professions are represented? How many active retirees? How many unemployed? How many couples without children? How many formally trained in ministry skills? How many finishing their schooling in the next five years? How many gifted in evangelism? How many mission-minded? How many retired and returned missionaries? How many open to a short-term trip? If we asked, "How many new missionaries could we send by the year 2000 or 2010?"—what would be the answer?

*Finances.* What is the total income of our fellowship? The total disposable income? How does the giving in our church represent these amounts? What percentage of our fellowship's income is spent on ourselves? What percentage on impacting our own people group? What percentage on other cultures—and what percentage to reach unreached cultures? Are we giving to support the home-front staffs of mission societies? To support mission mobilizers? What annual amount could be generated if we monthly gathered all the loose change left in our pockets and purses at each day's end? Are we open to the "Faith-promise" method of giving for outreach?

What blessings—resources—has God put into your fellowship for the sake of His name among all nations?

Terry Hofecker, pastor of Northwest Chapel in Dublin, Ohio, has adapted the baseball diamond analogy used by Saddleback Valley Community Church in Mision Viejo, California. It too has progressive levels Christians need to take in order to become World Christians.

To help you understand the diagram, you'll need a few explanations. The "4:12 Level One" refers to a basic Christianity course seeking to teach believers to apply the Scriptures in their everyday relationship with God and others. The "4:12 Level Two" does the same, but goes deeper. "Operation Vision" refers to a four-week curriculum on the World Christian perspective.

It is the strategic intent of the Church for every person to go through this model—that is, to get around all the bases. Obviously, some will be on third base while others are getting up to bat. Yet this diagnostic tool helps the church staff (and members of the church themselves) to see where members of the congregation are.

The problem, though, is that people get stuck in between the bases for any number of reasons. It is the goal of the staff to remove those barriers and provide resources (motivation, accountability, and biblical illumination) to move them along. Once a person reaches home base, then they need to reevaluate everything else they've learned and see how it applies to God's global plan.

Now that you have these two models, think through what your fel-

# NORTHWEST CHAPEL
## Discipleship Strategy

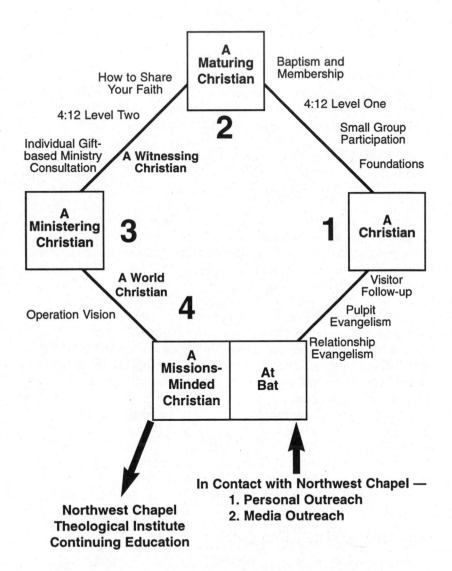

Note: Baseball diamond metaphor is taken from the Saddleback Strategy (1983, Mission Viejo, CA).

lowship is like (if there are already a few concerned about the same things you are, get together with them). You'll want to ask such questions as

- Who are a part of the 20%?
- Where do they fall in these levels?
- Who is considered a leader of the group?
- Who are the decision-makers for this group?
- Which women have a vision for the world?
- Are there any mission prayer groups going on that you're not aware of?
- Who are the key children's workers?
- What is the leader's vision like?
- How am I/are we viewed in this fellowship?
- Have I/we established any credibility with my/our fellowship?
- What kind of a relationship do I/we have with any of its members?

The last three questions are vital because people accept a radical global paradigm shift much more easily from people who have their trust. If you have good relationships with key people, God may have given you that asset for His Kingdom purposes. If you don't have any, remember a mobilizer's key word "Serve!" and do it in love. (Giving yourself in service is how you can win over pastors who don't have a vision beyond their own church.)

If you're out of the ballpark as you think through this, there is help. Larry Walker of ACMC has a seminar designed for people like you called "Seven Dynamics for Advancing Your Church in Missions." You may want to contact him directly (see Training Helps in Resources section) to see when his next seminar is scheduled and find a way to get there. Or see if ACMC (or a group like ACMC) has a regional meeting for helping individuals just like you. Call someone (the Caleb Project, ACMC, AIMS) and ask if they know of any other mobilizers in your area that you could learn from, or even team up with! Seek to be mentored by another more mature mobilizer!

## Stage One: A Vision That Catches

When you first encourage a fellowship to catch a vision of the overall mission of the Church, you're not asking for much commitment. And so even believers at levels one and two on the commitment scale usually respond enthusiastically. Frankly, with all that God is doing globally, it's simple to get folks excited.

But if excitement is the platform from which a church commits itself to serious global battle, its vision will never endure in the long haul. A large church in Pasadena, California, with a mission pastor extraordinaire at the helm adopted an unreached people in 1986 or '87. (No one quite remembers which year.) The commitment was made in the glow of a mission emphasis that helped folks catch the vision. Three years later only the mission pastor even remembered the name of the people group!

Leaping from catching a vision to acting on that vision isn't giving a church enough time to shift worldviews. Getting excited about God's global breakthroughs and then, for example, responding by adopting an unreached people is like watching the film *Chariots of Fire* (a film about running) and then entering a marathon. A few unusual individuals might complete the course, but most won't—and they won't try it again. A church that sees a new level of mission interest merely as another program added to all the other programs of the church will probably fail in its mission vision; and failure will prevent a whole-church mission vision from materializing.

How can you serve a fellowship as it catches a vision? Believers first need to understand God's heart for every people. So the message that begins to mobilize them asks for no commitment or low commitment, sharing the welcome message of the wonderful breakthroughs of what God is doing worldwide. And that should be your first step! For starters we all need to hear good news:

"Like cold water to a weary soul, so is good news from a distant land" (Proverbs 25:25).

Moreover, the idea that God is alive and moving in mighty ways—though perhaps not in our quiet corner of Christendom—is both encouraging and challenging. ("O that God would do that here!")

"Give thanks to the LORD, call on His name. . . . Praise the LORD in song, for He has done excellent things; let this be known throughout the earth" (Isaiah 12:4–5).

So what can you do to accomplish the first step?

1. *Pass on to the pastor(s) anecdotes from around the world* for appropriate inclusion in sermons. Make several of these breakthroughs available weekly to whoever designs church announcement sheets, bulletins, newsletters. They can be used as "fillers," filling in a block of unused space with vision-expanding news!

2. *Give global-scope praise and prayer requests* to existing prayer

groups—even if these items have nothing to do with your church or denomination.

3. *Use FrontierScan monthly bulletin inserts or design your own.* If you don't use a bulletin, simply pass these out monthly.

4. *Use all the tried-and-true reminders that God's heart is for the whole world:* Post maps, charts, photos of other cultures. Hang up flags, discreet travel posters showing the faces of peoples. Invest in a giant globe.

5. *Monthly host a book table* display of global-scope materials—such as packaged in the World Christian Display Table offered by William Carey Library.

6. *Host special speakers,* realizing that some missionaries are themselves not good communicators to our home front cultures. Make sure the speaker gives a "catch the vision" presentation; dramatic challenges to high-level mission commitment can come later! Schedule these specials during regular meeting times. Hosting the meeting at a special time means extra effort is being asked for—and the ones needing vision-expanding probably don't have the mission commitment to make that extra effort—yet!

7. If you have a ministry in the fellowship, *refer consistently to Scripture's emphasis on God's heart for all peoples* and the biblical concept of a vision beyond ourselves. Avoid using the "M-Word": Missions. It's too loaded with connotations.

8. *Make available a "Catch the Vision" brochure.* Leadership of the church can in a one-month period read through the brochure and gather once informally for discussion about its content.

9. *Plan on-the-field awareness trips* with those few key individuals from the "20%." Short-term mission trips are sometimes confused with short-term mission awareness or exposure trips. Participants on a mission awareness trip don't have to even pretend to be ministering—a demanding activity that doesn't easily happen on short-term trips anyway. The idea here is to get the leadership of your church on the field to see, smell, taste, feel, and remember. The trip can be to sites where your missionaries are already active or to peoples you're only dreaming of targeting. Send your pastor away on such a trip. Tell him to take lots of photos, tape recordings, and videos.

After six months to a year of carefully disseminating catch-the-vision messages to a fellowship, urge a one-Sunday emphasis if your group doesn't already have one. As a significant number of individuals make a corporate move up the scale of mission-vision commitment, it's good to mark such a step with a one-time, all-church event. Hopefully this will become an annual event! Take advantage of these yearly rituals by presenting an overview of what God is doing in the big picture today.

What is your objective in this Sunday emphasis? It isn't to get a group to jump up into mission action. It's to allow them corporately to come to a point of asking, "How can we find out more about this?" This can be done by using a packed presentation already created, or by presenting one yourself.

Fantastic packaged programs already exist. In the U.K., the Evangelical Missionary Alliance has a superb packet called *Missing Faces in the Worldwide Church*. It has good information on learning activities for almost every age group in the fellowship. Jay Randall's Caleb Project presentation *A View From On High* is a high-impact tool that can give a fellowship an interesting, humorous and yet powerful splash of vision in a church service setting. Videotape the session for those not able to attend. (The condensed overview was presented in Chapter 2.) *A Sunday for the World* (see Resources) is specifically designed for this step.

Or you can have a one-Sunday emphasis that is a do-it-yourself presentation. Try to refrain from calling it a "mission" day; instead, use a title that suggests something about God's purpose or our destiny. ACMC and other organizations offer many good resources with creative activity ideas for meetings of various age groups and Bible studies for the day. Tape-record or even videotape sessions to pass around to anyone not able to attend.

Now it's time to move into a higher commitment level as people in your fellowship (or key individuals) build their vision of God's heart for all nations.

## Stage Two: A Vision That Builds

This is the critical step. If key individuals or even your whole fellowship catches excitement about what is going on in the world but don't get the biblical foundation along with it, it will be a short-lived excitement. Folks need to be systematically guided toward a biblical worldview that differs substantially from that of your typical Christian culture, or a few hardy mission fanatics will end up carrying the burden of world evangelization alone.

How can you serve a fellowship as it builds its global vision?

Teach *Catch the Vision, Destination 2000,* or *The World Christian* (see Resources), or another cutting-edge mission course. Some of these can be done for your fellowship as a whole, or they can be done for small groups of individuals.

Why not consider having a dinner party for some key people in the

"20%" and pop in video number one from the *Destination 2000* series after the meal? Or ask your leader if you can have an hour of his time (schedule it far in advance for his sake and for the sake of prayerful preparation) and go over the first chapter of *Catch the Vision* and see what he thinks.

If you are teaching for your fellowship as a whole, at all costs don't call it a "missions course." Call it by the course title and describe it as a look at God's great purpose and our significant part in it. Even the authors of these courses don't mention "the M-word"—missions—until the course is nearly half completed! A solid, three-month weekly course should give enough input to encourage individuals in small groups to pursue additional worldview-shifting studies.

Train other teachers to offer these courses. Don't be stuck with having to do everything in this educational phase yourself! And remember, if God sends you overseas you will want to have a replacement behind you continuing on in the work.

Foster world-class prayer:

1. *Infuse existing prayer groups with harvest-focused praises and prayer requests*—whether these items deal with your own missionaries' ministries or not.

2. *Provide learning opportunities* for those new to serious prayer and for veteran prayer warriors to gain new skills in strategic prayer. Inquire about the seminars, small-group studies, or individual books recommended by your denomination or other fellowships in your stream of church tradition. There are volumes and volumes of good prayer training materials; all too often these materials are seen as incidental because prayer itself has become incidental in too many fellowships!

During this build-the-vision stage, the zeal generated in the "catch the vision" stage must be maintained. This needs to be done, because in the time it takes for this new paradigm shift to solidify, the evil one has many ways of pouring on cold water to stop that growth.

This needs to be done in several ways. First, continue to feed the church more information all the time. Help them discover more of God's heart through the Scriptures to new and exciting breakthroughs that happen all the time—things you are learning about.

Giving them easy-to-handle projects will also keep them growing in their vision. It could be something simple like reading a missions magazine and cutting out interesting articles, or calling a mission agency and doing some research, or preparing for a short-term vision trip by helping raise funds or calling to purchase tickets.

Prayer will keep their vision strong. Praying through *Operation World* is a great way to pray effectively for missions. But don't let its size intimidate your children. They could meet with others weekly or monthly and pray through a region or religion. They could call their missionaries overseas and ask for special prayer requests. Continuing to pray for the nations will add fuel to the fire God has put in their heart.

A final way to keep their zeal alive is to have them pass their vision on to someone else. This is part of God's design in discipling. Once they teach it to someone else they'll really learn it for themselves. It could be as easy as reviewing the memory picture found in *Destination 2000* with another person. Another idea would be to invite friends for a dessert and conclude with a short talk and/or skit.

## Stage Three: A Vision That Takes Action

Although new believers are in many ways just as prepared to step out in faith to minister cross-culturally as are mature believers—they have the same Holy Spirit in them as do others—the average believer needs and deserves adequate preparation and training before he or she steps out. How can you serve a fellowship as it begins to act on a vision of blessing every people on earth?

That question will best be answered by the fellowship itself as it expands its informed vision through a congregation-wide Build the Vision stage. It may be astounding to watch the opportunities, the complexities, the unusual custom-designed outreach a fellowship enters into as it responds intelligently to God's direction. As Mary instructed the servants at the wedding in Cana, "Whatever He says to you, do it."

Still, this action-packed stage of a church's growth in global vision seems to be fairly consistent from church to church in three key action-steps: establishing some form of world Christian accountability pair or group such as a monthly mission fellowship, developing short-term training and outreach opportunities, and focusing in some way on an unreached people.

### An Act-on-the-Vision Step: Facilitate a monthly mission fellowship.

A monthly mission fellowship seems essential in the demanding realities of partnering with God in serious cross-cultural ministry. Some fellowships find that a core of zealots who have survived the Building-the-Vision stage want to gather *weekly*. But a quality session is difficult to maintain on a weekly basis; and even if the session is spent in solid prayer, a weekly meeting means most of these mission-minded folks won't be rubbing shoulders with the non-mission-minded during regular church get-togethers. And since global vision is more caught than taught, the weekly mission zealots become more and more isolated as another compartmentalized interest group of the fellowship. A monthly meeting is probably ideal for a healthy, quality mission fellowship.

What happens at a monthly mission fellowship? A typical 90-minute schedule might include:

*Ten minutes*—Global reports about your own missionaries as well as the general harvest force.

*Ten minutes*—A brief Bible study discussion on God's plan for all nations. (Can be a review or elaboration on one of the biblical points of your Build-the-Vision courses.)

*Thirty minutes*—New information. This might be a video, a guest speaker, a cross-cultural game, a special presentation by alternating group members, a whole-group discussion of an article or essay assigned last month, a course study such as *Serving As Senders* (see Materials and Courses in Resources section), an ethnic meal, mission book reviews, or a mini-project that will go to a missionary or be used in an outreach. (In other words, this isn't mission committee-type planning or policy discussion time; a mission committee, not a monthly mission fellowship, handles the logistics of the fellowship's mission involvement.)

*Ten to thirty minutes*—Prayer for the world. Praying across a huge map provides plenty of prayer fuel when teamed up with *Operation World*. Alternate praying in small groups and in the larger group. This will make the time more manageable.

*Ten minutes*—Refreshments and fellowship. (If this is at the end of the meeting, people can stay as long as they wish.)

Avoid doing church mission "business" at what you're calling a "global" prayer meeting. That business end of a church's mission involvement is best handled by a slim corp called a "mission committee" or "mission task force" who are responsible for the logistical decision-making of the fellowship's mission involvement. Your denomination—or mission service organizations such as EMA or ACMC (see Organizations in Resources section)—have good, tested manuals for forming and maintaining a smart, efficient mission committee/task force.

It seems typical that out of monthly mission fellowships arise the key players in the church's mission committee or task force, those that will coordinate special emphases such as focusing on an unreached people and missionaries themselves—who usually begin their going as short-termers.

### An Act-on-the-Vision Step: Facilitate a short-term training program and short-term outreach opportunities

Short-term training and outreach opportunities are another standard action-step as a fellowship acts on its vision for all nations. Your mission committee must consider the pros and cons of short-term missions as highlighted in our discussions on trends in the harvest force. Then, in conjunction with your mission leadership, with missionaries involved, and with your fellowship's educational leadership, design a strategic training program.

The details of sending short-term teams is well outlined in several good publications such as *Vacation With a Purpose* (see Materials and Courses in Resources section). How do you do it? The basic "how" is to begin with just one project. A full-fledged mission program for your youth and adults can then build on the success of that first effort. How do you implement that one project?

1. *Consider* and evaluate project ideas. (Contact outside groups for help.)
2. *Plan* all the details.
3. *Implement* mission outreach training.
4. *Develop* an outreach support group.
5. *Do* the outreach and mission ministries.
6. *Evaluate* and return to Step 1.

What's not so readily available is solid material on how to train those teams in Step 3. Local-church training that includes youth as well as adults, that equips short-termers with realistic skills and not just more education, and that has a revolving curriculum is, frankly, not well documented yet. The materials closest to answering this problem are found in several self-published booklets and manuals of groups or large churches that are sending short-term teams—booklets that usually focus on the logistics of sending, and yet which sometimes include an overview of training topics.

How do you seriously train for increasingly competent local-church outreach—in your own people group and beyond?

One of the great things about training believers for outreach ministry is that they're automatically motivated. When Diana realizes that a ten-year-old boy will soon be asking her in Spanish how to start reading the Bible, you don't need a "hook" to interest her in studying Spanish phrases. When Kendall finds out he will be giving his testimony on a national radio broadcast in Bulgaria, you won't have to wonder whether or not he's listening to a "How to Give Your Testimony" lecture.

Sometimes, for the first time in their church lives, ordinary pew-sitters rapidly acquire a sense of responsibility to learn—when they know they will be held accountable for the knowledge in actual ministry.

The following suggestions on training are directed toward a training coordinator, who is not necessarily the resident church mission mobilizer (who is blessed with dozens of other urgent projects). Actually, a mobilizer may have to initiate the first year's program in order to train others for subsequent years' training and outreach ministries.

1. *Start small.* Choose a single project to train for the first year. Generally, an annual, large-group training program is followed in most churches by individual outreach team practice-and-prayer sessions.

Most local-church training programs are open to believers grade ten through adult. Combining age groups in one training program is adequately effective, although with large numbers of trainees, breaking into youth and adult levels is preferable.

Seasonal training usually works best. For summer ministries, conduct your training during the three or four months before school is out. A training program that runs through the summer is difficult because of inconsistent attendance due to vacations, camps, and other special activities. A three-month, once-a-week training program is a good rule of thumb for most serious outreach projects.

Find a time during the week that is satisfactory for all your trainees. Be sensitive to their time restraints. Don't conflict with regular church programming.

One option that has worked effectively for some groups is having the weekly training session one morning a week at an early, ghastly hour. Conflicts with after-work or after-school activities as well as evening family times or church programs will be avoided. The older saints in your church might want to minister on a rotating basis by providing an inexpensive breakfast for the trainees. Or a nearby doughnut shop might be willing to provide a group discount on "continental breakfasts." Trainees pay for breakfasts on a donation basis.

2. *Training sessions should be brief and intensive.* Plan a ten-minute cushion of time for quizzes and late arrivals, followed by no more than 30 minutes of instruction. A tight, well-planned, 40-minute session should be sufficient each week.

Your session isn't going to be a relaxed discussion period; the purpose is not education and awareness but instructions for action. So the room should be set up for lectures. Make sure the temperature will evoke neither yawns nor goosebumps.

3. *Instructional Methods.* Since you have a lot of information to relate in a short amount of time, you may need to adjust your usual method

of teaching. In fact, you're not teaching; you're training. Keep in mind the following guidelines:

Teach intensively. Sessions should be fast-paced and show you mean business. Emphasize the basic, essential information team members need to know.

Don't be afraid to use a lecture method in this first part of training; on-the-job application comes later on the outreach trip. Still, use plenty of visuals and handouts that emphasize the points you are making verbally. Use guest lecturers often.

Quiz your trainees to encourage accountability. At the beginning of each session, give a quick quiz on the previous week's material.

Duplicate quizzes with three to five basic questions. Choose questions that are vital to the previous week's learning objectives and are difficult enough to ensure that trainees continue to take good notes during the lectures. If you assign weekly Bible reading sections, include a question on the quiz to cover current assignments.

With a quiz each week, you won't have to take attendance during the sessions; you can keep track of each person's progress; and you will have a system of regular makeup activities for absentees.

4. *Duplicate yourself.* You can multiply your training if you record your sessions on cassette tape, label them, and start a file. The tapes can then be used in a number of ways:

- Team review of especially crucial information.
- A "correspondence course" for those unable to attend.
- A training tape to be improved upon by next year's lecturer—who is probably a trainee this year!
- Coupled with the weekly quiz sheets, tapes form an effective package for trainees to make up for a missed training session.

5. *Give realistic assignments.* Give weekly assignments such as

- Study this session's notes and prepare for next week's quiz.
- Read a certain section of Scripture.
- Pray for our church's mission vision with one elderly person.

Give monthly assignments such as

- Complete a month-long prayer chart.
- Visit church or youth-group absentees and newcomers.
- Teach a Sunday school class, children's ministry session, Bible study.

- Lead a meeting at a soup kitchen ministry, a jail, or homes for the elderly, orphans, delinquent youth.

- Help the training leader (on a rotating basis) prepare for meetings, grade quizzes, or other leg work.

Assign a single long-range project such as

- Meet regularly with an older prayer partner who will commit him/herself to pray for you and this outreach project.

- Research and write a report on a topic of mission significance (a people group, a mission agency, an outreach strategy).

- Conduct several personal interviews with people active in full-time ministry (pastor, evangelist, goer, welcomer). Ask: What's the best and the worst of your ministry position?

- Explain the plan of salvation to at least one person during the training period.

Various groups from Youth With A Mission to World Evangelical Fellowship insist that training must develop basic discipleship as well as practical skills. The reason such groups have seen the need to include basic personal discipleship in their training is that local churches have been lax in that area. Mission organizations can't expect any real ministry if they simply tack practical skills on to a believer who hasn't been properly discipled.

This reality highlights the distinct advantage of outreach training going on within the local church—the training time can focus heavily on ministry skills development alone. Because in a local church, virtually every ministry strengthening the church develops a believer's basic discipleship. And that discipling must be effective.

But time usually spent in teaching basic discipleship by mission training organizations can be saved in a local church as it teaches the believer the Word, as it leads the believer in worship and prayer, as it, in the form of dozens of saints, mentors the believer in a lifestyle of accountability, as it counsels the believer in its pastoral role, as it evaluates and teaches a believer's interpersonal abilities within its supportive community. For example, the time usually spent in training courses to study the mission theme of the Bible is saved since your fellowship is already teaching those concepts in your Build-the-Vision Bible courses.

The local church is the perfect place for serious ministry training!

Implement a three- or four-year revolving curriculum. Each year can include a month of basic ministry topics, a month of focus on the harvest field your projects will impact, and a month of very practical skills training that applies in all projects. Additionally, ongoing team preparation meetings should lead right up to, into, and through the short-term outreach itself. An example of a first-year training schedule might be:

### Session/Topic

Month One: Ministry Basics
1. Orientation to This Year's Project(s)
2. Updates and Trends in the Harvest Force and Fields
3. The "Call" to Ministry and Your Spiritual Gifting
4. Finding Your Niche in the Harvest . . . For Now!

Month Two: Our Harvest Field
5. Looking to the Fields: God's Heart for Our Own People
6. Looking to the Fields: God's Heart for a People Whose Church(es) We Are/We Plan to Be Partnering With
7. Looking to the Fields: God's Heart for an Unreached People We Are/We Plan to Be Approaching
8. Looking to the Fields: Key Approaches and Key Prayer Strategies for These People Groups—Our Own, a Reached and an Unreached People

Month Three: Personal Skills
9. Age-Group Characteristics in Our Project Target Areas
10. How to Introduce a Person to Faith in Christ
11. Basic Principles of Ministering Through the Arts
12. Character Issues Which Need to Be Addressed

Be sure to use your trained workers as trainers and future team leaders. "The things which you have heard from me in the presence of many witnesses, these entrust to faithful men, who will be able to teach others also" (2 Timothy 2:2). Multiply the experiences of every participant.

Serious, ongoing evaluation of your short-term training and outreaches is crucial. Career missionaries and other full-time ministry workers who come out of this training must be given a good foundation of training that won't have to be contradicted by later formal training.

Evaluation and fine-tuned improvements are also important because what you're ultimately doing is growing a visionary core of church members who know how to implement the vision of your entire fellowship. And one of the facets of your vision of God's heart for all peoples might be adopting one!

### An Act-on-the-Vision Step: Focus on an unreached people

As your fellowship or church eases into acting on the vision of blessing every people, they'll often find that focusing on a particular unreached people group—even if in prayer alone—helps clarify their vision.

Focusing and pooling resources has long been a key military tactic, as attested by the German military strategist Clausewitz:

> The best strategy is always to be very strong at the decisive point. There is no more imperative and no simpler law for strategy than to keep the forces concentrated. All forces that are available and destined for a strategic object should be simultaneously applied to it, compressed into one act and one movement.

It would make sense if churches would realize the impact of unified effort (see John 17:21) and "keep the forces concentrated." Many churches apply the shotgun approach to missions, scattering their efforts in all directions. But it's time for a wiser approach to using our resources for the advance of the global Kingdom.

There are now more than 1,200 congregations of committed believers for every identified unreached people group in the world. What would happen if those hundreds of churches would pray for one group? What if they were to take up an offering for that people? What if those hundreds of congregations polled their members to join a team to plant a church in that unreached group? If we concentrated and coordinated our resources, having church-planting teams within every remaining unreached culture in the world would be a simple task. Not easy, but at least simple.

And that is exactly what is happening in the worldwide Body of Christ. Churches large and small are focusing their prayers and mission efforts on an unreached people, linking up with other congregations and mission agencies to see that people reached. (See case studies mentioned in Chapter 5.) Some of these partnerships are calling their project *Serve a People, Adopt a People, Reach the Unreached,* or *Focus on a People*. Regardless of the name, the idea is simple: Concentrate your mission efforts.

A church of a few dozen members in the remote, small town of Mossman in northeast Australia asked their denomination for an unreached people to pray for. The suggestion was the Deccani, a Muslim people of India. Now, just two years later, little children and the elderly join in prayer vigils for the Deccani. The church has discovered there are Muslims within their own region, and are helping support an evangelist to Muslims locally. And this small church, located in the far coast of Australia, is linking up globally to partner with other countries' churches and missionaries to see that the Deccani soon have a church of their own.

A congregation in Cincinnati in the U.S. and another in Christchurch, New Zealand, both viewed a brief video about the Naxi people of China. Now both are exchanging prayer guides and ideas on how to mobilize their fellowships to pray, learn more, and partner to reach the Naxi. And not coincidentally, for the first time in history a small group of Naxi have turned to faith in Jesus Christ.

Your church can "adopt" an unreached people. Just as adopting a child is to care for him until he's able to care for himself, adopting an unreached people is to care for that group—praying, giving, learning about them, and sending and/or going—until a viable church movement is established and they can then "care for themselves."

*Steps to Adopting an Unreached People*. After a solid educational process of encouraging a fellowship-wide understanding of people-group thinking, be sure that your group doesn't approach adopting an unreached people in the frustrating steps of ready, fire . . . and then aim! Instead:

## 1. Ready! Choose an unreached people (in 90 days).

- Pray for God's linkup.
- Ask those already in your mission networks for suggestions—your current missionaries, the mission societies you know.
- Watch for logical connections—perhaps an unreached group in your city's cultural exchange programs, a people whose language is being taught in your local university, a people who are already represented in your community or country.
- Consult with your denominational or associational mission office; mission sending societies such as Frontiers, AIM, Wycliffe; or mission service organizations such as Youth With A Mission, Target 2000 offices worldwide, AIMS, ACMC, the U.S. Center for World Mission Mobilization Division, the Adopt-A-People Clearinghouse, the New Zealand Centre for Mission Direction.

With all this input, your fellowship is certain to have found at least one unreached people group needing your care. If not, simply pick a name of a group out of a hat! Seriously, one exciting linkup with an unreached people came as a result of jotting several unreached people groups' names on slips of paper, tossing them into a hat, and drawing one out. God has mysterious ways His wonders to perform!

After your time-consuming building-the-vision stage, do not spend more than 90 days deliberating which unreached people to adopt. Some churches' action plans have stagnated for more than a year while members nitpick about various unreached peoples. Imagine stepping onto an accident scene with hundreds wounded, and then spending hours deliberating about whom to help first!

## 2. Aim! Prepare for commitment.

- Pray.
- Link up with a mission society who will partner with your involvement. If your favorite mission society resists such an active partnership with a local church, encourage them to change their policy, or find an agency that is moving with this strategic trend instead of against it.
- Organize; choose a focus-on-a-people coordinator and team—usually from the ranks of your monthly mission fellowship.
- Expand your networks to other agencies and churches as well as secular organizations dealing with your adopted people.
- Research. Link up with other informal and professional researchers and information sources to compile a clear picture of God's heart for this people group. Prayerful research will guide you toward
  - Key prayer points for your people group.
  - Strategic approaches to reaching your people.
- Establish communication lines—between other churches and agencies reaching your people, between workers on the field and your church, and within the church so prayer information and insight is regularly, efficiently exchanged.

## 3. Fire! Focus on a people.

- Pray.
- Form a survey team to bring back videos and firsthand information and insights. Include your church leadership on this trip.
- Determine your commitment level. What you'll do, how much you'll give financially, whether you'll help send a team, how long you'll be involved—all these possible involvements are yours to decide since adopting a people is simply an idea, not a program.
- Plan specific action steps (with target dates) toward those commitments.
- Host a formal "adoption service," a time of signing as a group a

covenant to focus on your people group.

- Fasten your seat belts!

Your fellowship can look forward to rejoicing together with at least some representatives of that people—since sometime and somehow, they will be part of the crowd of every people, tribe, tongue, and nation before the throne of the Lamb!

## A Dose of Realism

Seeing a fellowship mobilized could be a five- to ten-year process, depending upon where they are beginning. Make sure you will be in this for the long haul. Included in the Appendix is a suggested time line for taking a church that does not have any global vision all the way to adopting an unreached people. Some steps may not be applicable to your fellowship. Look it over and prayerfully see which goals would apply to you, and what kind of time frame it could take.

Whether it's implementing a comprehensive training program or adopting a people, releasing a flood of funding or sending a mission team, acting on the vision of God's heart for every people is the measurable objective of mobilization.

## Beyond the Local Church

Finally, when things start to happen in your church, don't keep it to yourself. Join with others in your area to form a local mission task force. You can

- Pray.
- Get a local mission task force manual downloaded from the Genesys computer network (see Electronic Linkup in Resources section).
- Publicize local prayer groups' schedules and infuse into those prayer groups global prayer requests and praises.
- Feed breakthrough news to your local Christian radio stations and newspaper religion page editor.
- Encourage local Christian book shops to feature evangelism and mission materials.
- Promote area-wide Concerts of Prayer, Marches for Jesus, Perspectives courses, mission seminars. (Details and contact numbers available for such activities on the Genesys system.)

- Promote the adoption of a "sister city" from a list of the world's least evangelized cities, and the adoption of a particular unreached people that many churches in your area could focus on.

## Small Ambitions?

Whether you're a goer, a welcomer, a sender, a mobilizer, or a plumber with a heart for God, encourage others around you to a new vision of God's heart for the world. Stay connected with others in your area who are doing the same, and be sure to tie in with the national mission movements happening across the globe. It's time to think big. It's time to see how the events of your personal life are inextricably linked to events in Aqtau, Kazakhstan, or KwaZulu, South Africa—because you're part of a body that's flexing its muscles in a new sense of boldness worldwide.

Hundreds of years ago, the great French missionary Francis Xavier was dying. From establishing communities of believers in India (that are to this day thriving) to founding Christian education in Japan, this man of God had come to China. But as he awaited permission to begin ministry, he fell ill. A friend whispered to the great man lying thousands of miles from home, "Francis. . . . O that you could return home to Paris."

Xavier whispered back, "O Paris. If I could but be in Paris again! I would walk the streets of the city through the day and into the night. In the darkness I would swing my lantern and call out to the students on every street, 'Give up your small ambitions!' "

For the sake of the Name, give up small ambitions. For the night is coming when none of us will work anymore.

Run with the vision!

# Afterword

*"Give thanks to the LORD;*
*Call on His name.*
*Make known His deeds among the peoples;*
*Make them remember that His name is exalted.*
*Praise the LORD in song, for He has done excellent things;*
*Let this be known throughout the earth."*

—Isaiah 12:4–5

STUNG TRENG — Clusters of blossoms hang like grenades in the foliage. The vice-director's daughter has finally died. There were rumors of another robbery on board the Mekong River boat from Phnom Penh. And in the midst of a three-hour downpour that smells of mold and frogs, Christine sits under a tin-roof canopy getting her hair permed. Welcome to Cambodia.

Christine tries to smile genuinely through the heavy rain at members of the crowd—twenty Khmer children, several gaunt women, and a bald old man with no teeth—all of whom laugh and grin happily at Christine, wrapped in her bright yellow salon cloak, her short hair disappearing into perming rods. Her tiny, tough hairdresser spits into the rain, challenging the drenched crowd to keep its distance as they mull through the quagmire of the main street. Christine simply, sadly smiles.

Perhaps she can't forget—as every missionary in Cambodia can't forget—the searing images of the stories they've heard. Like the British sea captain who stood a few years ago on the Gulf of Tonkin's rocky beach, feeling what the Old Testament prophets felt when they wept aloud and tore their garments in anguish. Half-eaten bodies of hundreds of Cambodian boat people were washing up on the beach, bodies mostly of women and children, robbed and abused by pirates, then thrown overboard to the sharks.

The village where Christine lived was a sort of medical aid headquarters to the slowly healing Cambodian countryside. Just this morning the vice-director of the health school had sent a messenger to Christine with a carefully typed note: "Can you come speak with me?"

Christine was busy briefing a newly arrived short-term evangelistic team of Khmer youth, teenagers whose families had fled to Australia years before. The group had recently graduated from a YWAM Khmer Discipleship Training School in their new hometown of Sydney, and now they had come to the land of their cultural heritage to proclaim Jesus Christ. Finding a substitute to brief the Khmer/Aussie team, Christine and two others from the health-care ministry took each other's hands, stood just inside the black screen door of the clinic, and prayed, "Lord, it's time for this man. Give us wisdom."

The hot blue sky suddenly turned charcoal gray, and the day's monsoon water began pouring over them as they waded through the mud to the vice-director's office. Christine stood in the rain on the veranda and resignedly swabbed off the worst of the mud from her shoes. Then, in soggy socks, she slipped inside the door to sit in a cool cane chair before the desk of this sad man in his crisp white shirt.

"Thank you for coming," he said. "And I want to thank you for what you have done here. My baby. . ." He coughed, pushed back from the desk, and crossed his arms in his lap. His baby had been twelve years old. "My baby's life was preserved for several months because you gave your blood."

Christine looked at the floor. The funeral of this man's daughter fell only a day after the funeral of a young man murdered just five days after his commitment to follow Jesus Christ.

He continued: "All of my life since I was a little child, I have wanted to know the true God. I was Buddhist because my father was Buddhist, and his father before him. I was taught I had no soul, that there was no God. I remember looking into the sky over our village temple, seeing the spire of that pointed into heaven, into nothing. I was nothing, and if I could endure the dream of this life of pain, I may again become nothing, as the tip of the golden temple spire, after rung upon rung, vanishes into the air." He again cleared his throat. "Then came the killing fields."

Christine's studies of Cambodia's Khmer people had, of course, included weeping through their recent history. After centuries of invasion by the Thai, the Vietnamese, the Japanese—and then four more recent years of hell, when communism invaded their thick jungles—the Khmer flinch at nearly everything, like abused foster children. In 1975, the demons in a madman named Pol Pot experimented with a shortcut to worker's utopia promised by communism.

Karl Marx had foretold that when the deadly ruling-class died off and the mindless middle-class finally disappeared, a true workers' paradise would emerge. Pol Pot decided to fast-forward through the century what this process would normally take by simply and immediately exterminating the upper- and middle-classes of Cambodian society. Bodies piled in the streets of every town and village in the country as anyone who wore glasses, any shopkeeper, anyone with an education, any nonmilitary leader, anyone not liked by the military or by rural peasants was mutilated by machete, or stood in lines of hundreds and was blasted backward by machine-gun fire into ditches become graves—"the killing fields." Everyone remembers. Everyone lost someone. No one kept count, but two million Khmer people, perhaps, were slaughtered during the Pol Pot regime. When the Vietnamese invaded to set up a puppet government in 1979, the capital, Phnom Penh—once a bustling city of one million—was populated by 75 survivors.

Christine took another deep breath. Over the years she has come to love this smiling, spirit-fearing people. The vice-director continued: "I now know that it was God who spared my life in those years. And I know it was God who spared my daughter's life for several more months. He was saving her from her leukemia through your blood. Thank you three for the many blood donations you gave to my lovely baby.

"And I finally understand what you mean when you say that Jesus as God in a body gave His blood to save the Khmer. To save me. I understand your purpose here. You are making the true God of the heavens visible. Thank you."

Now Christine Yates snaps from her reverie as three tiny women compete to pluck the perming rods from her hair. The strong smell of the ammonia wafts away into the cool rain to the crowd of Khmer that God loves so deeply. She smiles again, imagining the opening lines of her prayer letter home to Clitheroe, Lancastershire: "Now the vice-director, along with about 40 others, have been soundly saved during this last week alone! To God be the glory!"

———

Why is the world such an evil place, a world of suffering for so many? Because Satan and his demons have decided to live an existence of absolute evil. Because so many humans decide also on a life of evil. Because the accumulation of evil affects even the natural world.

And where is God? Why give thanks and call on His name in all this evil and its consequence of suffering?

Because He is here. He is the Redeemer. And He answers through His people. Through you.

> May God be gracious to you
> And bless you;
> And cause His face to shine upon you
> That His way may be known on the earth,
> His salvation among all nations. Selah.

The Authors:
Bob Sjogren
Frontiers
325 North Stapley Drive
Mesa, AZ 85203 USA

Bill & Amy Stearns
World Christian
Box 1010
Colorado Springs, CO 80901 USA

# Appendix

*You're Hired!*

Human resource experts suggest that for an organization to determine where or if a worker fits its staffing qualifications, the organization has to be crystal clear on its mission. Then it looks at the how-to—the tasks—of that mission statement. The tasks determine what skills and aptitudes are needed in the ideal employee. Then, finally, the degree to which an applicant demonstrates those needed skills and aptitudes determines whether he or she should be hired.

The fact that we're workers in our Father's Family business might allow us to use the same criterion in establishing our role as a goer or welcomer—or disproving our presumption that we're a goer-welcomer. Needless to say, our exercise won't be exhaustive or "thus-saith-the-Lord" accurate. There are days' and weeks' worth of considerations in this life-determining field; there are extensive diagnostic psychological tests you can pursue; there are thousands of cross-cultural experiences you can live through to help determine your niche in The Plan. But let's at least consider some basics to see where you fit.

## The Tasks

First, the mission of our enterprise is clear: We're in the business of seeing the blessing of redemption in Jesus Christ—in the fullness of the meaning of that blessing—offered to every people group on earth, including our own, reached peoples, and the unreached.

The tasks of the stage-three and stage-four phases of that mission require ministering in people groups other than our own. These cross-cultural tasks require workers who will be sent, who will go. What are those tasks?

Tom Steffen in *Passing the Baton* lists several practical tasks that outline the work of a church planter and to a large extent a pre-evangelism worker and an enabler to an established church in another culture. Envision yourself

- Studying the culture
- Studying the language
- Working with a team
- Building cultural (within the mission team) and cross-cultural relationships
- Leading culturally and cross-culturally
- Training culturally and cross-culturally
- Teaching the Bible and other subjects culturally and cross-culturally
- Mediating conflict culturally and cross-culturally
- Living/working/traveling in a possibly different climate
- Developing contextualized curricula
- Assessing demographics, making surveys
- Strategizing, implementing, evaluating
- Updating supporters
- Maintaining personal/family spirituality
- Mediating between government and society
- Dealing with subversives
- Building, repairing
- Providing basic medical assistance
- Changing roles constantly

## Qualifications for the Tasks

Requirements for serving as a goer include (not in any order of priority)

- Physical vitality
- Cross-cultural adaptability

- An ability to communicate
- Functional intelligence
- An ability to plan, with a goal/performance orientation
- An ability to take leadership, to demonstrate submissive leadership
- An ability to train using discipling, nurturing skills
- An ability to follow
- Evidence of a high level of spiritual maturity—usually demonstrated in emotional/mental/relational endurance
- Evidence of a high level of psychological maturity
- Evidence of concern for others' survival skills, vocational skills, and practical skills.[1]

We're obviously listing ideals here. We must be realistic about the fact that no one is perfect. If you're too perfect you may have a hard time fitting into other cultures, anyway. An example of the ideal of physical vitality being set aside is a paraplegic, whose physical immobility doesn't detract from his reputation as one of the most effective missionaries in Colombia! So don't disqualify yourself if you don't meet these ideal qualifications perfectly.

The Center for Organizational and Ministry Development in Southern California (see Organizations under Resources) has developed a profile that looks at the desirable qualifications for the specific missionary role of church planting. A church planter is

- A person of faith and prayer
- Committed to personal holiness
- A Kingdom builder
- A sovereignly submissive planner
- A servant leader
- Psychologically mature
- An effective communicator
- Maintaining a Christ-centered family

But how do you start seeing yourself in these tasks and qualifications? You take a series of self-tests.

## The Unfortunately Unreliable Self-Test

Until conclusively proven wrong, you're predisposed to consider yourself as a goer in God's great economy, right? (Keep reasserting that unconventional attitude!) The way to confirm that role is to ask whether you actually have the qualities we've listed.

And here is where we have to get ridiculously subjective, since the only one reading this book right now is you! You'll have to explore in your own life the evidences of those goer-qualities listed above. What may make this exercise especially skewed is your current image of yourself. That is, if you are feeling committed to Jesus Christ—regardless if that's a false feeling or not, you will tend to answer that, yes, you are highly committed to Christ.

But maybe you can circumvent some of that self-image self-talk and perhaps see yourself as others see you in this thought-question exercise. You can do this by attempting to answer these questions on the basis of your observable behavior—not on what you think of yourself, but on what you actually do that others would be able to observe. Give yourself a thorough pop quiz: Do you evidence the qualities of a goer?

*My Commitment*

1. Do I evidence a high commitment to God?
2. What steps have I taken toward living out my commitment to serve in God's Family Business?
3. What are my long-range plans? How do they correspond to God's long-range Plan?
4. What could stop me from living out my commitment to ministering in the name of Jesus Christ?
5. Do others confirm my commitment to ministry?
6. Who are my spiritual heroes? Why?

*My Spiritual Maturity*

1. Am I an anxious person?
2. What biblical principles are evident in my actions?
3. Have others seen evidence of the fruit of the Spirit in me?
4. Do I expect God's intervention in my life?
5. How do I react when I sin?
6. Does thankfulness characterize my life?
7. Do I encourage others into roles that develop their ministry gifts and skills?

*Managed Household/Singleness*

1. (If married:) Do I show respect for my spouse? Do I encourage

his or her spiritual, emotional, and intellectual growth?
2. Does my spouse show respect for me?
3. (If children:) Is there evidence our children fear either of us?
4. Are we overprotective of our children?
5. Is the fruit of the Spirit evident in our home life?
6. (If single:) How do I handle my singleness?
7. Do I see God's sovereignty in my singleness?
8. How do I find fulfillment in the growth and development of others?

*Psychological Maturity*

1. Do I focus on the past?
2. How do I handle group activities?
3. How tolerant am I of others? Am I a team player?
4. Do I encourage others to grow psychologically? Am I jealous of maturity in others?
5. Am I teachable? Or do I get defensive?
6. Do I rate my self-worth on the basis of competition?
7. Am I moody?
8. Do I have a balanced self-image?
9. Do I take risks?

*Evangelistic Experience*

1. How do I define the Gospel?
2. Do I pray for opportunities to witness?
3. Am I adaptable in how I present the Gospel?
4. Have I witnessed to someone in another culture? What problems did I encounter?
5. Do people like to talk with me?
6. What is my track record in witnessing and leading people to Christ?
7. Have I ever been involved in a team evangelistic effort? How did it work out?
8. Have I successfully trained others to witness?

*Discipleship Experience*

1. Who disciples me?
2. Do people look to me for spiritual advice and/or encouragement?

3. How adept am I at discerning a person's spiritual need?
4. Do I try to enhance my discipleship abilities?
5. Do I rebuke my friends when that is necessary?
6. Can I name those whose faith grew because of my interaction with them? Have they gone on to disciple others?

## International Political Awareness

1. When was the last time I voted?
2. How do I react to critiques of capitalism? Marxism? Liberation Theology? My culture's Christianity? My race?
3. Can I articulate the strengths and weaknesses of capitalism? Marxism? Liberation Theology?
4. Do I know the class structure in relation to the various ideologies?
5. How willing am I to train nationals so they can lead the churches? Am I a team player?
6. Is there evidence of uncritiqued (from a biblical perspective) capitalistic values in me?
7. How do I keep current on political affairs?
8. Do I work to delineate biblical Christianity from my culture's adaptations or veerings from truly biblical Christianity?

## Empathetic Contextual Skills

1. Have I effectively taught children?
2. Have I effectively taught adults?
3. Do I show a desire to learn other languages and cultures?
4. (If you have worked with people in another culture:) What problems did I encounter? How did I handle them?
5. Am I aware of my own style of leadership/followership? Am I willing to adapt them?
6. When in a group, do I listen respectfully to others? Do I observe nonverbal cues from others?
7. Do I show Jesus Christ to others in my methodology?

## Servant Leader/Follower

1. Do I have a mentor? Is he or she willing to be a follower?
2. Do my questions cut to the heart of the issue?
3. Do I take initiative in situations calling for leadership?
4. How do I handle competition? Am I a team player?

5. Do I willingly delegate responsibilities to others?
6. How do I handle conflict? Do I listen to others?
7. Am I an effective steward of my personal finances?
8. Do I show a hunger to learn from anyone?
9. Do I show a willingness to change roles so others can grow?

## Adaptability

1. Am I resilient?
2. Am I sociologically mobile? That is, can I be content in a different economic and social bracket from that in which I grew up or am in now? (If married:) Is this true of my spouse?
3. Am I a perfectionist? Do I demand it of others?
4. How have I handled separation from my extended family? (If married:) How has my spouse handled this?
5. What is my opinion of ethnic groups? My opinion of working on a team with other ethnic groups? (If married:) What is my spouse's opinion?
6. Am I controlled by cleanliness? time? food preferences? privacy? orderliness? (If married:) Is my spouse?
7. Am I willing to give up my rights so others can be reached?
8. Can I let go of things, people, relationships?

## Physical Vitality

1. Am I disciplined in the area of physical conditioning?
2. How often am I sick?
3. Do I participate in a personal exercise program?
4. When was the last time I took a vacation? For how long?
5. Do I make it a habit to eat a balanced diet?
6. Do I make it a habit to get sufficient rest?
7. Do I delegate when the workload is heavy?
8. Have I experienced burnout? What were the circumstances?

## Basic Medical Skills

1. Am I willing to learn basic hygiene and first-aid skills?
2. Am I capable of transferring my knowledge of hygiene, first aid, and medicine to others?

## Support

1. If I stepped into the role of a goer, do I have a base of senders who would support me in moral, financial, and prayer support?
2. Do I trust God to meet my daily needs?
3. Do I view "living by faith" as unrealistic?
4. Do I emotionally equate security with having money?
5. For the sake of my possible cross-cultural ministry, am I willing to face the fear of asking others for financial support?
6. Are others growing in their faith because of my example?
7. Am I willing to work extra hard to get completely out of debt so I can serve in the role of a goer? Why or why not?

## What Will Others Ask?

How are you doing in these self-testing thought questions? Are you a goer or welcomer? Of course, your potential as a missionary isn't simply up to you to determine. Others can help you evaluate your qualifications.

For example, below is a list of questions a mission agency or church mission committee would ask you before encouraging you in the direction of cross-cultural ministry. This particular list of questions is designed to help determine a person's potential as a tentmaking goer. It's adapted from the Tentmaker Research Evaluation Profile. If you'd like to get a professional assessment of your qualifications as a goer, contact TMR Research, 312 Melcanyon Road, Duarte, CA 91010 USA. Imagine yourself being asked:

What is your understanding of the scope, purpose, and strategy of God's plan for world missions?

What is the highest level of education you have completed?

How much experience have you had in your professional field?

What is the highest level of formal Christian training you have completed?

In your church activities, do you tend to be involved
   a. as a recognized leader
   b. as an active participant
   c. by attending, but without participation
   d. sporadically
   e. not at all

In your outside-the-church activities (business or social groups), do you tend to be involved

a. as a recognized leader
b. as an active participant
c. by attending, but without participation
d. sporadically
e. not at all

What best characterizes your interest in being sent as a goer or a welcomer across cultural lines to minister?
a. I have specific plans to go.
b. I would really like to go, but currently have no specific plans.
c. I am open to the idea, and I'm actively investigating.
d. I am not interested in going.
e. None of the above or don't know.

How would you characterize your relationship with God?
a. intimate and personal
b. occasional
c. one-sided
d. distant and anxious
e. none of the above or don't know

How would you characterize your attitude toward God?
a. a fiery zeal for His purposes
b. obedience, submission, and intimacy with Him
c. an on-again-off-again type of relationship with many ups and downs
d. somewhat impersonal or distant
e. none of the above or don't know

Which best characterizes you?
a. Much of the time I have an abiding fear of failure.
b. Much of the time I think about and fear physical or emotional pain.
c. I usually avoid people, because I fear hurt or rejection.
d. Guilt weighs heavily upon me, so I fear acute depression.
e. I don't seem to have debilitating fears.

What best characterizes your reaction to extremely stressful situations?
a. My lack of resources to cope most often leads me to depression.
b. I tend to block the problems from my mind in order to function.
c. I usually seek God for help and direction.
d. I usually avoid God and seek out friends and associates.
e. None of the above or don't know.

How often do you share your faith in Christ?

a. share Christ on many occasions with others
b. occasionally share Christ with others
c. seldom share Christ with others
d. almost never share Christ with others
e. never share Christ with others

How effective are your abilities in personal evangelism?
a. lead people to Christ on many occasions
b. occasionally lead people to Christ
c. seldom lead people to Christ
d. almost never lead people to Christ
e. never lead people to Christ

In what ways are you involved in Christian activities?
a. usually in an event, or programmed format (For example, I only seem to be involved in Christian activities at church-based meetings.)
b. in a repetitive regimen (For example, I visit the hospital every Thursday.)
c. on a free-form "needs" basis as the opportunity presents itself
d. in a role-developed basis (For example, I minister due to my job as a minister.)
e. on an active-pursuit basis, seeking out opportunities of ministry

When with a new group of people, do you tend to spend most of your time
a. validating who you are to them
b. seeking their point of view
c. defending your point of view
d. looking for their approval
e. accommodating to their position

How would you characterize your daily activities?
a. I live a dual role—one secular and one Christian.
b. I live a Christian lifestyle that leaves me sometimes feeling ill-at-ease around "secular" people.
c. Although I feel a tension between the secular and Christian world, I function at ease in both.
d. I sense no tension between secular and Christian worlds.
e. none of the above or don't know

What do you enjoy most?
a. managing projects
b. project-oriented, technical endeavors

c. managing people

d. one-to-one people contact

e. none of the above or don't know

Don't you hate idealistic self-tests? Obviously no one comes through even a cursory self-exam unscathed: If we say we have no shortcomings, "we deceive ourselves, and the truth is not in us" (1 John 1:8). So because you may not have felt proud of your goer-welcomer qualifications as you plodded through those thought questions—or especially if you did feel proud of yourself—never regard this subjective exercise as the sole determining factor in your destiny as a cross-cultural laborer.

# Resources

## Children's Resources

Arapesh to Zuni
A Book about Bibleless Peoples
Wycliffe Bible Translators
P.O. Box 2727
Huntington Beach, CA 92647

Children's Missions Resource Center, Gerry Dueck
1605 Elizabeth St., Pasadena, CA 91104
(818) 398-2236
Periodic free newsletter on mission materials and resource people available. She is revising her out-of-print *Kids for the World: A Guidebook to Children's Resources.*

Crossroads Publications, Ruth Finley
P.O. Box 111475, Campbell CA 95011
(408) 378-6658
Eight true-story missions curriculum available, eight- to ten-part stories, some expandable to thirteen lessons. Pakistan, China, Romania, India, Liberia, Malaysia, and Guatemala.

Destination 2000 Teacher's Training Curriculum—a video series designed to show teachers how to teach missions to kids in a fun, exciting way. (Frontiers: 1–800–60–SERVE).

International Clothing Closet/Self Help
704 Main St. Box L, Akron, PA 17501
(717) 859–4971
No cost for using the ethnic clothing: you pay shipping. Crafts may be purchased direct or on consignment.

Kids Can Make a Difference, Jan Bell
4445 Webster Drive, York, PA 17402
(717) 757–6793 Fax (717) 757–6103
Resource catalog of the best and newest missions materials available. Author of "Missions Brought to You by the Letter P."

Monarch Publishing, Bev Gundersen
245 Second Ave. N.E., Milaca, MN 56353
(612) 983–2398
Bev has written over 40 Christian Education and Missions books for kids. Her latest curriculum is: *World Focus*, which is a mini-Perspectives course for grades one through six.

Peters Projection Map—Available through *Destination 2000*, 1–800–60–SERVE

*You Can Change the World*, Jill Johnson
Available at Christian Book Stores and through *Destination 2000*.

## Videos

*The 10/40 Window for Children*—6 minutes.
Joey and Fawn Parish
6673 Sora Street
Ventura, CA 93003
(805) 650–3511

The videos below are available from Kids Can Make a Difference (see Children's Resources).

*God's Kaleidoscope*—12 minutes
Wycliffe Bible Translators

*Carlos of Colombia*—10 minutes.
   Colombia
*Kambari*—22 minutes.
   Nigeria
*Malay Kids*—10 minutes.
   Malaysia
*Patna Kids*—10 minutes.
   North India

The *Ee-taow* videos can be purchased from
   New Tribes Missions
   1000 E. First Street
   Sanford, FL 32771–1487
   (407) 323–3430
*Ee-taow*
*Ee-taow* sequel—*The Next Chapter*

The following video can be purchased through
   Wycliffe Bible Translators International
   P.O. Box 2727
   Huntington Beach, CA 92647
   (714) 969–4600
   FAX (714) 969–4661
*Word Like a River*

## Games, Crafts, and Recipes

*Fun Around the World*
   New Hope Publishing, Birmingham, AL
   Games, crafts, food, and dress ideas.
   Available from Kids Can Make a Difference (see Children's Resources).

*Guess What I Made?*
   New Hope Publishing, Birmingham, AL
   Recipes from around the world.
   Available from Kids Can Make a Difference (see Children's Resources).

*International Playtime*
   Filled with hundreds of games and dances from around the world.
   Available from Kids Can Make a Difference (see Children's Resources).

## Cultural Activities for Children

ARTISTIC EXPRESSION
Have the children make a craft from another land. Learn a folk dance. Play a game using ethnic music. Have a musician come in and demonstrate instruments from other parts of the world.

FOOD
Have the children prepare a dish from another country. Visit an ethnic grocery store (Asian, Middle Eastern, Indian) the children can see the different foods and smell all the smells. Bring in food from different ethnic restaurants for the children to taste.

LANGUAGE
Learn a song in another language. Learn to write their names in another language. Listen to a tape of someone speaking in a foreign tongue. Look at the Bible in different scripts.

SHELTER AND DRESS
Have the children try on clothes from other countries. Have an international friend come in and show traditional dress in their country. Build a storefront grass hut.

## Electronic Linkup

Brigada is an automated mission update service that comes to your (or a friend's) E-mail address weekly at no cost. Type "subscribe brigada" in a message to "hub @ XC.org" and you are signed up!

Global Glimpse is an electronic service of Caleb Project. It delivers weekly key breakthroughs to your E-mail address. Send a message to "jhanna @ cproject.com" to sign up.

The Genesys Computer Network is a key ongoing resource that can keep you updated on all of the best materials, opportunities, breakthroughs. Routed through British Telecom and MCI, the system has convenient local connections in hundreds of locations worldwide.

Unreached people information: Find someone with a computer and modem and have them tap into the People Group Consultant database of info on people groups. Your computer wizard can send a simple message of "Search _____" (Fill in the people group's name. Don't use quote marks.) to hub@xc.org or, if your friend can access the World Wide Web, he or she can call up http://www.xc.org/pgc.html to get the WWW homepage of the People Group Consultant.

Here are some of the things you can do on-line:

- Get updates of what God is doing under Global Reports.
- Learn what critical body-wide prayer needs are posted today.

- Watch for answers to those prayer requests coming from Kathmandu, Korea, or Carlisle.

- Exchange ideas with mission mobilizers worldwide.

- Read descriptions and sources of the latest mission materials.

- Download lists of unreached people groups—which need more research done for prayer bulletins, which have been "adopted" by churches and which have not.

- Track contact numbers of mission agencies, service organizations, and key individuals.

- Pick out opportunities for short- and long-term mission ministry.

- Get key articles and Bible studies you can use to encourage new vision in fellowships.

- Review case studies of churches and campus groups who are growing in new mission vision.

Send or phone for information on how you or a computer whiz you know can link you up into this Christian, nonprofit network: Genesys, 3686 King St., Suite 182, Alexandria, VA 22302 (703/750–0318; fax 703/658–0077)

## Materials and Courses

Videos, tapes, entire catalogs, and order sheets of similar items are available through hundreds of mission agencies and associations, and through mission service sources such as

- William Carey Library in the USA
  P.O. Box 40129
  Pasadena, CA 91114 USA
  (In USA: 800-MISSION or 818/798–0819; fax 818/794–0477)

- The Centre for Mission Direction
  P.O. Box 31146
  Ilam, Christchurch, New Zealand
  (0 3 342 7711; fax 0 3 342 8410)

- The Target 2000 Office in England
  Youth With A Mission
  13 Highfield Oval, Ambrose Lane

Harpendon, Herts AL5 4BX England
(0582 765481; fax 0582 765489)

The following are a few of the materials that can help you and your church run with new vision:

*Catch the Vision 2000* book (Bethany House) and *Leader's Study Guide* (World Christian, Inc.) by Bill and Amy Stearns. A book-based study course for individuals and small groups. Order from your local Christian bookstore or through William Carey Library (contact numbers above).

*Destination 2000* video course, audio-tape course (Frontiers) or in book form as *Unveiled at Last* (YWAM Publications) by Bob Sjogren. An overview of the biblical basis of God's global enterprise. The sharp video study is particularly designed for small groups and Bible classes. Contact Frontiers, (address under Organizations) or order from your local Christian bookstore.

*FrontierScan.* Monthly bulletin inserts focused on the world's remaining unreached peoples. Order through the Global Prayer Digest offices of the U.S. Center for World Mission (address under Publications).

*The Great Comission Handbook* is the annual reference guide to mission groups and opportunities. Order bulk quantities from Berry Publishing Services, Inc., 701 Main St., Evanston, IL 60202 USA (708/869–1573; fax: 708/869–4825).

*Heart of God Ministries*, (3500 N.W. 50th, Oklahoma City, OK 73112, (405) 943–8581, FAX (405) 943–8604) is a new nondenominational mission agency that focuses on three emphases to increase the mission force in the 10/40 Window. They offer a three-hour Heart of God Seminar, a Bible study showing how God desires all peoples to come to Jesus. HGM also features teaching and preaching on the call of God to revive the Church. The third emphasis is a five-month training institute called Beautiful Feet Boot Camp, which prepares missionaries to go to the unreached peoples of the world.

*Living Proof* video series is available at NavPress, 7899 Lexington Drive, P.O.Box 6000, Colorado Springs, CO 80922. (719) 598–1212; (800) 366–7788; FAX (719) 598–7128.

"Missing Faces in the Worldwide Picture." An information-packed activity packet for a one-Sunday emphasis on the final tasks of the Great Commission. Contact Evangelical Missionary Alliance at Whitefield House, 186 Kennington Park Road, London SE11 4BT (071/ 735–0421).

*Perspectives on the World Christian Movement* is a life-changing course driving you through the biblical, historical, cultural, and strategic aspects of God's global plan. Contact the Perspectives Study Program for locations of extension courses and information on resident courses in Pasadena and the personal correspondence-course format for individual study. Write or call through the Perspectives Office, U.S. Center for World Mission (under Organizations).

*Serving As Senders* book and course (Emmaus Road Intl., OM Publishing). A simple, very effective eight-session study for sending teams, by Neal Pirolo. Order from your local Christian book shop or Emmaus Road International (under Organizations).

*Vacationing With a Purpose* book and leader's guide (David C. Cook Publishing Co.). A clear, effective guide to maximizing short-term ministry, by Chris Eaton and Kim Hurst. Order through your local Christian bookstore.

*A View From on High* (Caleb Project). A one-service, easily performed drama depicting the big picture of God's heart for every people written by J. Reed Randall and Caleb Project staff. Contact Caleb Project, 10 West Dry Creek Circle, Littleton, CO 80120 USA (303/730–4170).

*World Christian Display Table*. A broad package of books and brochures ideal for regular set-up in your church foyer. Contact William Carey Library (contact numbers p. 265).

*The World Christian* workbook (Lynx) by Robin Thompson can be studied individually or as a small group. Designed for young people particularly in the U.K., the book is slanted toward goers/welcomers, but is key for any mission-minded activist anywhere! Order through St. John's Extension Studies, Bramcote, Nottingham NG9 3DS England (0602 251117).

## Publications

The following are key publications for any serious goer/welcomer, sender, or mobilizer. Add to the list as many denominational, faith mission, and parachurch periodicals as you and your reading-research team can handle (see pp. 271–272). Be sure to include publications from cultures, countries, and church traditions with which you would otherwise have no communication link.

ACMC *Update* newsletter, PO Box ACMC, Wheaton, IL 60189–8000 USA. Helpful hints and strategies for church mission task forces.

AIMS newsletter, PO Box 64534, Virginia Beach, VA 23464 USA. Organizational; mission tips and strategies for renewal churches.

*AD 2000 Global Monitor*, PO Box 1219, Rockville, VA 23146 USA. Concise statistical analyses of secular and Christian data; also reviews of relevant articles.

*Asian Church Today/Church Around Asia*, 803/92 Deepali, Nehru Place, New Delhi, 100019, India. Good, non-Western look at what is happening in the Church in Asia.

*Asian Report*, PO Box 9000, Mision Viejo, CA 92690 USA, or Asian Outreach, GPO Box 3448, Hong Kong. Good overviews of what is happening in Southeast Asia, China, and the Pacific Rim.

*Centre for Mission Direction Newsletter*, PO Box 31–146, Christchurch 8030, New Zealand. Newsletter for mobilizers, reviewing the latest mission resources and opportunities for short-term service.

*Christian Mission*, 3045 Ivy Road, Charlottesville, VA 22903 USA. A sample of the many Western mission society periodicals with good information on the non-Western mission force.

*Church Around the World* (bulletin insert), Tyndale House Publishers, 336 Gunderson Dr., Wheaton, IL 60187 USA. Bulletin-insert sized, paragraph breakthroughs and prayer requests.

*DAWN Report*, DAWN Ministries, 7899 Lexington Dr., Suite 200B, Colorado Springs, CO 80920 USA. Reports of progress in the "discipling a whole nation" movement around the world.

EP News Service, 1619 Portland Ave., Minneapolis, MN 55404 USA. Journalism at its best!

*Evangelical Missions Quarterly*, PO Box 794, Wheaton, IL 60189 USA. Thought-provoking articles on relevant mission topics.

*Evangelical World*, PO Box WEF, Wheaton, IL 60189 USA. Regular report from World Evangelical Fellowship.

*Global Prayer Digest*, 1605 Elizabeth St., Pasadena, CA 91104 USA. Daily prayer guide for unreached peoples; monthly.

*IFMA News*, PO Box 398, Wheaton, IL 60189–0398 USA. Quarterly report on the Interdenominational Foreign Missions Association.

*India Church Growth Quarterly*, Post Bag No. 768, Kilpauk, Madras, 600100 India. Excellent source for what is happening in the Indian Church.

*International Bulletin of Missionary Research*, PO Box 821, Farmingdale, NY 11727–9721 USA. Quarterly research for scholars and serious researchers.

*International Journal of Frontier Missions*, 1539 E. Howard St., Pasadena, CA 91104 USA. Frontier missions quarterly with thought-provoking articles.

*Latin America Evangelist*, PO Box 52–7900, Miami, FL 33152. USA. Organizational overviews from Latin America Mission.

MARC newsletter, 919 W. Huntington Dr., Monrovia, CA 91016 USA. Good information for researchers from the Mission Advance Research Center of World Vision.

*Mission Frontiers*, 1605 Elizabeth St., Pasadena, CA 91104 USA. Bulletin from the US Center for World Mission, covering important frontier mission information and trends.

*Mission Outreach*, Indian Evangelical Mission, 38 Langford Rd., Bangalore 560025 India. Reports from church planters in India.

*Missions Today*, 701 Main Street, Evanston, IL 60202 USA. Annual magazine from the publisher of the *Great Commission Handbook*.

Newswire, PO Box 1122, Wheaton, IL 60189 USA. Bi-monthly reports from eastern bloc countries.

*Operation World*, Zondervan Publishing House, 5300 Patterson S E, Grand Rapids, MI 49530. A guide to praying for the nations. Revised frequently.

*Partnership Report*, Interdev, PO Box 30945, Seattle, WA 98103 USA. Reports and advice on strategic partnerships around the world.

*Praise & Prayer*, IFES, 55 Palmerston Road, Wealdstone, Harrow, Middlesex HA3 7RR U.K. Praise items and prayer requests from the International Fellowship of Evangelical Students.

*Prayer Special & Mission*, The Evangelical Missionary Association

(TEMA), CH–1032 Romanel, Switzerland. Organizational; European alliance of mission agencies.

*Pulse*, Evangelical Missions Information Service, PO Box 794, Wheaton, IL 60189 USA. A must for anyone serious about mission information. Journalistic reports from around the world.

*World Christian Magazine*, Periodical of an association of global activists for the cause of Christ. Info on publications, resources, conferences, expeditions for world Christians. Colorado Springs office: Box 1010, Colorado Springs, CO 80901 U.S.A. (719) 634–5310; FAX (719) 634–5316. E-mail: bill.stearns @ gen.org or Compuserve 73502,3126.

*World Christian News*, PO Box 26479, Colorado Springs, CO 80936 USA. Breakthroughs and key, concise analysis that covers the world with insights from YWAM, one of the largest and most diverse mission agencies.

*World Report*, United Bible Societies (UBS), Box 755, 7000 Stuttgart 1, Germany. Reports on the spread of God's Word around the world.

For more key publications, contact the following sample list of church associations—not necessarily mission associations—to plug you into other regions of the Body of Christ worldwide. Ask to be put on their mailing lists and include a contribution.

AFRICA: AEAM, Association of Evangelicals in Africa and Madagascar, PO Box 49332, Nairobi, Kenya.

Asia: ACCF, Asia Christian Communications Fellowship, c/o CCL, PO Box 95364, Tsimshatsui, Kowloon, Hong Kong.

Brazil: AMTB, Associa de Missoes Transculturais Brasileiras, c/o CP 582, 01051—Sao Paulo, Brazil.

Hong Kong: HKACM, Hong Kong Association of Christian Missions, 525 Nathan Rd., Bell House, Block A, Flat 2003, Kowloon, Hong Kong.

India: EFI, Evangelical Fellowship of India, 92/803 Deepali, Nehru Place, New Delhi 110019 India.

Nigeria: NEMA, Nigeria Evangelical Missions Association, U.I.P.O. Box 9890, Ibadan, Oyo State Nigeria.

Philippines: PCEC, Philippine Council of Evangelical Churches, Inc., PO Box 10121, Q.C.P.O., Quezon City, 3008 The Philippines.

Singapore: EFS, Evangelical Fellowship of Singapore, #04–05, Bible

House, 7 Armenian St., Singapore 0617.
South Africa: SAAWE, Suid-Afrikaanse Aksise vir Werlde-vanagelisasle, PO Box 709, Kempton Park 1620, RSA.

## Training Helps

*Catch the Vision 2000* seminar introduces your fellowship to the big picture of God's global plan. Contact World Christian (address on previous page under World Christian Magazine).

*The Destination 2000* seminar is a sprint through the Bible to discover the exciting theme of God's plan for all peoples. Contact Frontiers, address below.

*Run With the Vision Mobilizers' Training Workshops* equip mission-minded activists to impact their fellowships with new mission vision. Contact World Christian.

*Seven Dynamics for Advancing Your Church in Missions* is a clear, effective seminar that can gear your fellowship to practical, informed mission action. Contact Larry Walker, ACMC Southwest, 1670 E. Valley Parkway, Suite 145, Escondido, CA 92027 USA (619/746–4285).

## For Goers/Welcomers

Tremendous opportunities are available in most parts of the world for goers/welcomers.

Contact your mission agency, one listed in The Great Commission Handbook, or: Global Opportunities (address under Organizations).

Any mission society will be able to refer interested goers or welcomers toward short-term or long-term training. In addition, guidance is available through specialty ministries such as

The Center for Organizational and Ministry Development. Assesses and offers training for church-planters. 120 E. La Habra Blvd., La Habra, CA 90631 USA (310/697–6144).

TMQ Research. Guides you into realistic tentmaking ministry. 312 Melcanyon Road, Duarte, CA 91010 USA.

## For Senders

Serving as Senders is the only "generic" course we're aware of that practically launches senders into their ministries—which are actually more often than not learned "on the job"! See *Serving as Senders* under Materials and Courses. Many mission societies have great resources such as brochures to coach senders in how to pray for missionaries, how to care for missionaries upon reentry.

## For Mobilizers

There is currently no formal training available for mission mobilizers. A *Run With the Vision Training Workshop for Mobilizers* (minimum time necessary is three days) is offered through World Christian.

## Organizations

Among the thousands of key ministries worldwide, the following represent those that are especially helpful in dealing with the topics presented in this book.

ACMC. Provides materials and conferences for mobilizing churches. PO Box ACMC, Wheaton, IL 60189–8000 USA (708/260–1660).

The AD2000 and Beyond Movement. This is a loose network of hundreds of organizations working in their various areas.

Adopt-A-People Clearinghouse. Monitors the status of unreached peoples in the world and helps churches link with agencies. PO Box 1795, Colorado Springs, CO 80901 USA (719/473–7630; fax: 719/473–5907).

AIMS. Provides materials and conferences for mobilizing, particularly renewal churches. Association of International Mission Services, PO Box 64534, Virginia Beach, VA 23464 USA (804/523–7979; fax: 804/523–7509).

The Antioch Network. Helps link churches which are directly active in sending their own mission teams. 7854 Nichols, Lemon Grove, CA 91945 USA.

Centre for Mission Direction. Provides generic mission awareness resources and courses—particularly in New Zealand. PO Box 31–146, Ilam 8040, Christchurch, New Zealand (0 3 342 7711; fax: 0 3 342 8410)

Centre for Mission Resources. Offers resources and various specialized training seminars, retreats, and study opportunities. Contact Tony Horsfall, Bawtry Hall, Bawtry, Doncaster DN10 6JH England (0302 710020; fax: 0302 710027).

Emmaus Road International. Provides resources, training seminars, and opportunities for goers and senders. 7150 Tanner Court, San Diego, CA 92111 USA (619/292–7020).

Evangelical Missionary Alliance. Offers topnotch materials and ideas on mission involvement. Publishes *Facts* magazine. Whitefield House, 186 Kennington Park Road, London SE11 4BT England (071 735 0421).

Frontiers. One of the world's fastest-growing mission agencies with an emphasis on reaching Muslims. U.K. offices: P.O Box 4, High Wycombe, Bucks HP14 3YX England (0494 485917); USA offices: 325 North Stapley Dr., Mesa, AZ 85203 (602/834–1500)

Global Opportunities, 1600 E. Elizabeth St., Pasadena, CA 91104, (818) 398–2393. A nondenominational service agency of evangelical tradition, providing services in mission-related research/information and missionary orientation/mobilization through tentmaker jobs referral, counseling, and other activities.

Heart of God Ministries, 3500 N.W. 50th, Oklahoma City, OK 73112, (405) 943–8581; FAX: (405) 943–8604.

InterCristo, 19303 Fremont Ave., Seattle, WA 98133 (800) 251–7740, FAX: (206) 546–7483. An interdenominational service agency of evangelical tradition, providing guidance and information to help mission agencies locate salaried, qualified personnel.

Issachar Frontier Missions Strategies, PO Box 6788, Lynnwood, WA 98036, (206) 744–0400. A transdenominational service agency of evangelical tradition engaged in mission-related research/information services and mobilization for mission by assisting local churches in strategic use of their resources for world evangelization.

ISI International Students, Inc., PO Box C, Colorado Springs, CO 80901 (719) 576–2700. This organization is located on many college campuses. It exists to share Christ's love with international students and to equip them for effective service in cooperation with the local church and others.

Target 2000 Offices of Youth With A Mission (YWAM). These offices, located within the facilities of many YWAM bases around the world, offer mission awareness resources and expertise far beyond the specific concerns of YWAM itself. Contact the international office for a Target 2000 center near you: Target 2000, YWAM, 13 Highfield Oval, Ambrose Lane, Harpendon, Herts AL5 4BX England (0582 765481; fax: 0582 765489).

U.S. Center for World Mission. Promotes *Perspectives on the World Christian Movement* courses. Publishes *Mission Frontiers* and the *Global Prayer Digest*. Offers adopt-a-people guidance through its Mobilization Division. The Mobilization Division also tracks a worldwide network of centers for world mission. Write or call with *specific information requests:* 1605 E. Elizabeth St., Pasadena, CA 91104 USA (818/797–1111; fax: 818/398–2263).

WEC, Intl. (Worldwide Evangelization for Christ) Although WEC is just one of hundreds of strategic mission agencies, it is listed here for its remarkable research office that is open to public use. Request information for permission to visit the facilities. Bulstrode, Gerrards Cross, Bucks SL9 8SZ England (0753 884631; fax: 0753 882470).

World Evangelical Fellowship (WEF). Although the many other cutting-edge mission and evangelism associations are not listed here, WEF is particularly crucial because of its global links with the two-thirds-world mission movements. WEF is your link to the evangelical alliances throughout the world. Subscribe to WEF publications, support it financially, but be very reluctant to contact WEF offices with random requests since their role is in servicing evangelical associations and mission societies rather than individuals. In the U.K.: WEF, Le Emrais, Castel, Guernsey, Channel Islands (0481 54471; fax: 0481 711052). In the USA: PO Box WEF, Wheaton, IL 60189 USA. In Singapore: 141 Middle Road, #05–05, GSM Building, Singapore 0718.

# Sources Cited

ACMC. *Networker* newsletter, October 1992.

AD2000 Unreached Peoples Resource Network newsletter, March 1993.

AEF (Asian Evangelical Fellowship) *Focus Forward* 30th anniversary special edition. Singapore, 1992.

All Nations Mobilization. *Global Report.* (Note: For an entire set including the sources for each breakthrough item, write All Nations Mobilization, Box 416, Colorado Springs, CO 80901 USA. Please include a donation for copying, shipping and handling costs.)

Arab World Ministries *Update* newsletter. No. 4, 1992.

Around the World (HCJB), Spring 1993, p. 10.

Asian Outreach. "Asia's Maturing Church," *Asian Report*, March/April 1992, pp. 6–9.

Barnes, Seth. "The Changing Face of the Missionary Force," in *Evangelical Missions Quarterly*, October 1992, pp. 376–381.

Barrett, David B. "Statistics, Global," *Dictionary of Pentecostal and Charismatic Movements*, editors Stanley M. Burgess and Gary B. McGee. Grand Rapids: Zondervan, 1988.

———. *World-Class Cities and World Evangelization.* Birmingham, AL: New Hope Publishing, 1986.

Barrett, David B. and James Reapsome. *Seven Hundred Plans to Evangelize the World.* Birmingham, AL: New Hope Publishing, 1989.

Barrett, David and Todd Johnson. *Our Globe and How to Reach It: Seeing the World Evangelized by AD2000 and Beyond.* Birmingham, AL: New Hope Publishing, 1990.

Borthwick, Paul. "A Love Affair That Must Be Cultivated Three Ways," *Evangelical Missions Quarterly*, January 1991, p. 51.

Brumbelow, Gary. "Know Thy Sending Church," *Evangelical Mission Quarterly*, January 1989, pp. 54–56.

Bryant, David. "The Most Hopeful Sign of Our Times: A Growing National Prayer Movement Points America Toward Spiritual Revival" in *Special Report from The National and International Religion Report*, Media Management, 1992.

Bush, Luis. "How Can All Peoples Be Reached by the Year 2000?" *Mission Frontiers*, Sept.-Dec. 1992, p. 57.

Carey, Keith. "Pray for Muslims in China," *Mission Frontiers*, Jan.-Mar. 1991, pp. 10–11.

*The Church Around the World*. Carol Stream, IL: Tyndale House Publishers. January 1993, p. 1.

Christudas, Bhanu, "Reaching the Hindu World," *Mission Frontiers*, Jan.-Mar. 1991, pp. 18–19.

CoMission Press Conference. ACSI Convention, Anaheim, CA, November 5, 1992. Unpublished transcript.

Conklin, Deborah. "That Ishmael Might Live Under His Blessing," *Mission Frontiers*, Jan.-Mar. 1991, pp. 14–15.

Connections Guide brochure. Christian Info, #200, 110 11th Avenue S.W., Calgary, Alberta T2R OB8 Canada.

Cunningham, Loren with Janice Rogers. *Is That Really You, God?* Seattle: Youth With A Mission Publishers, 1984.

DAWN. *DAWN Around the World* newsletter, April 1993.

Dubert, Karen. "Ten Steps to Success: The Major Themes," *Evangelical Missions Quarterly*, April 1989, pp. 156–158.

Engles, James and Jerry D. Jones. *Baby Boomers and the Future of World Missions*. Orange, CA: Management Development Associates, 1989.

Fatsis, Stefan. "Corporate Makeover," *Gazette Telegraph* of Colorado Springs, CO USA. December 27, 1992. Section E, p. 1.

*Fresh News* newsletter. US Center for World Mission, Pasadena, CA. July 30, 1992, p. 1.

Frontiers. "Testimonies of God's Tenderness," in brochure *Muslims: It's Their Turn*, 1992.

Gallup, George. *Special Report for the AD2000 & Beyond Consultation* in Phoenix, AZ, August 31, 1992. AD2000 Office, Colorado Springs, CO USA.

Giles, Greg and Jean. "Well Worth the Effort," *Africa Now, SIM*, Nov.-Dec. 1979, p. 7.

Giles, Ray. "To Fulfill the Task" in *Unto the Uttermost*, editor Doug Priest, Jr., Pasadena, CA: William Carey Library, 1984, p. 303.

Glubb, John. *The Life and Times of Muhammed*. New York: Stein and Day, 1970.

Graham, Thomas. "How to Select the Best Church Planters," *Evangelical Missions Quarterly*, January 1987, pp. 18–21.

Hamilton, Don. *The Hamilton Tentmaker Survey*. Duarte, CA: TMQ Research, 1986.

Hawthorne, Steve, editor. *Stepping Out*. Monrovia, CA: Short-Term Missions Advocates, 1987.

IMTF. *Training for Cross-Cultural Ministries* bulletin of World Evangelical Fellowship. August 1993, pp. 4–5.

Jansen, Frank Kaleb. AAP (Adopt-A-People) definitions flyer and materials relating to the Adopt-A-People Clearinghouse list of identified unreached peoples. Colorado Springs, CO.

———. A Holistic Perspective on World Mission. Unpublished manuscript, 1991.

———. "Fifteen Trends Shaping Our Future." Mission Direction, newsletter of the Centre for Mission Direction, NZ, February 26, 1994, p. 5.

Johnson, John. Book review of *Tribal and Peasant Church Planting* by Tom Steffen (Center for Organizational and Ministry Development), *Evangelical Missions Quarterly*, January 1993, p. 95.

Johnstone, Patrick. Message at the Lausanne II Congress on World Evangelization, July 1989.

Kane, Herbert. *Life and Work on the Mission Field*. Grand Rapids: Baker Book House, 1980.

Kauffman, Paul. "From Asia With Love," in *Asian Report*, Mar.-Apr. 1992, p. 3.

Keyes, Lawrence. *The Last Age of Missions*. Pasadena, CA: William Carey Library, 1983.

Kornfield, William. "What Hath Our Western Money and Our Western Gospel Wrought," *Evangelical Mission Quarterly*, July 1991.

Kwok Pui-lan. "Claiming Our Heritage: Chinese Women and Christianity" in *International Bulletin of Missionary Research*, October 1992, pp. 150–152.

Lukasse, Johan. "It Takes Team Effort to Root Churches in Hard Soil," *Evangelical Missions Quarterly*, January 1986, pp. 34–42.

McAlister, Jack. "Why Is Prayer of Supreme Importance?" Unpublished transcript of message at Nations for Christ Congress, Riga, Latvia, May 1992.

McClung, L. Grant. "The Pentecostal Trunk Must Learn From Its Branches," *Evangelical Missions Quarterly*, January 1993, p. 37.

"Milestone Dates in the Growth of True Christianity" chart. *Mission Frontiers*, Sept.- Dec. 1992, p. 4.

Miley, George. *A Vision: Churches Sending Church-Planting Teams to Unreached Peoples*. Handout at an ACMC workshop, Denver, CO, October 1992.

*Mission Frontiers*. "People Group Definitions." Jan.-Feb. 1994, p. 10.

Montgomery, Jim. *DAWN 2000: Seven Million Churches to Go*. Pasadena, CA: William Carey Library, 1989.

Morehead, Bob. "Commitment as a Christian"—a tract from Hands for Christ, Roanoke, VA USA.

Nickel, Jim. Newsletter. "Adopting Unreached Peoples: Making It Practical."

Niemeyer, Larry.

Parshall, Phil. "How Spiritual Are Missionaries?" *Evangelical Missions Quarterly*, January 1987, pp. 10–16.

Pate, Larry D. *Bridging Peoples* newsletter. July 1989.

———. *From Every People*. Monrovia, CA: MARC and OC International, 1989.

———. "The Changing Face of Global Mission," in *Perspectives on the World Christian Movement: A Reader*. Editors Ralph D. Winter and Steven C. Hawthorne. Pasadena, CA: William Carey Library, 1992.

Pike, Jeff. Target 2000 Overhead Set. Target 2000 International Office, Youth With A Mission, 1992.

284

Radio Voice of Christ unpublished letter, March 1993.

Roberts, Dayton W. and John A. Siewert, editors. *Mission Handbook, 14th Edition: USA/ Canada Protestant Ministries Overseas.* MARC & Zondervan, 1989.

Samaritan's Purse Newsletter, July 1993.

Sheffield, Robert. "CoMission Update." An unpublished memo, November 4, 1992.

Sitton, David. "To Every Tribe With Jesus," *Mission Frontiers*, Jan.-Mar. 1991, pp. 16–17.

Steffen, Tom. *Tribal and Peasant Church Planting.* La Habra, CA: Center for Organizational and Ministry Development, 1992.

Stephens, James. "Buddhist Kingdoms in a Shrinking World," *Mission Frontiers*, Jan.-Mar. 1991, pp. 22–23.

Strategic Frontiers. Overhead statistics. Youth With A Mission, Colorado Springs, CO USA, 1993.

"Take a Giant Step: Be a World Christian. Mission Education." Board for Communication Services, Lutheran Church-Missouri Synod. St. Louis, MO.

Telford, Tom. *ACMC Update.* Winter 1993.

*The 10/40 Window.* Booklet produced by the AD2000 and Beyond Movement, Colorado Springs, CO USA.

Tribes and Nations Outreach. *Kindreds.* Vol. 4, No. 1, 1993

"Urbana Testimony: The Starting Point of a New Perspective" in *Urbana Update* newsletter. InterVarsity, Spring 1992.

Wagner, Peter. *Frontiers in Missionary Strategy.* Chicago: Moody Press, 1971.

———. "Praying for Leaders: An Underrated Power Source for World Evangelism," *World Evangelization*, Jul.-Aug. 1988.

Waldrop, Bill. *ACMC Networker*, June 1992.

———. "From the Executive Director." *ACMC Networker*, December 1993.

Walls, Andrew. "Toward an Understanding of Africa's Place in Christian History." *Religion in a Pluralistic Society*, editor J. S. Pobee. Leiden: Brill, 1976.

Watkins, Morrie. "Chinese Beliefs," an unpublished paper. All Nations Literature, 1994.

Windsor, Raymond, editor. *Training for Cross-Cultural Ministries* newsletter. International Missionary Training Fellowship/WEF, August 1992.

Wirt, Sherwood. *The Social Conscience of the Evangelical.* New York: Harper & Row, 1968.

Winter, Ralph. Community Night address at the U.S. Center for World Mission, Pasadena, CA USA. September 1990.

———. "Racing to the Finish!" *Mission Frontiers*, Jul.-Aug. 1992, pp. 4–5.

———. "Rejoice!" Mini-Poster. Pasadena, CA: William Carey Library, March 1992.

World Thrust. "Winning Strategies Seminar" brochure. Atlanta, GA, 1992, p. 3.

Yancey, Philip. *Praying With the KGB.* Portland: Multnomah Press, 1992.

Ziervogle, James. "The Chinese World: One People or Many Peoples?" *Mission Frontiers*, Jan.-Mar. 1991, pp. 20–21.

# Notes

## Chapter 1

1. Philip Yancey, *Praying With the KBG* (Portland: Multnomah Press, 1992), p. 23.
2. OMS Outreach, July/August 1995.
3. Ralph Winter, *Community Night*, U.S. Center for World Mission, Pasadena, Calif., USA, September 1990.
4. David B. Barrett and Todd Johnson, *Our Globe and How to Reach It*, Birmingham, AL: New Hope Publishing, 1990.

## Chapter 2

1. Winter, "Growth of the Gospel," *Mission Frontiers*, July/August 1995.
2. Jansen, Adopt-A-People.

## Chapter 3

1. *Operation World*, p.23.
2. Deborah Conklin, "That Ishmael Might Live Under His Blessing," *Mission Frontiers*, January-March 1991, pp. 14–15.
3. David Sitton, "To Every Tribe With Jesus," *Mission Frontiers*, January-March 1991, pp. 16–17.
4. Ibid.
5. James Ziervogle, "The Chinese World: One People or Many Peoples?" *Mission Frontiers*, January-March 1991, pp. 20–21.
6. Morrie Watkins, "Chinese Beliefs," an unpublished paper. All Nations Literature, 1994.

## Chapter 4

1. Strategic Frontiers, Overhead Statistics, Youth With A Mission (Colorado Springs, Colo., USA, 1993).
2. *Mission Frontiers*, "People Group Definitions," (January-February 1994, p. 10).
3. Ralph Winter, "Racing to the Finish!" *Mission Frontiers*, July-August 1992, pp. 4–5.
4. Larry Pate, *Changing Balance*, pp. D229–D230.
5. Tom Telford, *ACMC Update*, Winter 1993.
6. Items from *Global Report*, December-February 1994
7. Luis Bush, "How Can All Peoples Be Reached by the Year 2000?" *Mission Frontiers*, September-December 1992, p. 57.
8. Larry D. Pate, *From Every People* (Monrovia, Calif.: MARC and OC International, 1989), pp. 75–76.
9. Andrew Walls, "Toward an Understanding of Africa's Place in Christian History," *Religion in a Pluralistic Society*, editor J.S. Pobee (Beiden: Brill, 1976), p. 180.
10. AEF (Asian Evangelical Fellowship), *Focus Forward*, 30th anniversary special edition.
11. Larry D. Pate, *Bridging People* newsletter, July 1989.
12. David B. Barrett, "Statistics, Global," *Dictionary of Pentecostal and Charismatic Movements*, editors Stanley M. Burgess and Gary B. McGee (Grand Rapids: Zondervan, 1988), p. 811.
13. L. Grant McClung, "The Pentecostal Trunk Must Learn From Its Branches," *Evangelical Missions Quarterly*, January 1993, p. 37.
14. Steve Hawthorne, editor, *Stepping Out* (Monrovia, Calif.: Short-Term Missions Advocates, 1987).
15. Dayton Roberts and John A. Siewert, editors, *Mission Handbook, 14th Edition: USA/Canada Protestant Ministries Overseas* (MARC & Zondervan, 1989), p. 51.
16. Ibid., pp. 51–53.
17. Leith Anderson, *Dying for Change* (Minneapolis: Bethany House Publishers, 1990), p. 135.
18. Leslie Pelt, "What's Behind the Wave of Short-Termers?" *Evangelical Missions Quarterly*, October 1992, pp. 384–388.
19. Ibid.
20. Steve Hawthorne, editor, *Stepping out* (Monrovia, Calif.: Short-Term Missions Advocates, 1987), p. 13.
21. James Engles and Jerry D. Jones, *Baby Boomers and the Future of World Missions* (Orange, Calif.: Management Development Associates, 1989), pp. 32, 39.
22. Seth Barnes, "The Changing Face of the Missionary Force," *Evangelical Missions Quarterly*, October 1992, p. 381.
23. "Urbana Testimony: The Starting Point of a New Perspective," *Urbana Update* newsletter, Spring 1992, InterVarsity.

24. Kwok Pui-lan, "Claiming Our Heritage: Chinese Women and Christianity," *International Bulletin of Missionary Research,* October 1992, pp. 150–152.

25. Larry Niemeyer, "The Unmet Challenge of Mission to the Matrilineal Peoples of Africa," *Evangelical Missions Quarterly,* January 1993, pp. 26–31.

26. Stefan Fatsis, "Corporate Makeover," *Gazette Telegraph* of Colorado Springs, CO, USA, December 27, 1992. Section E, p. 1.

27. Ibid.

28. Arab World Ministries *Update* newsletter. No. 4, 1992, p. 1.

29. Ibid. p.3

30. David Barrett and Todd Johnson, *Our Globe and How to Reach It: Seeing the World Evangelized by AD2000 and Beyond* (Birmingham, Ala.: New Hope Publishing, 1990).

31. Frank Kaleb Jansen, AAP (Adopt-A-People) definitions flyer and materials relating to the Adopt-A-People Clearinghouse list of identified unreached peoples (Colorado Springs, Colo.).

32. Patrick Johnstone, quoted from a message at the Lausanne II Congress on World Evangelization, July 1989.

## Chapter 6

1. Peter Wagner, *Frontiers in Missionary Strategy* (Chicago: Moody Press, 1971), p. 68.

2. Herbert Kane, *Life and Work on the Mission Field* (Grand Rapids: Baker Book House, 1980), pp. 11–13.

3. Bob Morehead, "Commitment as a Christian," a tract from Hands for Christ, Roanoke, Va., USA.

## Chapter 8

1. Arab World Ministries *Update* newsletter, No. 4, 1992.

2. Ibid.

3. Karen Dubert, "Ten Steps to Success: The Major Themes," *Evangelical Missions Quarterly,* April 1989, pp. 156–158.

## Chapter 10

1. Jim Montgomery, *DAWN 2000: Seven Million Churches to Go* (Pasadena, Calif.: William Carey Library, 1989), p. 119.

## Chapter 11

1. CoMission Press Conference, ACSI Convention, Anaheim, Calif., November 5, 1992.

2. George Gallup, *Special Report for the AD 2000 & Beyond Consultation* in Phoenix, Ariz., August 31, 1992. AD 2000 Office, Colorado Springs, Colo., USA.

3. "Take a Giant Step: Be a World Christian. Mission Education." Board for Communication Services, Lutheran Church-Missouri Synod. St. Louis, Mo.

4. Peter Wagner, *Frontiers in Missionary Strategy* (Chicago: Moody Press, 1971).

5. David Bryant, "The Most Hopeful Sign of Our Times: A Growing National Prayer Movement Points America Toward Spiritual Revival" in *Special Report from The National and International Religion Report*, Media Management, 1992.

6. Ibid.

7. Jack McAlister, "Why Is Prayer of Supreme Importance?" Unpublished transcript of message at Nations for Christ Congress, Riga, Latvia, May 1992.

8. ACMC, *Networker* newsletter, October 1992.

## Chapter 12

1. David Barrett and James Reapsome, *Seven Hundred Plans to Evanglize the World*, (Birmingham, AL: New Hope Publishing, 1989), pp. 8–14).

## Appendix

1. Thomas Graham, "How to Select the Best Church Planters," *Evangelical Missions Quarterly*, January 1987, pp. 18–21.

CE National, Inc.
1003 Presidential Dr.
P. O. Box 365
Winona Lake, IN 46590